The Practice of Making Strategy

The Practice of Making Strategy

A Step-by-Step Guide

Fran Ackermann and Colin Eden
with Ian Brown

SAGE Publications
London • Thousand Oaks • New Delhi

First published 2005

 SAGE Publications Ltd
1 Oliver's Yard
55 City Road
London EC1Y 1SP

SAGE Publications Inc
2455 Teller Road
Thousand Oaks, California 91320

SAGE Publications India Pvt Ltd
B-42, Panchsheel Enclave
Post Box 4109
New Delhi 110 017

British Library Cataloguing in Publication data
A catalogue record for this book is available from the British Library

ISBN 0 7619 4493 1
ISBN 0 7619 4494 X (pbk)

Library of Congress Control Number available

Typeset by Keystroke, Jacaranda Lodge, Wolverhampton
Printed and bound in Great Britain by TJ International Ltd, Padstow, Cornwall

Contents

1 Introduction

The Book . . .

This book aims to make theories about strategic management work in practice – taking seriously Lenin's point that 'theory without practice is pointless, practice without theory is mindless'. Thus throughout the book reference is made to a variety of points of view about aspects of strategic management through consideration of a portfolio of major texts. The purpose of these references or cross-links is to pull together commentary about the theory and concepts that guide, reinforce, or in some cases contradict, the approaches to practice described in this book in order to enable you to place the approaches in the wider context of the strategy literature. These texts are: De Wit and Meyer (eds), *Strategy: Process, Content, Context: an International Perspective* (1998), Johnson and Scholes, *Exploring Corporate Strategy* (2002) and Lynch, *Corporate Strategy* (2003).

   The purpose therefore is to introduce a package of process tools and techniques developed and tested through over 200 strategy interventions in a wide range of organizations. They are expected to guide and help a management team (at any level of the organization) construct a workable strategy that is politically feasible and yet exploits the distinctiveness and capabilities of the organization. Although these tools and techniques have been used at the top management team level, we shall assume that you are not necessarily the CEO of a large organization, but rather that you might be managing, or be a part of, a work-group, department, division or operating company, or alternatively you are a consultant/facilitator to a manager.

   What differentiates this approach from that of others?

- A focus on the realities of management in the organization: what drives the attention of managers – the major issues and concerns that managers believe they face.
- An acceptance that, in most circumstances, incremental change is more practical than wide-ranging and fundamental change.
- The demand that a robust business model is constructed and tested, and so

it involves the discovery of core distinctive competences through a designed process, rather than their being stated.

Many strategic planning efforts come to nothing because a) they do not directly involve the power brokers but rely on support staff, and b) they take an idealized view of the organization and what it can achieve. These two points are related. Urgent strategic issues engage senior managers. Their time is largely devoted to trying to avoid possible future disasters, manage their own ambitions, protect their own reputations and ensure projects keep on track. Some issues are urgent, some are interesting, some are strategic and some are tedious but require immediate attention. If strategy making does not at least pay some attention to these dominant drivers of the organization then it will not be seen by the power brokers to connect with the real world. Strategic planning becomes an 'annual rain dance' of no practical import. It is an idealized notion. Unless power brokers are directly involved then these issues are not surfaced and addressed. Through negotiation they may be reviewed and seen as less important for a sound strategic future, or they may rise to become central, but unless they are at least surfaced then the attention given to strategy making will be at best an arid intellectual exercise and certainly not emotionally engaging.

The issues that managers actually address determine the strategic future of the organization, not the published strategic plans which often collect dust on shelves rather than having any impact on purposeful activity. The published material may influence the issues that are addressed, but often only at the margin. Some situations become addressed as strategic issues and other potential issues are not noticed. The way managers think about what goes on around them determines what is noticed and what is not. So, one of the outcomes of strategy making is a change in the way issues are defined. And so the way managers think about what is problematic, and what is an opportunity, has to change as a result of strategy making. Thinking belongs to people in the organization and not the organization, and the thinking that matters is that of the power brokers. They must be actively involved in the process of making strategy because ways of thinking cannot be changed other than incrementally. (From a psychological standpoint this is known as 'elaborating a person's construct system', or 'scaffolding'.)[1]

Thus, understanding and acknowledging the 'reality' of an organization is crucial to making the strategy deliverable. The starting point must be to detect **emergent strategizing**. This is how an organization determines its strategic future through managers habitually defining some situations as important and the ways in which they address these issues.

Emergent strategizing addresses the way in which most organizations demonstrate patterns of decision making, thinking and action. Often 'taken for granted' ways of working and problem solving come from the habits, history and 'hand-me-downs' of the organization's culture. Whether the organization members are aware of this or not, even if they define themselves as 'muddling through' rather than acting strategically, such enacted patterns inevitably take the organization in one strategic direction rather than another. Organizations do not act randomly, without purpose. It is this process of going in one strategic direction rather than another, based on patterns, or what are sometimes called 'recipes', of perceiving and acting,[2] which we call emergent strategizing.

Thus, we contend that any organization, big or small, *will* be acting strategically whether the emergent strategizing is quite unselfconscious, or rather more deliberate. As, for example, when there is a knowing reinforcement of the existing ways of working by key members of the organization in pursuit of a particular outcome or purpose. In either case the emergent strategic direction[3] and implicit or explicit goal and purpose, are detectable and, to a greater or lesser degree, amenable to change. It is in understanding the implied direction (based on the issues thought to be important) that change can be determined. Of course, for some organizations this implicit or emergent strategy may be determined as best for that particular organization. When this is the case then the organization has moved from a patterned and emergent 'muddling through'[4] to delivering a deliberate emergent strategy.

Starting strategy making by detecting emergent strategizing involves: respecting the history of the organization, understanding its ways of thinking and acting in practice rather than that espoused (chapters 3 and 4), and understanding the role of systems and structures (chapter 8). These are all aspects of understanding the culture of the organization.[5]

As we have implied above, in practice the best way of gaining an understanding of the emergent strategic future of the organization is through an exploration of the ways in which the power brokers define and address strategic issues (chapters 3 and 4). In doing so it is also more likely that these managers will become engaged in the strategy making – both emotionally and intellectually.

This approach to strategy making implies that the new strategy will make demands on changing the way issues are defined and addressed – that is ways of thinking and acting in practice will need to change. But, these changes will be determined in the light of the existing ways in order that the chances of successful change can be assessed. The approach also implies that changing the strategy of an organization demands **incremental change** from emergent strategizing to a deliberate, but realistic or realizable, new strategy. The incrementalism invariably involves changing structures and systems, as well as recognizing that the strategy-making process itself is designed to promote change by renegotiating ways of understanding the purpose of the organization, and creating and testing a new business model or livelihood scheme through a thorough exploration of patterns of distinctive competences. It is both a rational and social process.

Figure 1.1 shows our view of the key aspects of strategy making. Figure 1.2 shows those covered in this book and the tasks required to write a powerful and

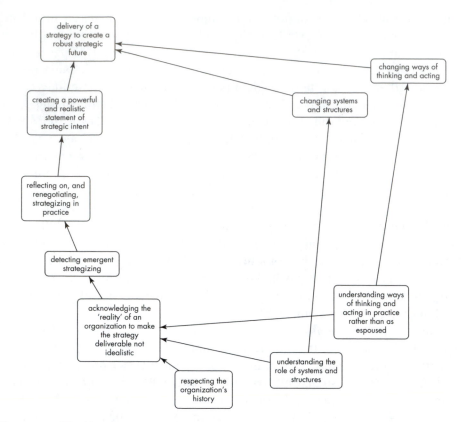

Figure 1.1 The Key Aspects of Strategy Making

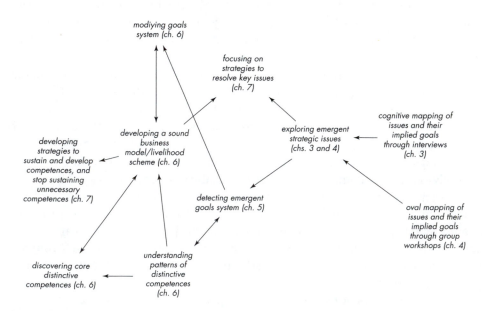

Figure 1.2 The Strategy-making Tasks

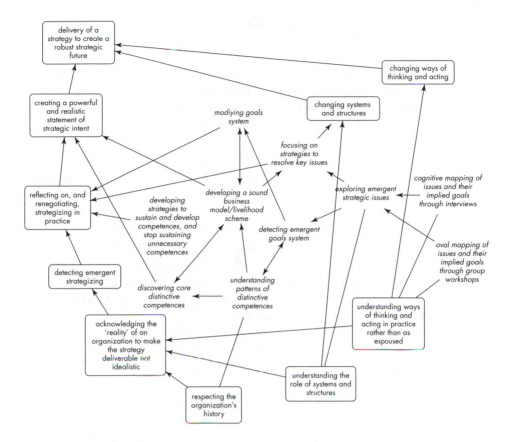

Figure 1.3 The Relationships Between the Tasks and Key Aspects

realistic statement of strategic intent (chapter 8), and Figure 1.3 shows how these tasks relate to the key aspects of strategy making.

Strategic Management

As we have implied above, the book represents a practical guide to making strategy. It is based on two key definitions, first, that effective strategy is

a coherent set of individual discrete actions in support of a system of goals, . . . which are supported as a portfolio by a self-sustaining critical mass, or momentum, of opinion in the organization. (Eden and Ackermann 1998, p. 4)

And second, that strategic management is

a way of **regenerating an organization**, through continuous attention to a vision of what the people who make up an organization wish to do. It is a pro-active process of seeking to change the organization, its stakeholders (in as much as they are different from the organization) and the context, or 'environment', within which it seeks to attain its *aspirations*. It is, particularly, about **stretching the organization** (see Hamel and Prahalad, 1993) to **gain leverage from its individuality** – its distinctive competences and ability to change them. (Eden and Ackermann 1998, p. 3)

As we suggest early in this chapter, the guiding principles for developing the tools and techniques (presented as tasks) derive from seeking the **political feasibility of strategy**[6] by focusing on process management and design as much as on content management. To gain political feasibility the wisdom and experience and therefore the ideas and views of each member of the strategy-making team are attended to – thus there is a focus on either, or both, interviewing each participant using cognitive mapping (chapter 3), and using a group process of issue surfacing through the oval mapping technique (chapter 4). The processes introduced pay attention to the need for strategy to be a negotiated product of a group process that is designed to gain a sufficient degree of consensus for strategy delivery to follow. Power, politics, procedures, psychology, social psychology, group behaviour and negotiation are key background concepts that guide the process management and content management.

Fundamental to this attention to process is the attention to procedural justice – the idea that process can be more important than outcomes in gaining commitment. Recent research[7] clearly indicates that there are three important principles of procedural justice. These are engagement, explanation and expectation clarity. **Engagement** means involvement in the decision making. **Explanation** means ensuring an understanding of why final decisions were made. **Expectation clarity** means ensuring that the targets, reward systems, and milestones for the new situation are understood. The key outcome of this recent research is to highlight that good outcomes are less important than the process of getting to the outcome – and this is the key aspect to making strategy.

This book focuses on creating a workable basic strategy. However, there are some other important tasks that must be addressed: the implication of existing systems and structures; quantitatively testing the business model developed through the process; stakeholder management; adapting to alternative possible futures; and the development of appropriate performance indicators. These tasks are introduced and discussed briefly in chapter 8. Figure 1.4 shows how these additional strategy-making tasks relate to the key aspects of strategy making set out in Figure 1.1.

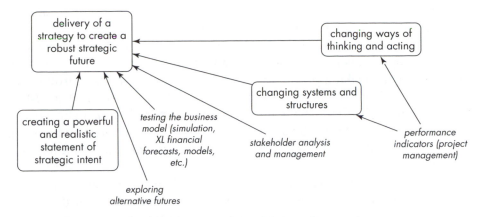

Figure 1.4 Additional Tasks to Refine the Strategy and Their Relationship to the Key Aspects

The Structure of the Book

The book aims to guide you through a series of process steps in strategy making. Included in most chapters are a series of tasks (sometimes forming a workshop), examples of what is expected from undertaking the tasks (steps), exercises to help you know whether you are developing a good understanding of the tasks, and most importantly some real cases. Each case study reports a real intervention, and each report has been signed off by the client. The tasks are to be undertaken by the strategy-making team, guided by a member of that team, or by an external or internal facilitator. These tasks are set out at the end of relevant chapters. Notes at the end of each chapter provide further indicative material and full references are provided at the end of the book.

Although the interview process using **cognitive mapping** (chapter 3) is crucial in a real exercise (it provides the means of eliciting in-depth and relatively open data which can then be merged with that from others and used as the focus), this is difficult to simulate and so is excluded from the tasks. However, using strategy mapping for direct work with a group (the oval mapping technique (OMT) – chapter 4) cannot be undertaken effectively unless the interviews and mapping chapter are well understood – hence its inclusion. In order to develop a good understanding of mapping, the chapter contains exercises rather than tasks.

All chapters, other than chapter 3, are laid out to provide 'commentary and issues' on the tasks and also 'hints and tips' that identify how to work through common pitfalls. The tasks are also available at *www.journeymaking.net* and the hints and tips will be updated on a regular basis as a result of feedback from teachers and practitioners. The web site also contains some material to help those teaching some or all of the approaches presented in this book. In addition a CD is available which has a) a live interview to watch/learn from, and b) slides explaining mapping. The tasks provide, in step-by-step detail, the means for carrying out the processes discussed in this book.

The tasks introduced in the book are immensely practical and can be undertaken by practising managers, consultants and MBA scholars who wish to form a strategy-making group 'for real' with their own department/division/ organization, or for readers wishing to simulate a strategy-making team. MBA scholars completing their degree on a part-time or flexible learning basis can 'experiment' with their own organizations directly, whereas those undertaking the degree on a full-time basis can envisage its use in their past or future organization.

Furthermore, for many years MBA scholars have successfully used the approaches in this book to help some part of their organization develop a strategy. In most of these cases their adventure into facilitating a management team (often a team for which they were the manager) led to a realistic and yet demanding strategy for their department, division, group or operating company. In some cases the approaches have been applied to 'start-up' groups where two to three individuals, along with their sponsors, have identified a realistic business model that has guided the development of their embryo organization. Indeed, one of the case studies in this book (support 3) reports on Ian Brown's use of the journey-making process as his company went through a management buy-out. The strategy not only guided the buy-out but also provided the framework for the business plan used to raise necessary funds.

Many MBA scholars undertake their qualifying project using the process in a real setting. Some recent projects have been with a division of Scottish Power, BBC Scotland, a department of the Bank of Scotland, a palm oil plantation in Malaysia, a technology start-up in Japan, a Swiss software company, a BP operating company in Azerbaijan, and a management buy-out in the music industry. The students have combined the approaches presented here with other aspects of their MBA programme.

Undertaking strategy making without a facilitator is difficult because there is a need to act as both facilitator and interested party. However, for internal and external consultants the approaches are particularly attractive because they enable significant progress in strategy making through a one- or two-day workshop (see, for example, case studies 5.1, 5.2 and 6.1). There are, however, different issues for internal and external facilitators (see support 4 for some notes on these issues).

As the above examples imply, the tasks can be used in large or small, public or private organizations, as well as organizations in many different parts of the world.

The Layout of the Book

Chapter 1 – Introduction
What the book is about, what guides it, and its structure.

Chapter 2 – Getting Started: First Steps – Getting a Team Together
Who should be involved? Why it is important to get this right.
TASK 1

Chapter 3 – Getting at Beliefs About Possible Strategic Futures: Using Cognitive Mapping to Capture Interview Material
Interviewing individual strategy group members. Using cognitive mapping to map out the beliefs and values of an individual with respect to their view of the strategic future for the organization. Bringing the interview maps together to build a draft 'strategy map'.

Chapter 4 – Surfacing and Structuring Strategic Issues in Groups
Using the oval mapping technique with groups, as either a next step workshop after building a draft strategy map using interviews, or as a first workshop.

■ **Case Study 4.1 Understanding the Issues: Seeking to Make a Major Services Contract Successful!**
A series of one-day strategy workshops using the oval mapping technique.
TASK 2

Chapter 5 – Building Up a Distinctive and Realistic Goals System
Detecting emergent strategic goals and creating a draft distinctive goals system.

■ **Case Study 5.1 Understanding the Issues: Seeking to Make a Major Services Contract Successful!**
In a multi-organization setting, determining the goals system and key strategies in a two-day workshop.

■ **Case Study 5.2 In Pursuit of a Direction: Clarifying Our Goals**
A charity focusing on poverty has the involvement of many representatives of a range of organizations. They wanted to involve them in establishing a clear and agreed sense of purpose.
TASK 3

Chapter 6 – Developing a Business Model or Livelihood Scheme: Identifying Distinctiveness and Core Distinctive Competences
It's all very well having some distinctive goals, but can they be delivered successfully within a competitive environment?

■ **Case Study 6.1   A Question of Turning Around**
A two-day workshop involving issue surfacing (chapter 4), the creation of a draft goals system (chapter 5) and the development of a viable business model for a small ($45m turnover) company.
TASKS 4–6

Chapter 7 – Agreeing Strategies: Sustaining the Business Model or Livelihood Scheme and Resolving Key Strategic Issues
Establishing the priorities for strategic action in order to ensure the business model is delivered and sustained into the future.
TASK 7

Chapter 8 – Making a Statement of Strategic Intent and Other Aspects of Making Strategy
Including commentary on additional tasks that may be undertaken in order to increase the robustness of the strategy and the probability of successful implementation.
TASK 8

Chapter 9 – Managing an Incomplete Process to Achieve Strategic Change
Sometimes making strategy needs to be finished when it is incomplete, against an ideal process. In these circumstances, how can the maximum added value be achieved in relation to the stage reached?

■ **Support 1   Analyzing Cause Maps**
How to work with maps – getting at the important characteristics of individual cognitive maps, or strategy maps.

■ **Support 2   The Formalities of Mapping**
For mapping to work well in making strategy it is important to follow some 'rules' or guidelines. These are set out here.

■ **Support 3   MBA Student Project Case Study**
A strategy for management buy-out: what is it like to use the approaches in your own organization as an active part-time MBA scholar? This case includes examples of using cognitive mapping (chapter 3).

■ **Support 4   Issues in Working With External or Internal Facilitators**
There are advantages and disadvantages in using external facilitators. Some of these are considered here so that an informed choice can be made.

■ **Support 5   On the Folly of Rewarding A, While Hoping for B by Steven Kerr**
An article that is particularly good at discussing some of the problems in developing performance and reward systems.

■ **Support 6   Additional Resources**
What resources may be used to help in the process of strategy making?
Including software, hardware and CD.

References

Working With This Book

Although this book is designed to follow a logical progress towards strategy
making, there is a choice at the issue surfacing stage. This is between starting
the intervention using interviews employing cognitive mapping (chapter 3) and
starting the process using the oval mapping technique (chapter 4) or using both
if wide coverage is required. This choice will be to some extent determined
by the nature of the group, the issue and organization. Each of the two issue
surfacing chapters contains material exploring the different benefits accrued
from each technique, for example, using interviews is recommended where
there are possible interpersonal issues, or members unfamiliar with airing
their views in public. Regardless of which of the techniques is employed,
it is recommended that you read the cognitive mapping chapter, as OMT is
dependent on good mapping skills.

Notes

[1] These are terms used by Kelly (1955) and Vygotsky (1962) to suggest that we change
    our mind, our way of understanding events, gradually through adding new under-
    standings – a process of elaboration or extending a scaffold.
[2] These are discussed in more detail by Calori et al. (1998) and Spender (1989).
[3] The idea of an emergent, rather than deliberate, strategy is explained in Mintzberg
    and Waters (1985).
[4] The term 'muddling through' was introduced by Lindblom (1959).
[5] An approach favoured by Johnson and Scholes (2002) is to understand the 'cultural
    web'.
[6] Johnson and Scholes (2002) argue that organizational politics 'has to be taken seriously
    as an influence on strategy development' (pp. 66–9).
[7] The significant research in this field has been undertaken by Chan Kim and Renée
    Mauborgne (1995; 1997). The topic is discussed in chapter 3 of Eden and Ackermann
    (1998), and is seen alongside the importance of procedural rationality – using a process
    that is seen as rational.

2 Getting Started: First Steps – Getting a Team Together

Introduction

In this chapter we will take the first three steps in strategy making: identify the organization (or part of it) which will be the focus of the strategy, choose a client, and bring together a group of people to form the strategy-making group.

While many organizations pay lip-service to strategic management, relatively few take it seriously enough to invest time and energy in it. In particular, strategy making at lower levels and in small units of the organization tends to go by the board, as more urgent issues constantly sidetrack managers and other key individuals. Yet sectors, divisions, departments and other small units need to develop their own strategies, as well as contributing to the organization's overall strategy.

This chapter of our strategy-making process begins by pointing out that making and updating strategy is seldom if ever the work of a single manager. It is usually pointless when undertaken by a staff planner[1] because the power brokers who drive the organization have no ownership of the strategy. Strategic change is achieved by groups of managers who gain ownership because they are a part of the thinking process – the journey.[2] The challenges can be considerable, and include a whole range of difficulties that typically confront change agents. The composition of the strategy-making group, and the roles that its members adopt, are critical issues, especially when we consider that it is rare for there to be no casualties as a result of effective strategy making.

The strategy-making group may be a subgroup within a unit, department, division or operating company. It does not have to be the top management team of the whole organization.[3] The group may be managing a relatively small part of a much larger organization. In such a situation, the wider organization forms part of the group's external environment: a powerful and very interested stakeholder, but not necessarily the sole determinant of the strategy that the group will develop.

Thus the role and composition of the strategy-making group is crucial, because it is the powerhouse of change. So, ideally who should be a part of the group? The key people are those who have the most power and influence[4] –

the power brokers – who can therefore contribute most to driving the delivery of the strategy, but also those with the knowledge, experience and skills that should influence the process. Of course, any individual may possess both attributes, just as they may play more than one role within the group. Therefore, there are two main reasons why someone should be a part of the group: a) they have the power to sabotage or support effective delivery of the strategy, and b) they know something that could ensure the strategy is better thought out.

Strategy-making Outcomes

■ Choose the organization (or part of it) for which the strategy is to be developed.
■ Select the client for whom the strategy is to be developed.
■ Carefully determine the membership of the strategy-making group so that the strategy stands a good chance of being implemented.

Choosing Where in the Organization to Focus

While most managers believe that doing some strategy making is important, they also find it difficult to prioritize it against urgent 'burning' issues. This means that it is usually crucial to make sure that any strategy-making events are both productive and enjoyable. For many managers strategy workshops are events that act as a useful social gathering but there is no expectation that the discussions will seriously affect them or the organization.

> A common experience for many managers is that the strategic planning process takes on the form of an 'annual rain dance'. The activity is taken to be important enough to devote some limited time on it because the intellectual arguments for doing so are difficult to argue with – 'of course an organization must have a strategy'. However, often the reality is that the activity will simply result in 'the usual annual budgeting battle' which is focused on short term issues and the retention of the status quo. Some managers will come off badly and others well, but this will be related more to their political clout and negotiating skills than any consideration of the longer term impact of the budgets on the strategic future of the organization. These budgeting rounds will have a real impact on the strategic future of the organization as a part of the emergent strategizing of the organization, but not in a thoughtful or designed way. (Eden and Ackermann, 1998, p. 47)

For the purposes of this book we are going to assume that getting strategy making started is not going to be easy. We shall assume that you are not the CEO of a large organization, but rather that you might be managing, or be a part of, a work-group, department, division or operating company, or alternatively a consultant/facilitator to a manager. In accepting the challenge of doing some strategy making we expect you to target a strategy-making group which stands a reasonable chance of success. We do not expect you to consider becoming the champion of strategy making for the whole of your organization if you do not have access to the power brokers at the level of the organization that this would demand. We need you to consider carefully, and from the standpoint of pragmatics, who might be the client for the work you are about to undertake. In so doing you will need to consider the boundaries of the organization for whom the strategy will apply.

Go to task 1a

Decide for which organization the strategy is to be developed.

Commentary and Issues

You will be drawing a boundary between the organization for which you will want to secure a sound strategic future and the setting for that organization. If your organization is set within a larger organization then we shall be treating this larger organization as a part of the environment of your organization. You will only be interested in the aims and intentions of the wider organization to the extent that it is a powerful player (stakeholder) which influences the strategic future of your organization (see chapter 5 for a specific consideration of the emergent goals in relation to the wider organization's goals). The nature of your interest in the wider organization will follow from strategic analysis of the whole of your environment (stakeholder analysis and management,[5] and considerations of alternative futures,[6] not from a presumption of its importance).

In almost all cases we expect that you will be an internal (rather than external) facilitator. Being an internal facilitator provides both disadvantages and advantages (see support 4). In some cases you may be both facilitator and client. However, a large number of MBA students have successfully managed to combine both and have produced effective and insightful strategy making.

Hints and Tips

Example 1

You are the manager of a computer services department – a department that supplies a service to a large organization with sites all around Europe. You may have some access to the senior management team of the whole organization, to the extent that you report to one of the vice presidents. However, your ability to influence the senior management team with respect to their strategy making for the whole organization is negligible. Your input to the strategic thinking of the whole organization does not go beyond expressing a specialist view – you are a source of specialist information. You are also aware that there remains a continuing risk that the main organization may choose to out-source computer services. As a services department you put a strategy on paper a couple of years ago, and the senior management team accepted it.

In this case, we would expect you to take on the challenge of using strategy making as the basis for developing, reviewing and renewing a strategy for the computer services department. The strategy you develop may, or may not, replace your published strategy. At this stage your strategy making is designed to secure the strategic future of your department. We would not expect you to use this book to simulate you facilitating the senior management team in their development of strategy.

Here, you are both facilitator of the strategy making and client. This dual role for yourself is likely to be problematic.

Example 2

You are a member of staff in a sales office consisting of eleven others including your local manager. You have reasonable access to your manager and are well regarded by most of your colleagues. Your colleagues know that you are undertaking studies in the field of business and management. Although you have met the sales manager to whom your manager reports, you are not well placed to persuade her that you could help her undertake strategy making for the whole of the sales team.

In this case, we would expect you to take on the challenge of developing and delivering a strategy for your sales office. Your client is likely to be your

continued

own manager. The manager has never thought about developing a strategy for his small team before, and is likely to resist the need for it. It is unlikely that you will be able to demand that the work is undertaken, rather you will need to work towards small gains in commitment to thinking about strategy. Your reasonable expectations are to gradually develop an enthusiasm and involvement in strategy making.

Example 3

You are part of a group of four friends in the process of starting up a new company offering consultancy in the development of web-based learning material. You are all currently in employment but intend to start up within the next six months using a bank loan that has yet to be negotiated. Here it is going to be difficult to identify a single person as the client. It is most likely that all of you will be the client, assuming that you each have equal shares in the new company. There is no wider organization to consider as a part of your environment.

Figure 2.1 represents the boundary notion.

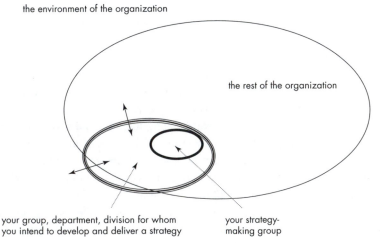

the environment of the organization

the rest of the organization

your group, department, division for whom
you intend to develop and deliver a strategy

your strategy-
making group

Figure 2.1 The Context of Your Strategy-making group

> **Go to task 1b**
>
> Choose a client and five key power brokers in that organization who will form the strategy-making team.

Commentary and Issues

Choosing a Client

It is important to establish who will be the client for the strategy making. They will be the person whose views will matter most to you when there is a choice to be made about one set of views as against those of others. The client cannot be an organization, because an organization cannot express views. The client must be a person (or at least a small group of people with very similar interests).[7] The client for the strategy making may change over time, although this is unusual. The client is the person who will drive forward the strategy making and delivery with your assistance. Although they may not, at this time, regard themselves as the client, it is your intention that they take on the role of client as you succeed in persuading them of the importance of the task you wish to facilitate.

Choosing the Strategy-making Group

> Never doubt that a small group of committed citizens can change the world. Indeed, it is the only thing that ever has. (Margaret Mead)

An organization changes as a result of the commitment and energy of the people within it to make changes. Rarely can a single person create strategic change or a desired strategic future.[8] A group of powerful individuals can create strategic change and manage strategic stability. Of course, organizations also only cope with a changing world because there is enough creativity, differences of view and new and alternative points of view (entropy,[9] as thermo-dynamicists would call it), to recognize and 'do battle' with uncontrollable turbulence.

As we argued in the introduction, strategy making is not just about agreeing strategy, but it is also about stretching the organization, so that it is prepared for action, recognizes and levers its strengths and therefore manages its own future interactively.[10]

Thus, we must think hard about who needs to be involved in the strategy making beyond the client. On the one hand there is a powerful argument for involving everybody – but then that is usually impracticable (at least to start with). On the other hand the smaller the group the easier it is likely to be to reach agreements (although there will be less ownership and commitment to the strategic outcome). To start our exercise we are going to consider a group no larger than five people. We may expand the group if it becomes clear that we should do so.[11]

Why do we start with five? Because the ideal group size is five to seven people, and in practice we find that even if we start with five people we shall find ourselves under pressure to increase the group size, and so we will leave some flexibility to do so. Research on team performance suggests a need for eight roles within an effective team, however, any one person is usually able to draw from a repertoire of several of these roles and so an ideal team size does not have to be eight people.[12]

As we noted earlier in the chapter, there are two reasons for including people in the strategy-making group:

1 They need to be committed to the strategy because they are powerful players in its delivery.[13]
2 They have the wisdom, experience or knowledge that is needed to inform the strategy.[14]

Those included may be supporters or they may be saboteurs. We hope, of course, that they will finish up as supporters because the strategy will have been negotiated with their involvement in processes that pay attention to **procedural justice** (doing things a sensible way) and procedural rationality (attending to sensible analysis).

Each of these reasons for including a person in the strategy-making group you are about to form represents a power base,[15] and so the key to membership of the strategy-making group is that each person is a power broker of one sort or another. But here the power base that is of interest is that which is related to strategy making and delivery.[16] An understanding of the different bases of power in organizations is therefore crucial in selecting a strategy-making group. Consider, for example, formal position, ability to reward others, direct control over others, specific expertise, access to information, who they know, who is likely to be willingly influenced by them, and so on.[17]

The following interconnected leadership tasks are important if strategy making and implementation are to be effective:[18]

■ Understanding the people involved, including oneself.
■ Sponsoring of the process (considering who needs to be a supporter of the process in order to protect both the client and subsequently yourself).
■ Championing of the process (in this case you are likely to be the champion at the start).
■ Facilitating the process.
■ Fostering collective leadership.

Any serious strategy making will question and probably change the current power structure[19] of the organization[20] (the 'social order and negotiated order'[21]). There will be some in the organization who will believe that they will come off worse and some who will believe that they will come off better from strategy making – **anticipated losers** and **anticipated winners**. Anticipating losing or winning will, rightly or wrongly, set up a political dynamic[22] and power struggle. As we noted earlier, it is rare for there to be no casualties from the results of strategy making.

> It must be considered that there is nothing more difficult, more dangerous or more apt to miscarry than an endeavour to introduce new institutions. For he that introduces them will make enemies of all those who do well out of the old institutions, and will receive only cool support from those who would do well out of the new ones. This coolness is caused partly by fear of their opponents, who have the old laws on their side, and partly from the natural scepticism of mankind, who have no faith in new arrangements until they have been confirmed by experience. (Niccolo Macchiavelli in *Il Principe* (1513), chapter 6)

Hints and Tips

When considering the make up of a strategy-making group consider the possibility of powerful players taking on the following roles:[23]

■ Anticipated loser.
■ Anticipated winner.
■ Genuine cynic (often a senior and powerful person who has 'been through this sort of thing before, and nothing comes of it').
■ Opinion former (when this person expresses a view in the organization it tends to be followed by many others without their investigating the validity of the view. They might, for example, assert that the strategy making is a 'good thing' and so influence many others in the organization to think positively about it).
■ Ideas generator.[24]
■ Saboteur (this person often overlaps with the anticipated loser).
■ Sit back and wait and see before jumping (this person often, literally, sits at the back in group sessions and does not become involved – might overlap with a 'genuine cynic').

In many cases a person will take on several of these roles. As shown, often an anticipated loser will also be a saboteur, or a genuine cynic will sit back and wait and see before jumping. Forming strategy-making teams may be helped by considering the eight team roles, mentioned above, that are regarded as important in creating effective teams. It is not usual to submit possible team members to a Belbin team role questionnaire[25] or a Myers-Brigg Type Indicator (MBTI) questionnaire![26] Using the team role or MBTI categories as a framework for considering the team is often helpful for clients who are accustomed to these profiles.

During this first stage of strategy making our aim is to increase the probability of the strategy being successful. This early decision about the nature of the group will play a very important role.[27]

■ Often the consideration of possible candidates for the strategy-making team is best undertaken jointly with the client – providing the client has accepted the role of client.

■ Remember that the need for a sponsor can be crucial.[28] The sponsor will not be a member of the strategy-making group and will not have a specific interest in the outcomes of the strategy, rather they support the effort – possibly being required to give permission for resources to be spent on the exercise. If time is to be spent in strategy workshops they will need to be supportive of the potential value of time spent in this way, and will legitimize your initiation of the process as well as the client's and others' involvement. Sometimes the client and sponsor may be the same person, but this can be dangerous, because the client has no protection from the dynamic that can be set up by such an exercise, and you have no protection from being labelled as the instigator, or as the time waster. Determining when and how to involve the sponsor is best done with the client so as to help the client understand the rationale for their involvement.

This completes the first set of tasks. The next section of the book discusses the nature of the first steps to be taken with members of your strategy-making group. This may be either interviewing each participant using cognitive mapping to record the views expressed, or the design and delivery of the first strategy workshop.

Where Next? Interviews (Chapter 3) or Directly to Your First Strategy Workshop (Chapter 4)?

We are presuming that you cannot take up the time of your strategy-making group with ease – that they will be resistant to giving up even two to three hours for such an event organized by you. Burning issues and immediate concerns are usually higher on the list of priorities than strategy making.

One option is to go straight to an oval mapping technique/issue surfacing workshop. This might provide the opportunity to 'earn' their time by facilitating a first workshop that is enjoyable and productive, with clear added-value outcomes. Therefore we need to consider ways of getting commitment from the participants to attend a first workshop, whether or not interviews are the first step.

Interviews might be an easier entry method that additionally gain commitment to a first workshop. After each person has been interviewed a part of the closing statement will be to discuss what will happen next. The interview material for each person will remain as a confidential body of views, but they will be merged into a single interconnected strategy map where it is not possible for any participant to be certain of which views belong to which participant (even though they will probably attempt to guess). As this process is discussed with participants they usually become very curious about the nature of the strategy map – how their own views fit with those of others, what issues come forward, and so on. This curiosity provides the basis for getting the participants together for a workshop to agree goals, and work on distinctive competences and the business model. Arranging individual interviews is often much simpler, as is managing a one-to-one intervention.

We acknowledged earlier that the client might not yet be prepared to take on the role of client (unless you are the client as well as the facilitator – and you may need some convincing of the worth of the strategy you are about to embark upon!) Facilitation is a demanding skill – particularly when both process and content have to be managed simultaneously. For many consultants the role is so demanding there will be more than one facilitator, where one concentrates on process issues and the other on content issues.[29]

Facilitation becomes easier the clearer the facilitator is about the link between theory and practice. Workshops never turn out the way we expect, even with very good planning and design – therefore a facilitator must be able to operate contingently but within a well-understood theoretical framework. This statement is not intended to suggest that workshops do not need to be well designed and planned, rather it suggests that a plan should be the framework for a workshop and we should not fear moving away from it when appropriate. Therefore having a good understanding of the processes of strategic management is important.

We will plan on the first workshop, and other subsequent ones, being about two to three hours in length. This might mean that your planned outcomes may be incomplete, but you should have engaged your group to such an extent that they will commit to another workshop. In the worst case you may wish to encourage the group to meet on the grounds that 'you know I am undertaking a course/reading in strategic management, and I am asking you if you would help me in these studies by meeting with me for a couple of hours to try out some methods I am learning – the focus of the event will be for us to explore some of the strategic issues we think we will be facing over the next few years. I hope the time spent will be useful to us all, and certainly hope that it will be interesting – but I cannot guarantee it – I've never done this sort of thing before, but I do have a "book" to guide me!' In this way you are asking a favour without any guarantee of success, and you are reducing the risk to yourself by doing so.

Your aim is to make the event useful enough for the group to want to meet again, under your guidance, to continue the strategy making further, by moving on to decide on a goals/aspirations system (chapter 5), an exploration of distinctive competences and the business model/livelihood scheme (chapter 6), developing a statement of strategic intent (chapter 8) and gaining closure (chapter 9).

Notes

1. Johnson and Scholes (2002) discuss the role of planners in an organization, suggesting that 'planners can overlook the importance of the experience of those in an organization' (p. 64).

2. 'Journey' is used as an acronym by Eden and Ackermann (1998) where it relates to JOintly Understanding Reflecting and NEgotiating strategY: the process of making strategy. Johnson and Scholes (2002) state that 'a successful (strategy) workshop process works through issues in face-to-face debate and discussion, drawing on and surfacing different experiences, assumptions, interests and views. In this respect it is seeking to tackle the design of strategy, whilst facing up to the realities of the cultural and political processes of the organization' (p. 65).

3. De Wit and Meyer (1998) pp. 93–4 suggest that objectives setting should be carried out by the top management in the organization. This contradicts our view that it can be done at any level in the organization. Johnson and Scholes (2002) support our point of view that strategy can be developed at any level in the organization, saying, 'it could be that the direction of strategy that emerges from lower in the organization is more appropriate to the needs of the organization' (p. 78).

4. Johnson and Scholes (2002) pp. 212–15 discuss the sources and indicators of power in an organization.

5. For an introduction to stakeholder analysis and management see chapters C7 and P4 of Eden and Ackermann (1998).

6. For an exploration of 'alternative futures' analysis and 'scenario planning' see chapters C8 and P4 of Eden and Ackermann (1998), and van der Heijden (1996).

7. See chapters P9 and P5 of Eden and Ackermann (1998).

8. When referring to the 'design school', De Wit and Meyer (1998) Mintzberg states that 'ultimately there is only one strategist, and that is the manager who sits at the apex of the organizational hierarchy' (in De Wit and Meyer (1998) p. 71). Our view is that it is rare for strategic change to be created by a single person. Lynch (2003) p. 364 suggests that many would argue that the vision should be created by the CEO but also gives the alternative point of view that it should involve many in the organization. He suggests that the method used will be dependant on the culture of the organization.

9. Stafford Beer (1966) reflects on the important role of entropy in keeping an organization alive. The idea also fits with current proposals about organizations needing to be on the edge of chaos (see Pascale et al., 2000).

10. Russell Ackoff (1974) discusses an interesting approach to the nature of interactive planning in the public arena.

11. Lynch (2003) pp. 580 and 643 argues that while involving more people in the formulation of strategy may slow it down, it may speed up the implementation process. De Wit and Meyer (1998) support greater involvement, stating that 'all of the major

interests throughout the company should be invited to participate in the strategic business-planning process' (p. 115).

[12] Meredith Belbin (1981) has undertaken considerable research on the make-up of effective teams. He suggests that an effective team needs to cover eight roles, although this does not imply that a team needs eight people – each person will typically take on more than one role.

[13] Lynch (2003) suggests that people who have not been involved in the development of the strategy are less likely to be committed to it.

[14] De Wit and Meyer (1998) Chakravarthy and Lorange discuss the possibility of involving those with expert knowledge in the goal development process, saying, 'it is not uncommon for key managers to be invited to participate in the objectives-setting step . . . as experts in a corporate task force' (in De Wit and Meyer (1998) p. 95).

[15] Johnson and Scholes (2002) p. 560 introduce a useful table identifying power mechanisms in organizations.

[16] Lynch (2003) pp. 270–2 and 786–8 discusses the need to take account of politics and power in strategic change.

[17] De Wit and Meyer (1998) Mintzberg suggests that it is important to harness the expertise that exists within the organization when developing strategy where 'there is too much information to be comprehended in one brain' (in De Wit and Meyer (1998) p. 77).

[18] From Bryson (1995) and Bryson and Crosby (1992).

[19] Johnson and Scholes (2002) pp. 558–62 discuss power and political processes in the context of managing strategic change.

[20] Johnson and Scholes (2002) argue that 'there will be a need for the reconfiguration of power structures in the organization' (p. 558) as a consequence of strategy making. Thus, not surprisingly, participants and other stakeholders anticipate such possibilities.

[21] The idea of organizations being a balance of social order (maintenance of social relationships) and negotiated order (problems being resolved by negotiation rather than by rational analysis and optimization) is an important aspect of considering political feasibility in strategy making – see C48–50 in Eden and Ackermann (1998).

[22] Johnson and Scholes (2002) p. 9 and 66–9 discuss organizational politics in the context of strategy development, making the point that 'strategies develop as the outcome of processes of bargaining and negotiation among powerful internal or external interest groups' (p. 66).

[23] Lynch (2003) p. 788 identifies three important tasks that need to be undertaken when seeking agreement to a new strategy. These include identifying potential and influential supporters, seeking out potential opponents and building the maximum consensus. We believe that it is better to build these tasks into the strategy-making process through the careful design of the group.

[24] Akin to Belbin's (1981) category of a 'Shaper' or 'Plant'.

[25] Belbin, 1981.

[26] See www.keirsey.com.

[27] For considerations of the issues of group work in strategy making see chapter C3 of Eden and Ackermann (1998).

[28] Bryson (1995) and Bryson and Roering (1988) discuss the significance of the role of a sponsor in public sector strategy making; also see chapter P9 in Eden and Ackermann (1998).

[29] An interesting article by Andersen and Richardson (1997) who argue for five roles. For other material recommended on facilitation see: Bostrom et al. (1993), Schwarz (1994) and Ackermann (1996) in relation to computer-supported groups.

Task 1 Getting Started

a   Decide for which organization the strategy is to be developed:

■   With a realistic view of where you can intervene: define the boundary of your organization (department, group, division, operating company, etc.).

Task 1 Getting Started

a Decide for which organization the strategy is to be developed:

■ With a realistic view of where you can intervene: define the boundary of your organization (department, group, division, operating company, etc.).

b **Choose a client and five key power brokers in that organization who will form the strategy-making team:**

■ **It is likely that you will count yourself among this group, indeed you may also be the client.**
■ **Try to keep to five members, however, up to seven (including yourself) is reasonable.**

3   Getting at Beliefs About Possible Strategic Futures: Using Cognitive Mapping to Capture Interview Material

Introduction

In chapter 2 you were asked to envisage the role of a consultant/facilitator, working on behalf of a client, a person rather than an organization, whose needs and constraints you need to understand clearly. Your task was to begin creating a strategy-making group through which you and the client can develop strategy and begin to drive it forward. In this process, you will have confronted the classic realities of group dynamics, and it is vital to develop an understanding of how these dynamics manifest themselves.

In the nature of things, the strategy-making group will not start out as a unified, disciplined and committed team. Some members are likely to be hesitant, others cynical or even deliberately obstructive, anticipating that nothing will come out of the work, or that their personal interests may be harmed. The reason for recruiting certain people to the group may indeed be to win them over through their participation. Turning the group into an effective body may, therefore, make considerable demands on your leadership and facilitation.

This chapter takes us into the detail of building a strategy. The cognitive mapping technique is one route to beginning the process of uncovering what the group's emergent strategy is – though not the only or even the most appropriate one, as chapter 4 will show. It is important to note that while this chapter introduces cognitive mapping, based on theories of cognition, cognitive mapping is used as a small part of a group process approach to strategy making. This use does not imply that the whole approach is founded on what is usually referred to as the **cognitive school**[1] of strategic management.

This chapter does not involve the execution of tasks. Cognitive mapping is introduced because it can be the most effective method of surfacing the real strategic issues that the organization will expect to address,[2] and so it is usually the best way of detecting the emergent strategy of the organization.[3] However, it is inevitably more time consuming than starting with a group workshop.

Cognitive mapping, which resembles the well-known mind mapping technique for making notes developed by Tony Buzan,[4] is a supple and powerful tool for analyzing the ideas, concerns, values, hopes and fears of your colleagues.[5] To master it, you will need practice. Compared with typical linear approaches, cognitive mapping links ideas and issues together in a logical and dynamic way, in a structure resembling a spider's web. Thus it has the major advantage of generating a relatively simple visual representation of the interrelationships of the statements. For analyzing interviews, this is a more realistic approach than the linear one, since people's ideas seldom emerge in a logical progression (and indeed are often complex and interrelated), particularly in the kind of open-ended interviews and workshops that we recommend for this stage of strategy making. In this chapter you will find several practice exercises (with further exercises and a live interview noted on the CD available), and, of course, real-world opportunities for practice are innumerable, as the technique can be used to analyze almost any spoken or printed text.

Strategy-making Outcomes

■ Create a cognitive map for each member of your strategy-making group.
■ Surface issues and aspirations from the individuals that have an impact on the strategic future of the organization.
■ Merge individual cognitive maps to form a group **strategy map** which is the starting point for developing the strategy model for the organization.
■ Gain access to the knowledge and wisdom of the individuals in the strategy-making group about the strategy setting of the organization.
■ Create a curiosity about what others have said which lays the foundation for a future workshop that addresses the group strategy map.

The Role of Cognitive Mapping for Issue Surfacing and Structuring

People, not systems, deliver strategy. The way each person thinks about problems and strategic issues (their cognition) will influence how they act to create a strategic future for an organization. Their thinking and acting will, alongside the systems, structures and reward systems embedded within the organization, deliver the future. In making strategy it is, therefore, important to change thinking and acting as well as systems and structures.[6]

Cognitive mapping is a technique designed to capture the person's values and embedded wisdom in a diagrammatic format.[7] Based on a well-established body of psychology theory,[8] it is designed to capture the rich thinking about strategic issues – their causes and consequences – of each key person within an organization. It seeks to map out how each person 'makes sense of their organizational world'.

With linear notes, statements are jotted down without consideration of their ramifications, multiple interrelationships and implications for other statements.

This 'disconnectedness' makes it difficult for the interviewer, the interviewee and any other third party to gain a clear understanding of the full nature of a discussion at a later date. With cognitive mapping, however, statements are not only captured but are linked together using arrows that represent a cause and effect relationship.

These arrows show implied possible actions and possible outcomes. Moving up the arrow, means 'may lead to', 'has implications for', 'influences', 'causes' or 'supports'. Arrows may be negative (indicated by a minus sign on the right hand side of the arrowhead). Here, the meaning of the arrow is inverted and so moving up the arrow means 'may lead to [not]'. Statements can therefore have multiple consequences (**laddering up** arrows) or multiple explanations (**laddering down** arrows).

Mapping demands from the interviewer a fuller and better understanding of the issues (as seen by the person who is being mapped) because meaning is given to a statement not only by its content, but also from the causal relationships surrounding it.[9] We need to be less concerned by dictionary definitions for understanding a statement, and more concerned with the action implications: what would need to be done or to happen for the statement to occur (arrows in), and what would happen if it did occur (arrows out)? Consequently, capturing information this way allows us to make better sense of large amounts of complex information that are regarded as relevant by the interviewee. The resulting map should be seen by the interviewee as a good representation of how they wish you to understand *their* world. The example in Figure 3.1 shows how a bullet point list when converted to a map gives greater clarity to the action implications and so provides the fuller meaning of the statements.

A cognitive map will never be totally accurate – a person's thinking is continually changing (in part because of the interview and mapping process), and people are never completely open to an interviewer. Nevertheless, mapping

The following notes were taken from an interview with the managing director of a theatre lighting company:

- Schools have drama classes and clubs
- Schools hire their halls to drama clubs
- Shows are held regularly in schools
- Schools are a potentially profitable niche market
- Demonstrate how the quality of shows can be enhanced by quality lighting
- Increase our share of the schools market
- Increase the number of installations
- Increase sales of consumables
- Increase the number of equipment hires

Compare this to the map of the same interview. The map adds a great deal of clarity by adding context to the content, thereby enhancing our understanding of the discussion.

Figure 3.1 Using a Map to Attain Greater Clarity of Meaning

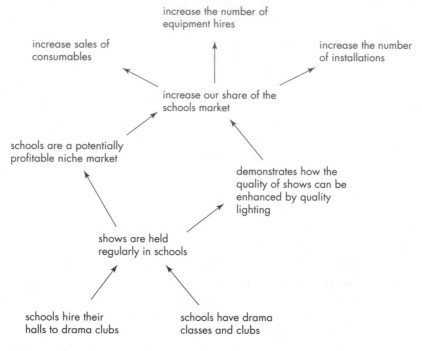

Figure 3.1 continued

usually manages to capture significant aspects of the way a person thinks. The cognitive map captures, in a mostly hierarchical format, how a person explains why they see things in a particular way, and why situations (strategic issues) might matter for the strategic future of the organization (eliciting goals, objectives, values).

Mapping is usually undertaken by a facilitator and is normally based upon an interview, although it could be based on an analysis of personal documents or reports.[10]

Why Use Individual Interviews?

There are three situations in which individual interviews are effective. First, where the culture of the organization is not one of openness or where interpersonal or internal issues prevail. In these circumstances, the underlying tensions may result in various issues not being aired in a group situation. Second, where the culture of the organization is such that people are not familiar or comfortable with participative methods and are not used to being consulted. In these circumstances, the participants may find the group process a bit unnerving. Finally, where a deep and rich understanding of the issues (as perceived by the participants) is required.

Equally, there are situations in which the oval mapping technique (OMT), which is discussed in chapter 4, is more effective. You may consider initiating the intervention using OMT in circumstances where the culture of the organization is such that people are comfortable with group working. OMT is also useful when there is a need to obtain faster results, capturing a large number and range of alternative views from a group, albeit in less detail than would be obtained from interviews. OMT also allows for team building, individual learning and a holistic view to be gained. In any event, group workshops using OMT are likely to occur even if the overall process is started with individual interviews.

Individual interviews have a number of advantages over OMT, including:

■ The relative anonymity encourages participants to discuss important issues more openly than can be the case in a group where participants may want to avoid 'rocking the boat' and may fear reprisals from more senior participants. This assumes that the interviewee believes assertions about the confidentiality of individual maps!

■ In group situations participants are always influenced in some way by peer pressure. There is, therefore, more chance of getting a personal perspective in interviews, albeit influenced by the politics of the strategy making.

■ Interviews help to avoid **social loafing**[11] where views are expressed by some in a group while one or more participants remain silent. Although silence can be interpreted as an implied form of consent, it is not always the case and there is the risk of missing valuable contributions.

■ Interviews help to avoid what is called **group think**.[12] This occurs when members of the group believe that their view is 'out of step' with the rest of the group, and they feel they may be subject to ridicule for expressing an alternative view (it is possible that everyone in the group feels this way). Members may have 'trading agreements' with others in the group which would be broken if they opposed the views of their trading partners; to do so would have consequences for support on other issues. To dissent from the view of the group may risk team cohesiveness – the camaraderie of being a team.

■ It may be easier to 'buy' the 1 to 1.5 hours required for an interview than to persuade a senior person to give up a day or even half a day from their diary for a group workshop. In addition, the group workshop may then follow more easily because of the curiosity raised about what all of the other participants will have said in their interviews.

■ Interviews allow the individuals involved to have much more 'air time' than they would have in a group situation where less socially skilled participants may be inhibited from contributing.

■ Interviews give the participants the opportunity to think the issues through more thoroughly.

■ Good interviews are usually rewarding experiences for the interviewee. These rewards derive mostly from the flattery that comes from 'being on the stage' – someone listening carefully to what is being said is an unusual occurrence for many people – and from the value which mapping gives to an understanding of what the person is saying.

■ Interviews are a relatively less risky starting point, as it is often easier to work on a one-to-one basis rather than in a group setting.

The disadvantages of using interviews include:

■ Interviews can be very time consuming for the facilitator, with each interview requiring 1 to 1.5 hours, a further 1 to 2 hours to make sense of the interview and then the attempt to finalize the map after all the interviews.

■ The time taken up by the interview process can be a drawback if the management team wants to make progress quickly. In these circumstances, a group workshop using OMT may yield faster results at the expense of less detail. (It is possible for two experienced facilitators to undertake 4 interviews each per day, and so complete the interviews for a 'large' workshop of 16 people in 2 days).[13]

■ Unless the interviewee is to be involved in subsequent group workshops, they will not see any of the alternative perspectives of the other participants. This will inhibit knowledge transfer and may also have a negative impact on 'procedural justice'.[14]

Do the exercise in Figure 3.2.

1   Think about a meeting or meetings in which you have been involved and consider how your contribution and the contribution of the others present were inhibited or enhanced by the following factors:

■ The people who were present – those more senior to you, those more junior to you, your friends, and your peers.
■ The way in which the meeting was directed by the chairperson (e.g. the topics discussed, the control of interruptions, the time that people were given to speak, the people who were allowed to take up most of the discussion time, etc.).
■ Any other factors that you consider to be relevant.

2   From what you have learned about cognitive mapping thus far, consider how your contribution might have changed if an independent facilitator had interviewed you on a one-to-one basis.
3 ˙ Consider the effect that interviewing each person individually might have had on the outcome of the discussion.

Figure 3.2 Exercise

Some Guidelines to Cognitive Mapping[15]

When capturing material for a cognitive map during an interview, you should try to:

- Separate sentences into distinct phrases. Where two or more possible options are implied, ensure that the statement is split up. For example, separate statements such as 'increase and improve services', as options for increasing services, might not necessary improve them. As a rule of thumb, six to eight words for each statement on the map seems to work well.
- Write each statement as a rectangular block of text rather than as a single line – this enables the chains of argumentation to be seen easily.
- Avoid 'should', 'ought', 'need', etc. and make each statement into a proposition. For example, 'we ought to hire more sales people' becomes 'hire more sales people'.
- If there is likely to be ambiguity then consider including 'who', 'what', 'where' and 'when' in the statement (although this requirement can make the statement too long).
- Without doing violence to what was said, add an action orientation to the phrase by using a verb where relevant but be careful to retain the interviewee's own language (or intended language).
- Build up a hierarchy by identifying which, in the interviewee's opinion, is the option and which is the desired outcome (see Figure 3.3). It is important to record what the interviewee means, or wished they'd said, rather than what they say, so, if in doubt, ask.
- When a statement includes several considerations, as for example: 'postponing the reorganization of production, employing a new production

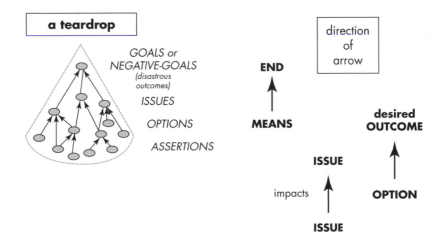

Figure 3.3 The Hierarchy of Maps

manager and promoting a line supervisor', then it is important to decide whether the statement should become several nodes. Ask whether:

- Each has different consequences.
- Each has the same importance.
- Each might involve different types of actions/explanations in order to create the outcome.

- Thus, in the example:

  - Employing a new production manager may be more important than postponing the reorganization of production or promoting a line supervisor, in which case the statement should be separated into two parts.
  - Postponing the reorganization of production may have different consequences because it involves other colleagues, in which case it should be separated.

- Watch out for desired outcomes (goals) and strategic issues that are important to the interviewee and mark them in some way (using an asterisk, for example). Changes in non-verbal behaviour, such as voice levels and intonation, will usually give an indication. Often such statements are made several times for emphasis.
- Consider introducing **trigger** issues that have been identified in previous interviews or by your client. This ensures that everyone gets an opportunity to respond to emerging themes, but does tend to give an advantage to those involved in early interviews. In addition, the use of triggers can help to simplify the process of merging individual maps to form one group map (see support 1) since there will be clear overlaps in the subject matter.
- Take care when dealing with assertions:

  - We presume that when someone makes an assertion they have a reason to do so, and that it is intended to suggest an implied action is required.
  - Thus, if someone states that 'Glasgow has a population of over 500,000 people' then we ask why this assertion is being made – what is its meaning?
  - For example, they might know that it was 600,000 last year and so the statement 'obviously' implies that the 'council will be short of taxes next year', which also is stated as a 'fact' with implied consequences.
  - Thus, assertions tend to be at 'the bottom' of a map, with consequences following from them.

■ Watch for instances of feedback – where arrows can form a loop.

   ■ These may appear as 'double headed' arrows. Where possible it is worth 'unpacking' these by asking how does A→B and vice versa (the → can be read as A may lead to B). This either confirms (or not) the validity of the feedback loop and provides further intervention points.

   ■ They can be 'controlling' (negative) or self-sustaining vicious or virtuous circles (positive).[16]

   ■ Often they are the result of poor coding about the direction of arrows, rather than representing true feedback (see the following example in figure 3.4).

   ■ When 'true' feedback loops are discovered they are usually very significant, because they can dominate the nature of the map. For example, a vicious circle can mean that almost any other actions (outside the loop) have only short term impacts.

■ Review the material that has been captured with the interviewee on a regular basis. Make use of natural breaks during the interview to gain confirmation of the emerging map by playing the material back. For example, you might say, 'If I understand you correctly . . .', and then provide a replay from the map you have constructed.

■ When linking constructs, if you are unsure as to the direction of the arrow, in other words, if you are not sure which statement is the option and which is the outcome, ask the interviewee for help. They will often welcome the opportunity to think through what they meant. Sometimes, you may judge that it is better to let the interview continue and put in a simple link without an arrowhead in order to indicate a potential link and revisit the question of its direction later.

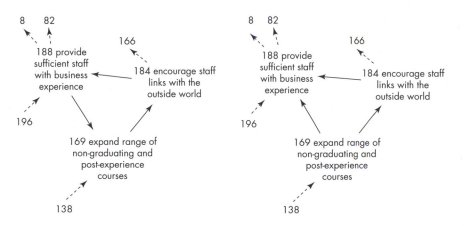

Figure 3.4 Three Statements Coded as Either a Loop or as a Hierarchy, Depending on the View of the Interviewee About the Link between 169 and 188 (dashed arrows show that links to other statements exist)

Frequent review has a number of advantages, including:

■ Enabling you to validate the information that you have captured, thereby ensuring that the links between concepts are correct.
■ Demonstrating that you have been listening carefully to what has been said. This, in itself, can be very valuable since this may be the first time that the participant feels their views have been truly listened to.
■ Giving the opportunity to clarify the meaning of what has been said and to elicit further material from the participant by stimulating their thinking.
■ Providing the means for 'catching up' as you are able to write down material still in your head but not yet on the map.

If possible, try feeding back with some 'added value' such as, 'so and so seems to be particularly central to your thinking', 'the following issues seem to be emerging as important and these . . . seem to be well linked, whereas . . . is out on its own'. Do not worry about getting the feedback wrong, the interviewee will usually be impressed with your listening and understand why you might have formed your views, and then go on to elaborate and correct.

Tidy up your map by looking for orphans – isolated ideas with no inward or outward links. Also examine end points (heads and tails). A *head*, which has no arrows out and so no stated consequences, should sound like a *goal* or *negative goal* – something the interviewee would be clear about aiming for or avoiding (see chapter 5 and support 1). When heads do not seem like goals or negative goals, invite the interviewee to elaborate on the consequences of the statement (laddering up). Similarly *tails* can be elaborated by inviting further explanations or 'beliefs' about why the situations may come about, have come about, or what options might change the situations (laddering down).

Figure 3.5 shows how laddering up and down helped expand the map shown in Figure 3.1.

Once you think you have a reasonably good understanding of what you think are goals and negative goals, then consider feeding back this part of the map. Starting with goals at the top (with no outward links) and gradually working down the goals, presents a hierarchy of means-ends. If your writing is not completely illegible to others then it can be useful to share your map with the interviewee – often the interviewee is curious about the unusual form of note taking, so capitalize upon this. If this is done then you will probably need to declare your 'peculiar note taking' and why you find it helpful. Surprisingly, but understandably, the interviewee is rarely disturbed by a 'mess of a map', providing it does reflect what the interviewee meant.

'You suggested that demonstrating how the quality of shows can be improved by the use of quality lighting would help you to gain access to niche markets. How might you demonstrate this?' (Laddering down)

'We could hold a series of open days for local schools, colleges and drama clubs.'

'Why else might that be useful?' (Laddering up)

'It would help to educate people as to what equipment is available, what they may need and how they might use it. It would also show how the proper use of lighting can enhance the appearance of a stage show.'

'How might that help the company?' (Laddering up)

'Open days will increase our "visibility" in the marketplace, which should help us to get a foot in the door and will help to increase sales in all areas.'

'That's very interesting, are there any other ways in which the value of professional lighting might be demonstrated?' (Laddering down)

'We could include "before and after" type photographs in our brochure or we could put a video or CD ROM together which shows each of the lights in action.'

Exercise

1 Add the content of the above discussion to the map shown in Figure 3.1.
2 Consider what other questions you may ask in order to elaborate on some of the outcomes of the discussion shown above.
3 Consider what other questions you may ask in order to get at some of the actions that the company may take in order to achieve these desired outcomes.

Figure 3.5 An Example of Laddering Up and Laddering Down

(following from the map developed in Figure 3.1)

Practising Cognitive Mapping

Mapping in an interview requires substantial effort since you must listen intently and capture not only what is being said, but also how the statements relate to one another. However, the demands of mapping do mean that we listen carefully and really understand what is being said. It is, therefore, useful to practise your mapping skills in low risk environments before using them in a 'live' situation. This will not only enable you to capture more of what is being said but it will also increase your confidence, which will be picked up by the interviewees, thereby making them more comfortable with the process.

To begin with, try mapping without arrow links as this will help you to become accustomed to breaking up what is being said into statements scattered around the notepad as rectangular blocks of text and linking them roughly with lines. Positioning related statements close to each other is helpful. Next, try to add an action orientation to the statements. Finally, practise mapping with arrows working on getting the causality right.

Mapping a piece of written text (such as a company report or a newspaper article) will help to improve your understanding of causal relationships and will allow you to practise extracting individual statements from blocks of text. It may also provide an amusing insight into how the author has written the article – you will often find that there are many 'holes' in the chains of argumentation.[17] Recording the text and playing it back can help to develop your listening skills. Mapping television or radio programmes such as news broadcasts will add some time pressures, and also try mapping the interview that is on the CD (there is a mode of operating the CD for practising interviewing).

Once you feel that you have gained confidence in your ability to listen and map, you should move on to practising your interviewing skills. Again, it is important to practise in a safe environment so you may consider interviewing a friend, colleague or relative. Explaining what you are doing and why and allowing them to choose the subject matter for discussion may help them to feel more comfortable and may also lead to a more in-depth discussion.

Working within your own organization can help with this process since you will tend to have a better understanding of the issues and will, therefore, be better able to understand the causal relationships. However, the downside is that it becomes easy for you to impose your own views on the map rather than those of the interviewee. When we have trained consultants in mapping we have found that often the consultant will construct a map that does not 'connect' with the interviewee. In these circumstances it is usual to find that the map does not reflect the views of the interviewee, but rather those of the consultant.

Based on experience, the following practical hints can facilitate the process:

■ Consider using A3 sheets of blank paper. This will help ensure that you are able to get the entire map on one sheet of paper. Artist's pads work well as they provide a solid base upon which to rest the paper.
■ Try working in landscape rather than portrait format. This is because maps are usually teardrop shaped (see Figure 3.3).
■ Use mechanical or propelling pencils as using pencil will allow you to make changes easily during the mapping process and having a mechanical pencil will ensure that the tip stays sharp.

Try the exercises outlined in Figure 3.6a, and try creating a map from the text in Figure 3.6b. This exercise will be more difficult than if you were listening to the person speaking, as intonation helps in determining the links in the map.

1   Consider an issue that is currently important to you and spend 15 minutes creating a map of your thoughts surrounding that issue, then reflect upon the process and how it differed from how you would otherwise have thought about the issue.

2   Map some stories from TV or radio news programmes and then reflect upon how it felt and what might be different in a live interview. Consider questions which you would have asked had it been a live interview.

3   Spend 15 minutes interviewing a friend or colleague on a subject which has some relevance to them or their business and then feed the results back to them. How did they feel about the process? Did they feel that you listened to them? Did the process enhance their thinking about the issue?

Figure 3.6a Exercises in Mapping

Create a map of the following text:

To influence the attitude and policy of others to care for the natural heritage, SNH (Scottish Natural Heritage) could well be advised to use those protected areas owned by SNH as demonstrators for good care of the natural heritage. To meet this need and to secure practical management of the natural heritage (another of SNH's goals) SNH must develop and deliver a strategy for protected areas. Various ideas such as gaining a general awareness of global resource depletion, SNH addressing sustainability (they are currently the only organization doing so), and using their knowledge of how the natural heritage is changing with time, may go some way towards achieving a strategy for protected areas. Management of the marine environment, and of those species which cause conflict, for example deer and seals, may go some way towards balancing maintaining natural heritage features whilst addressing increasingly complex environmental problems, which adds to the knowledge of the natural environment.

The answer is shown in Figure 3.10.

Figure 3.6b An Exercise in Mapping Text

Designing the Interview Process

Understand Your Client's Needs

It is important to meet with your client in order to gain a clear understanding of what they expect to obtain from the intervention and if there are any particular issues that should be explored. They may, for example, want to uncover the aspirations that individuals have for the business and for themselves within the business. They may also want you to elicit ideas on how these goals may be achieved and, as we discussed above, identify strategic issues that each person believes need to be addressed, and why.

It is equally important to gain some understanding of what issues, if any, the client would prefer *not* to have discussed. In these circumstances, you should advise your client that while you will endeavour to circumvent certain subject matter, it is not always possible since overtly avoiding issues may have a detrimental effect on the perceived value of the process to the participants. It may, therefore, have a negative impact on both **procedural justice** and **procedural rationality**.[18]

Finally, issues of confidentiality will need to be discussed with the client. Interviews work best when the interviewee trusts that you will keep each individual map confidential and, after merging of maps, will keep the identity of those making particular statements confidential. You should, therefore, make it clear that you will not divulge the identity of the person who makes any particular statement.

Figure 3.7 illustrates a part of a discussion about the interviewing process to be undertaken in a small company.

When asked what he wanted from the intervention, the managing director of the theatre lighting company said: 'We have found ourselves in the situation where our market is being eroded by an increase in competition in the market which we once dominated. We have been slow to react to the threats posed by new competitors and we find ourselves in a situation where profits are falling and we are struggling to find work that we were once obtaining without even trying. It is important that we get some direction for the business and start to regain our market share. I want to involve all of my management team and my key staff in this process, both because I want them to feel that they have a part to play in the future of the company and because they each have unique knowledge and ideas that I would like to capture. I would like to gain some understanding of where they would like to see the business in three to five year's time. I would also like to gain some understanding of what they see as our strengths and weaknesses and also where they see opportunities for us in the marketplace.

From this discussion, we may open the interview with the following statement: 'I have been asked to discuss with you the ways in which you believe that the business ought to develop over the next few years. I am keen to learn about the ways in which you think that this may be achieved and what may get in the way'.

Figure 3.7 Example of a Discussion Prior to Interviewing

Formulating the Topic for Discussion

Each interview should be based on a common starting theme in order to ensure that all of the participants are working on the same subject matter, albeit with different perspectives. This is achieved by asking the interviewee to consider a specific topic. The wording of this topic is very important since it sets the scene for the whole interview. You may find the following guidelines useful when formulating the topic:

■ Ensure that you have a clear understanding of what your client wants to obtain from the process.

■ Word the topic in such a way that it sets the focus and, if relevant, any boundaries for the discussion and yet does not unnecessarily constrain the interviewee.

■ The topic should be future orientated and should spark the interviewee's imagination.

■ Check the wording with your client to ensure that they are happy with it.

Scheduling Interviews

Senior participants will tend to have a more visionary and/or holistic view of the organization, often covering a wider range of issues. They will also usually have more power to act on the results of the intervention. The interviews may, therefore, be scheduled to take account of political weighting, with the most powerful people (**key actors**) within the organization being interviewed first. This will enable you to feed some of the key issues (**triggers**) raised by the strategy-making group into the subsequent interviews, which will help to ensure that the final group model will, to some extent, at least address their thoughts. This is deliberately manipulative but it reflects the different power bases of the participants and may enhance the chances of the resulting strategies being implemented successfully (**political feasibility**).

Remember, there were two reasons for including people in the strategy-making group (chapter 2) and in the interview round: they are key actors who will have a major impact on the political feasibility of strategy; they have expertise that will make an important contribution to strategic thinking within the strategy-making group.

Preparation

As with any intervention, good preparation is an important element in the success of the process. Individual interviews are no different and adhering to the following guidelines will help to ensure that the interviews run smoothly.

■ It is important that you should be able to read the material captured during the interview. You should, therefore, take care not to cram the statements on to the paper and should write as legibly as possible. A self-propelling pencil with a built-in eraser is ideal for this purpose.

■ The size of paper used can also be important and will generally be influenced by the size and legibility of your writing. Some facilitators prefer to use A4 paper while others will use A3. Blank paper is best as this is a graphical mode of capturing material.

■ If possible, you should arrange the chairs so that you are sitting at a 90-degree angle to the interviewee (as shown in Figure 3.8). This will not only help to build a degree of mutual confidence, it will also ensure that the interviewee will be able to see what you are writing thereby enabling validation and joint exploration. Having the interviewee and interviewer sitting opposite each other can result in a 'competitive' dialogue, which is not conducive to the development of an open discussion, and interviewer and interviewee next to each other reduces eye-to-eye contact (which tends to be unhelpfully reduced as a result of note-taking anyway).

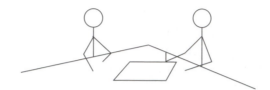

Figure 3.8 Representation of the Preferred Seating Positions Used During the Interviews

■ Holding the interviews in a relatively neutral location may help – a conference room or a meeting room away from the interviewee's office. This helps to reduce the possibility of interruption and, perhaps more importantly, to move the participants out of their own environment, or 'comfort zone'. Using a neutral location also aids facilitation since you can set up the room in advance, making it as 'user friendly' as possible.

■ Schedule first interviews to last between 1 and 1.5 hours with a minimum of a half an hour break between each to allow you to collect your thoughts and make additions/corrections to your map while the interview is fresh in your mind.

■ Participants should formally be invited to take part in the interview, by way of a memo or a note from the client. The memo should set out the reasons for the interview (or discussion) and should make it clear that each discussion will remain confidential. It should also confirm the time and location of the interview in order to avoid any confusion. A brief outline of the next steps, explaining how the information will be used, can also be useful.

Try the exercise in designing an interview programme outlined in Figure 3.9.

Design a series of interviews with six people from an organization with which you are familiar. Your design should include:

- A summary of the anticipated outcomes of the intervention as requested by your client, along with any subjects which should be avoided.
- The statement (or theme) that you will use to open each interview.
- Pen portraits of each of the participants (based on the discussions that led to choosing the strategy-making group – chapter 2).
- Identification of any 'problem' interviewees and any 'special measures' that you would intend to take for each.
- A schedule of interviews, including dates, times and locations. Remember to build time into the schedule for tidying up and reviewing the maps.
- A note that can be used by your client to invite the participants to come along to the interview.

Figure 3.9 Exercise in Designing an Interview Programme

During the Interview

Opening the Interview

When opening the interview, it is useful to give the interviewee a brief introduction to the whole process, setting out what you hope to achieve and how their contribution will be used to inform the strategy-making process. It is also worth reassuring the participants that the information generated from your discussion will be kept confidential. A good introduction will help to set the interviewee's mind at rest and will increase the chances of capturing more of the relevant material.

Watch for Non-verbal Signals

Non-verbal communication amounts to about two-thirds of all communication and so you should be alert to the non-verbal signals exhibited by the interviewee.

A negative attitude towards the interview may be indicative of a number of problems which might exist within the organization. You may, therefore, consider using the interview to uncover the nature of these problems.

As an interviewer, you may find some of the interviewee's non-verbal behaviours frustrating and you must work hard to avoid this having a negative impact on your performance.

Managing the Interview

The interviewee will, quite naturally, be inclined to start the interview by discussing topics that are at the forefront of their mind. Also, as the interview settles down the interviewee might take time to 'set the scene' for what they are about to say. It is usually important to map this background material even though it does not seem central to your task. The way background and context are introduced often provides an explanation to statements made later that are more important, and so the context may provide strategic options.

Interviewees often arrive with some preconceived ideas of what they are going to discuss and have done some preparatory work in advance of the interview. You should, therefore, consider whether you might obtain better results if the participants are given information that will allow them to think about relevant issues before the discussion. This will give them time to think about the issues and may, therefore, yield a greater depth and quality of information.

A delicate balance is required here since too much preparation may stifle the spontaneity of the process and may not allow you to uncover unscripted thoughts and ideas. It may also restrict the flow of the conversation, with the interviewee following a predetermined thought pattern. However, asking for elaboration as the map develops often takes the interviewee away from their set script, and allows more of their cognition to emerge.

It is common for interviewees to stay within their areas of expertise and to resist attempts to persuade them to discuss more general business or organizational issues. There are two reasons for this. First, they may not fully trust that confidentiality will be adhered to. This problem may be intensified if you are working within your own organization since you may, rightly or wrongly, be seen to have a conflict of interest in some of the issues being discussed. Second, the interviewee's knowledge will be bounded by their own experience so they may simply lack knowledge about the business in general and may, therefore, not be confident enough to discuss wider issues for fear of exposing their weaknesses. However, in some circumstances interviewees use the opportunity to comment on everything but their own area of expertise. They use the interview as a cathartic process which takes advantage of confidentiality.

In the first case the data from an interview tend to be narrower in scope but much richer than would be the case with data generated from a group workshop. The restricted scope is not necessarily a problem because breadth is created when the individual maps are merged to form a group map (see support 1). This essentially allows you to get the best of both worlds and results in a well-articulated model, which can provide a strong foundation on which to build a robust strategy.

Remember that it is unusual for any manager to have been listened to carefully and be given enough air-time to make their points fully. This is a crucial advantage in using interviews over an OMT workshop and makes the resulting maps subtle and rich in content.

Uncovering Goals and Aspirations

As discussed above, and in chapter 4, it is important to try to uncover the goals/negative goals and aspirations of the participants. Interviewees are encouraged to start by surfacing issues that are of key concern to them. One way of eliciting the goals is to use the technique of laddering discussed above. Here, the interviewee is invited to elaborate on the issues that they raise by asking 'so what?' type questions, such as 'why is this an important issue?', 'what are the consequences of this issue occurring?', etc. This process may have to be repeated several times before goals are detected. These then can be further explored and developed as noted in chapter 5.

Another useful technique is what is known as the '**oracle question**',[19] where the interviewee is asked to consider what questions they would ask someone who is able to foretell the future. The answers to this question will reveal something about the key uncertainties that are important to the interviewee. From this information it becomes possible to understand something about the nature of their beliefs (the data requested from the oracle are believed to influence outcomes for the organization) and aspirations (the answer to the question can be assumed to matter and so facilitate laddering to goals).

In addition, be alert to the interviewee continually repeating an issue or statement as it may mean that it is very significant. When repetition is because the statement is important, then allowing the interviewee to explain it fully and visibly marking it as a key issue on the map will ensure the map shows a centrality which may not be detected using structural analysis only.

Closing the Interview

You should set aside about 10 per cent of the interview time to provide the interviewee with a sense of closure. This will allow you to:

■ Provide a 'value-added' summary of the interview map (as you see it). This will help to ensure that you have captured the material accurately and will reinforce the fact that you have listened to what the interviewee has said.

■ Explain the next steps in the process. For example, whether a workshop will follow, what will happen to the cognitive map next and whether or not there will be an opportunity for the map to be reviewed once it has been 'tidied' after the interview.

■ Thank them for their time and contribution, restate what will happen to the information and reaffirm that the discussion will be kept entirely confidential. In addition it is important to describe the process of merging maps together in such a way that individual statements cannot be identified.

After the Interviews

The design of the intervention will, to a large extent, determine what the next steps in the process will be. The following are, therefore, general guidelines as to what action might be taken after the interviews have been completed.

■ Provide the interviewee with a copy of their map soon after an interview. This not only provides them with a concrete record of the interview, but also shows the structured representation of their thinking. This map could be either neatly handwritten or produced using the Decision Explorer® software.

■ If second interviews are to be held then the map may be further developed by providing more in-depth data, encouraging elaboration of those areas not yet well covered, and checking the relationships between statements.

Next Steps

Although, when designing the intervention, you will have considered what the next steps will be, this may change once you have created the individual maps as you will be better informed about the emerging issues. You have a number of options, some of which are briefly discussed below and are examined more fully in chapter 8.

It is important to enable those who have been interviewed to start jointly to understand and reflect on each other's thinking and on the strategic issues believed to influence the strategic future of the organization. Consequently, an important next step is to merge the individual maps to form a group strategy map before conducting an analysis on the resulting group model (see support 1).

The most effective way to follow up a series of interviews is to hold a group workshop. There are two options for running a group workshop. One is to make use of OMT (see chapter 4) as a follow on from feedback from the merged map, for example by using OMT to confirm and expand the emerging goals system (see case studies 5.1 and 5.2). Alternatively, the second obvious option is to use the group map in a computer-supported workshop (using it as the introduction to a workshop similar to that described in case study 6.1).[20]

However, it may not always be possible to conduct group workshops. In these circumstances, it is possible to attempt closure of the strategy-making process by creating a draft strategy document or a statement of strategic intent that can be circulated to the people who were involved in the interview process (see chapter 7). It should be noted that this places a great deal of responsibility on the facilitator, who has to analyze the merged map in order to pull out key issues, goals and aspirations. It also requires that the client is prepared to place a significant amount of trust in the facilitator to draft such a document.

Whichever steps are taken, it should be noted that, when practical, follow-up of some sort to all interviewees should take place within a period of ten working days from the initial interview – a **psychological week** (from the start of one week to the end of the next). This will ensure that the participants are still engaged in the process.

The MBA Student Project Case Study (support 3) describes a strategy for management buy-out (MBO) and this discusses what it is like to use cognitive mapping in your own organization as an active part-time MBA scholar.

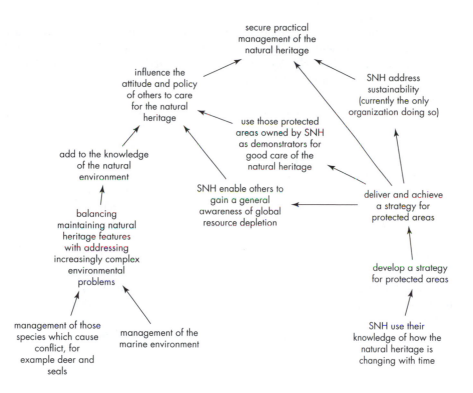

Figure 3.10 An Answer to the Mapping Exercise Shown in Figure 3.6b (note that without interaction with the interviewee there is doubt about some of the relationships)

Notes

[1] Mintzberg et al. (1998) devote chapter 6 (pp. 149–73) to a review of the cognitive school of thought in relation to strategy formation. While this is not directly relevant to the method that we propose, it does give some very useful background information which readers may find helpful.

2   Mintzberg et al. (1998): strategists 'develop their knowledge structures and thinking processes mainly through direct experience. That experience shapes what they know, which in turn shapes what they do, thereby shaping their subsequent experience'. This gives rise to two different views – one 'treats the processing and structuring of knowledge as an effort to produce some kind of objective motion picture of the world' while the other sees it as being subjecting and that 'strategy is some kind of inter-pretation of the world' (pp. 150–1).

3   Mintzberg et al. (1998): 'Managers are, of course, map makers as well as map users. How they create their cognitive maps is key to our understanding of strategy forma-tion. Indeed, in the most fundamental sense, this is strategy formation. A strategy is a concept, and so, to draw on an old term from cognitive psychology, strategy is "concept attainment"' (p. 162).

4   Tony Buzan (Buzan and Buzan, 1993) created a BBC series explaining his approach to mind mapping. See also *www.mind-map.com*.

5   Senge in De Wit and Meyer (1998) p. 137 discusses 'the leader as teacher' bringing to the surface people's mental models of important issues – here this process involves mapping these mental models. And Johnson (Johnson and Scholes (2002) p. 63) refers specifically to the 'cognitive maps' of managers.

6   Johnson and Scholes (2002) discuss these issues within the context of experience, bias and culture, in the sense of 'collective taken-for-granted assumptions' (see pp. 44–5).

7   See Eden and Ackermann (1998) p. 285. Here the authors discuss how maps allow the depiction not only of statements but also their relationships, enabling a more effective management of the particular issue under discussion.

8   In his Theory of Personal Constructs, Kelly (1955) considers how humans make sense of their world through examining a system of constructs accrued through experience, comparing and contrasting them with current situations so as to be able to act more effectively.

9   See Eden and Ackermann (1998) p. 95 for more detail on how the additional infor-mation yielded by incorporating contrast and context can add meaning to a statement.

10 Axelrod (1976) and colleagues used a form of cause mapping to analyze political documents. Eden and Ackermann (2003) used mapping of several documents for policy analysis.

11 'Social loafing' is a term used to describe a member of the group relying on the efforts of others rather than contributing fully themselves (see Williams et al., 1979).

12 'Group think' is a term introduced by Irving Janis (1972) reflecting the situation whereby social pressures exerted through, for example, wishing to remain part of an elite group, prevent critical material from being raised and discussed.

13 For an example of a 'fast' two-interviewer process see the NHS vignette in Eden and Ackermann (1998).

14 Procedural justice is concerned with fairness in organizational decision making – see Eden & Ackermann (1998) p. 53 for further discussion.

15 Bryson et al. (2004b) introduces causal mapping guidelines through a series of examples taken from personal problem solving in organizational settings.

16 Also referred to as 'cycles'.

17 The authors have been involved in a number of occasions where an organization has wanted to check the thoroughness of their argumentation when making a submission

to a commission of enquiry. Also mapping is used to develop careful and persuasive arguments in litigation, see Williams et al. (2003).

[18] Procedural rationality shows concern for a process to be explainable – see Eden & Ackermann (1998) p. 55 for further discussion.

[19] The oracle question was developed to be used in the interview procedure as a part of scenario planning – see Eden and Ackermann (1998) p. 92 and van der Heijden (1996).

[20] Computer-supported workshops are more fully described in chapter P3 of Eden and Ackermann (1998).

4   Surfacing and Structuring Strategic Issues in Groups

Introduction

Much of chapter 3 was devoted to reviewing an interview technique (mapping) that will ensure that a fair and thorough account of the individual's standpoint is obtained. Based on practices that are widely used by psychologists to establish the unique pattern of an individual's 'personal constructs', this technique is capable of great sensitivity and depth. In particular it can capture the relationships between a person's concerns (issues) and aspirations – as well as conflicts between them. As you saw in chapter 3, a skilled facilitator or interviewer soon learns how to probe issues, clarify the person's thinking and obtain confirmation that this analysis is correct. High on the list of gains you can make by practising these techniques is the ability to listen, take notes, clarify and engage in feedback. Thus the cognitive mapping technique itself may also be useful in many other areas.

Usually (particularly when first using mapping), it is a good idea to feed the individual maps back to the participants for comment and review (you can capture any material missed and check the accuracy of that depicted). Moreover, you will be able to construct a group composite map through merging the individual maps together (see support 1).

Interviewing as a starting point, however, is only one option – and a relatively time-consuming one – for developing a strategy. There are two other possibilities. The first is that it is also possible to carry out cognitive mapping on the basis of documents and reports about, and by, the person[1] (though in this case the ability to probe further and engage in a developing dialogue with the person is obviously lacking).

The second option is group mapping – where the map is built up in front of the group based on their contributions. This can be done either manually using what we refer to as the oval mapping technique (OMT)[2] or, through using computer support, namely the Decision Explorer® software.[3] Group mapping meetings or workshops have some initial similarities with more traditional brainstorming sessions – however, the use of mapping powerfully extends their function. In addition, group mapping workshops have advantages and disadvantages compared with individual interviews. In principle, group mapping utilizes group dynamics and creativity and can play a role in building a team,[4] whereas cognitive mapping in interviews deliberately subtracts the individuals from the group context, in order to allow the emergence of information that may be suppressed, influenced or contorted by group pressures.

You may find that interview-based mapping can be usefully followed up by a group mapping workshop, with the group map (or a selection of the issues elicited in the interviews) provided as a starting point. If, however, you do decide that starting with a workshop is the best option (due to time pressures, personal or organizational inclination, etc.) it is nevertheless important to have read and understood the individual mapping chapter first. This is because group mapping is based on the cognitive mapping technique (hence group **mapping**[5]) and knowing and understanding the rules of the technique are important.

This chapter will take you in detail through the process of running an issue surfacing workshop, right down to matters such as flipchart paper management and the use of pens. Do not underestimate these apparently trivial matters: such details can make or, more likely, break an otherwise useful working session. Like the capturing and structuring (linking) of the contributions, these planning and preparatory processes are things that you, as a consultant or facilitator, will need to practise. Over the years that we have been using mapping to support the strategy-making process we have increasingly found that getting the basics right can make a big difference.

The key issue with both forms of the group mapping (computer based or OMT) is to surface the issues, and subsequently create a structure by reviewing, structuring and clustering the material as it emerges from the participants. This may present practical difficulties 'on the day', particularly if the numbers of participants taking part are relatively large and very large numbers of contributions are generated. Time outside of the workshop may be needed to complete the map (along with help from participants if available). But the fact that running a successful workshop task is a challenge is by no means the whole story. As you will see towards the end of this chapter, facilitation can be extremely rewarding as participants benefit from the workshop meeting. The advantages of group mapping over brainstorming are considerable, because participants are able to crystallize useful outcomes as the workshop sessions progress. As group mapping is goal-oriented to a degree that brainstorming is not (as highlighted in case study 4.1 at the end of this chapter) it provides a powerful means of starting the strategy-making process.

Strategy-making Outcomes

Substantive Outcomes

■ Surface issues (both positive and negative) that reflect current and future potential managerial concerns. Through eliciting these you are dealing with the realities of managerial life.

■ Structure the resultant issues first in a hierarchical structure and subsequently through understanding how one issue might support, or be supported by, another (building the group map and thus further elaborating the structure). This will enable patterns to be detected through the resultant network revealing emergent properties.

■ Identify those issues that are central, busy or superordinate showing their relative importance and therefore providing a means of prioritizing them.

■ Provide a basis for developing the goals system and distinctive competences.

These outcomes relate to task 2 a–e.

Process Outcomes

In addition to the above strategy-making outcomes, there are a number of group-process outcomes. These are relevant not only for this task but also the subsequent tasks noted in chapter 5 (building the goals system), chapter 6 (determining distinctive competences and building a business model or livelihood scheme), chapter 1 (determining strategies) and chapter 8 (producing a statement of strategic intent).

■ Gain ownership of the strategic issues from the group, as members are involved in the process and therefore more committed to the outcomes. Using mapping not only allows material to be surfaced but does so in a way that is natural and transparent and therefore stimulates a more open dialogue, so participants can develop a shared understanding of the resultant outcomes.

■ Help build the team, as members appreciate the different concerns and opportunities each other faces, and begin to work together to resolve or capitalize upon them. The process is inherently social.

■ Stimulate cross-functional learning, as those in one part of the organization can see how strategic issues interact across the organization, how their work impacts on other's work and vice versa.[6]

The Role of Surfacing and Structuring Issues

Group mapping can be seen as similar to brainstorming and seeks to surface contributions from all those attending. However, group mapping used for strategy making has a number of important differences from brainstorming. To begin with the focus is on surfacing strategic issues and concerns – usually those activities or events that are potentially attacking or supporting organizational aspirations (see chapter 5) – rather than on creativity as an aim in its own right. The aim is to surface current wisdom and experience[7] rather than off-the-wall ideas.

Starting with issues enables managers to put on the table all the events, activities and concerns that they expect will demand their attention and time and will have an impact on the strategic future of the organization (the realities of organizational life). This not only gets at what is driving the organization – as these issues are the focus of managerial attention – but also allows managers to experience some relief as they bring them out into the open and can begin to explore and understand them (another important difference from brainstorming). Until these issues are openly presented and discussed, attention on the rest of the strategy-making processes will be clouded by their continual presence, as managers seek to find ways of making coherent links between their day-to-day concerns and the future. Realistic strategy making thus starts with issue surfacing (see figure 4.1).

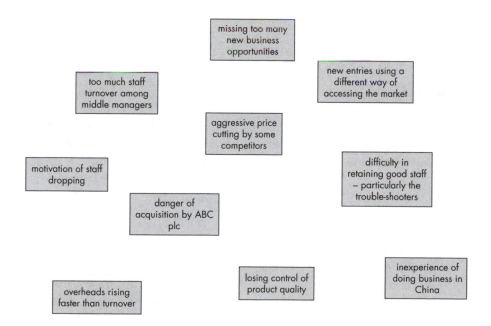

Figure 4.1 An Example of Some Strategic Issues (usually about 50–90 from a management team)

Group mapping encompasses the surfacing of assumptions, concerns, facts, assertions and constraints along with their relationships. This enables the material to be structured by reflecting causality (another key difference from traditional brainstorming). Structuring gives the meaning of each statement by setting it within a context: why it matters (consequences), and what needs to be done to change it (explanations). Instead of interpreting the statement by reference to a dictionary, meaning is determined by action and purpose. Encouraging participants to avoid arguing over the precision of the words and concentrating on the action context of a statement helps with the development of a shared understanding.[8] It provides some clarity in terms of next steps – answering the 'so what?' question (chapter 5). The process of detecting how issues impact upon one another is found by most mangers to be an activity that they can relate to easily – this is because we all use causality in order to make sense of our world. Group mapping thus aims to release deep knowledge and wisdom to get beyond the apparently similar descriptions of situations and into the subtle, but important, differences of what has to be done and why. The process raises alternative formulations and therefore opens up new options. See case study 4.1 at the end of this chapter for further illustration.

Go to task 2a and b

Identify the time horizon and begin to consider what are the issues that are currently facing your organization. Capture these either manually or electronically.

Commentary and Issues

■ Thinking about the relevant time horizon of the strategy-making exercise is necessary before surfacing issues. Where the organization is operating in a highly turbulent industry, for example telecommunications or IT, then a two to three year time horizon is probably as far into the future as can be seen sensibly. However, public sector bodies might wish to work with a three to five year time horizon.

■ Given the relatively short tenure for many senior managers there is a tension between the strategic planning horizon for their careers (one to three years) as compared to that of the organization (say, five to ten years). Indeed many CEOs do not expect to be in post for more than three to five years, and so will think strategically over that time period where their performance will be judged. In these circumstances it is important to be conscious of the tension and recognize that short term issues and strategy will be important and will need to be acknowledged within the context of a genuine, or espoused, concern for the longer term.

■ When capturing the issues surfaced it is possible to use either the Decision Explorer® software projected on to a public screen or oval Post-it® notes[9] displayed on a wall covered with flipchart paper. Both have their own advantages and disadvantages.

■ Manual techniques allow everyone to contribute directly, see the entire picture, and focus on the areas of interest to them when generating contributions. However, these are static representations and so cannot be easily edited or analyzed. Computers, on the other hand, provide search and analysis routines but due to screen size lose sight of the big picture and rely on a facilitator to capture the contributions[10] thus potentially altering what is generated.[11]

■ During the surfacing process, position the contributions to make sure that there is plenty of space between the different statements (regardless of whether a manual or electronic mode is being used). This is because participants tend to stop contributing material when they feel the space has been 'filled up'. Therefore it can be helpful to use either lots of flipchart paper if working manually (see below) or several different views when using the software.

■ Causal mapping places emphasis on the wording of contributions, so that an action orientation is sustained. Added value is gained when sufficient detail in the wording is provided to help participants understand what one another means by their contribution. This is encouraged by asking participants to follow a small number of 'rules' for contributions:

■ One action statement for each contribution.
■ Use around six to ten words per contribution.
■ Adopt a 'who, what, where, when' approach.
■ Avoid questions by turning them into propositions, for example, convert 'what is the size of the market' to a more action-oriented phrase such as 'investigate size of the market'.
■ Avoid 'should', 'ought', 'need to' by changing these statements into propositions. See examples in Figure 4.1.

■ As is often the case in meetings, time can be spent debating different possible meanings of particular statements. The issue surfacing process allows for this diversity by encouraging more than one meaning to be captured rather than, at this stage, expending time trying to resolve which is the 'right' one. The subtle differences may trigger further statements.

■ Participants usually start with a flurry of issues – raising those that are of immediate concern to them, which have usually been raised many times before. So, it is worth prompting for further issues to ensure the surfacing goes beyond 'obvious' and often repeated concerns. Getting participants to consider the issues already generated in the context of other parts of the organization and external environment often gives rise to further important material. When working with a team of 5 to 7 people, as suggested in chapter 2, it is usual to surface around 30 to 50 issues within the first 20 to 25 minutes of working.

Hints and Tips

Before Starting the Workshop

■ Get the **trivialities**[12] sorted out.

    ■ Get the room layout right. (See Figure 4.2 for an example of a room when working manually.) Having somewhere with lots of wall space is best (without wood panelling, textured wall paper or fixed furniture) if you are using the manual technique. Try to use at least 14 sheets (7×2 portrait). For those using computer support, a good quality projector (at least 1024×768 pixels, and at least 1100 lumens) will allow everyone to view the material being captured without the dangers of eyestrain and headaches.[13]

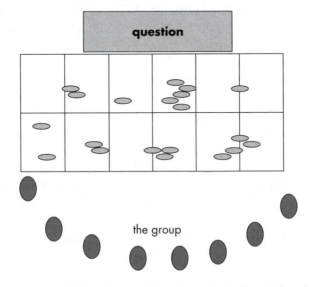

Figure 4.2 Room Layout When Undertaking Issue Surfacing Using the Manual Technique

■ Make sure you have all the equipment you need. The best flipchart pens are water based as these save on damage costs (as any marks can be cleaned off – particularly if the writing seeps through the paper on to the wall which occasionally happens with recycled paper). In addition, make sure you have a good stock of 'ovals' (minimum 30 for each person), or if getting hold of these proves problematic then use standard rectangular Post-it® notes (large size). Finally, if working manually ensure that participants' pens are all the same colour and nib size to increase anonymity. The best pens have a writing thickness that ensures no more than ten words can be written, and the words are, therefore, as large as possible.

Running the Issue Surfacing Workshop

■ Use the guidelines for cognitive mapping from chapter 3.
■ Make sure each member of the group offers at least four to five strategic issues.

   ■ If necessary, use a 'round robin' to ensure all those participating are able to contribute.
   ■ Ask participants to 'piggy back' off one another's views.
   ■ Avoid shutting down options and discouraging members – getting participants to think in terms of 'yes and' rather than 'yes but' can help.
   ■ Watch for group conformity – if all seem to be agreeing with one another and not surfacing issues beyond those that are relatively superficial, try throwing in some 'outsiders' view' issues that are designed to prompt responses (use some of the techniques noted in chapter 3, for example, the oracle question).
   ■ Prevent members from removing one another's contribution – even if they don't agree with it. Instead encourage the rationale behind the disagreement to be surfaced and captured.

■ Consider numbering contributions (when using the manual system, Decision Explorer® automatically allocates reference numbers) as it helps when linking the statements together (see later on in this chapter). To avoid duplication it often helps to note the last number used at the edge of one of the flipchart sheets.
■ Writing the statements in such a way that it is clear why the particular contribution is an issue will also help both when developing shared understanding regarding its content and also when later considering the goal ramifications of the issue (covered in chapter 5).

   ■ Often participants dump topics rather than issues, for example, 'HR', where there is no indication of what the issue about 'HR' is. This is noticed anyway because the contribution breaks the guideline about word length. This statement might become 'HR too slow in dealing with applications for jobs', or 'HR do not recruit the best staff', etc.

■ Include both internal and external issues and positive and negative issues. Don't worry too much if the group starts with lots of negative issues – this is typical and expected. Managers spend most of their time addressing problems and issues and rarely deal with opportunities. Encouraging participants to think of strategic opportunities may help surface positive issues.

Clustering and Structuring Issues as the Material is Gathered

Frequently when surfacing issues begins, those that are at the front of participants' consciousness emerge first. However, these are not necessarily the most significant issues (although they might feel so, at the time). Getting a better understanding of the relative importance or significance of the issues derives from understanding how these relate to each other.

From building up the network of issues, a clearer picture of the individuality of the organization's issues will also be revealed. Contrary to assertions in much of the strategic planning literature, organizations in the same industry do not face the same strategic issues. A unique set of issues based upon the history, skills and focus of the organization will be revealed. The focus of strategy making is to identify and exploit differences and distinctiveness.

Go to task 2c and d

Begin to position the issues into clusters and link them together to begin to form a network of issues.

Commentary and Issues

As noted above, clustering the issues (**chunking** into themes) in relation to their content can help start the structuring process and aid the group in managing the initial complexity of the material. These themes or clusters provide both a means of working with the full picture (through disaggregating it down into more manageable portions) and additional insights through the consideration of their content and thus 'label'. Deciding an appropriate heading for a cluster can often provide important clues to the nature of the cluster as well as prompting new material.

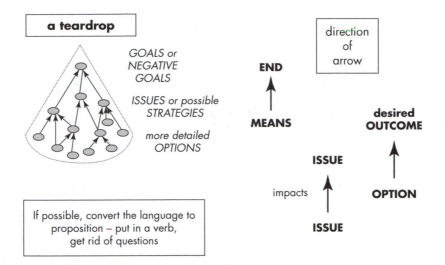

Figure 4.3 Getting the Hierarchy Right When Developing Cause Maps

However, be aware that these initial content clusters may prove to be misleading, as the linking process will mean that the final clusters will be based on an action rather than a content analysis. That is, it will be causality that will determine the ultimate clusters.

Structuring the material in relation to the hierarchy presented in Figure 4.3 also provides a means of making sense of the big picture and suggests the beginnings of causal clusters. Start by putting at the top those issues or concerns that are causally the most superordinate: representing final outcomes from the rest of the material in the cluster. A version of these statements can be seen as potential headings for clusters and will provide a useful starting point for later considering the goals and negative goals (see chapter 5).

As with cognitive mapping (chapter 3), beginning to understand how the different issues relate to one another will provide not only a means of managing the complexity and increasing a shared understanding, but will also trigger new thinking as different understandings are surfaced.

Linking the issues together enables the participants to begin considering how to manage each issue while recognizing implications for other issues – highlighting the point that these are not independent of each other. See Figure 4.4 for the beginnings of the linking process.

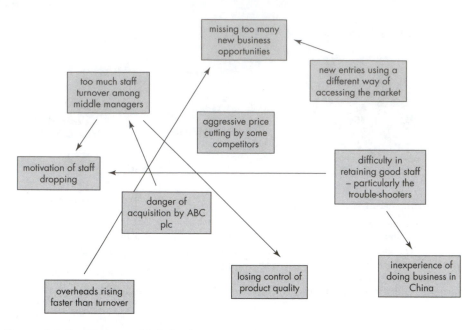

Figure 4.4 Beginning to Link the Issues

Hints and Tips

Clustering Material

■ Don't panic if you can't see any clusters forming as the material is gathered. At the beginning it usually takes a little time to see the patterns emerging. To help with this:

  ■ Be prepared to change the clusters if alternatives emerge. This might mean breaking down a big cluster into two or three subclusters.
  ■ If working in manual mode, ask participants to put the statements into clusters as best they can when they place them on the wall. However, this doesn't always work – it is often easier for them to simply put them anywhere on the wall! When working with the computer, try using different views.
  ■ Put those that don't seem to fit anywhere into a **query cluster**. These usually sort themselves out during the latter stage of the process.
  ■ Keep an open mind – don't get too fixed on early clusters.
  ■ Ask participants what they see as the emerging clusters rather than just relying on those you see – sometimes this surfaces new material as well as providing valuable help.
  ■ Don't get too concerned with the clusters being absolutely right – just try to get them into rough bundles of related material.

- Separate clusters into discrete bundles – with lots of white space (wall or screen) between them – this will help manage the potential cognitive overload experienced by participants. The more flipchart paper you have on the wall the easier this is – remember the earlier recommendation.
- Rearrange the statements so that the very broad-based outcomes are at the top of the cluster. Then place those more detailed options further down (but again don't worry about getting this absolutely right, when working through them the group will provide help).

- Clusters are generally teardrop shaped, as there are more detailed statements at the bottom of the cluster and less broad outcomes at the top. See Figure 4.3.
- A quick overview of the clusters or themes is a good way of giving participants a sense of what has surfaced (as it is helping them manage the complexity of surfacing a large amount of information).

Causality: Linking Contributions

- Ask participants how the different statements in a cluster relate to each other. This usually results in a range of different interpretations (showing how significant causality is in determining meaning!). For example, one participant might argue that statement A leads to statement B. To do this they add a chain of argument to defend their case. Ensure this extra material is captured and put up on the wall or screen with the links showing the line of argumentation. However, another participant might argue that statement A leads to statement D in another cluster – and to explain this they present their rationale. Capture this new material with the links. From this a shared understanding is developed and the map is elaborated both in terms of contributions and relationships.
- Watch for issue statements containing more than one phrase, each part with different causality. This makes linking difficult, as the relationship is only applicable to a section of the statement's text. Separate the two phrases and then explore the linking.
- Try to avoid double-headed arrows as these may mean that there is an implicit feedback loop (cycle) (see support 1), or alternatively a genuine difference of opinion about what is the means or option and what is the end or outcome. Try to get those proposing the links to elaborate how A might lead to B and vice versa. In fleshing out the relationships, a better understanding of all the information is gained. This might reveal that the implied feedback is not accurate. Alternatively where the feedback loop is legitimate, then fleshing out the relationships provides further possible action points.

■ Where issue statements contain phrases such as 'in order to', 'through', 'due to', 'to' then examine the statement to see if there are two statements embedded together. The above phrases can be interpreted as links between these two parts of the statement.

■ Watch for over-linking where redundant links mask the emergent patterns. It is very easy to add summary links. For example, the chain A→B→C→D which includes also A→C, B→D and A→D may have redundancy. Each link must express a different chain of causality. If it does not, then remove the links.

■ Always review the links with the group to check their validity. If you are working through cluster by cluster, don't worry if the first cluster takes a long time. Once participants get the hang of the process, the remaining clusters will go more quickly. It is usually a good idea to reassure participants that this is the case!

Reviewing the Emergent Structure

Often those issues that have energy spent upon their management are not the most significant to the organization's future (due to the issues being worked upon attacking the specific values or interests of a specific manager). However, once the issues have been linked together and a structure formed, new insights may emerge which highlight issues that are central to the overall structure or which encapsulate a range of issues (that is, one that is positioned at the head of a teardrop – see Figure 4.3). It is upon these insights that priorities can be identified.

Go to task 2e

Explore the emergent structure and determine priorities.

Hints and Tips

■ Compare content themes with the clusters that have emerged through the causal structuring process. Does this examination suggest any missing issues or links? Look for links across clusters.

■ Review the structure and see if there are any **islands** – issues that are not currently linked to any others. Where these exist explore whether with further material they could be incorporated into the network and if not, what this suggests for the organization. Are they, indeed, isolated issues that have no strategic impact elsewhere?

- Don't worry about the same issue being in more than one cluster – those that appear in a range of clusters are often more potent as they impact a number of strategic themes. For example, in Figure 4.5 the issue concerning the difficulties of retaining good staff appears in two clusters (China and motivation), whereas price cutting doesn't appear in any.
- Mark those issues that appear to be priorities. This can be simply done through using a ranking scale with *** depicting the most important, and ** and * being less important. These will be continually reviewed as the strategy making progresses.

Summary and Review

Issue management enables the first step of strategy making to take place. It does this by:

- Surfacing the issues and concerns facing managers.
- Exploring the relationships between the different issues.
- Revealing where the priorities lie according to the structure – often giving rise to new issues while some of the existing issues are put to one side.

The process results in a more holistic and integrated view of the influences on the organization and which, if not appreciated and acted upon, will drive the organization's strategy.

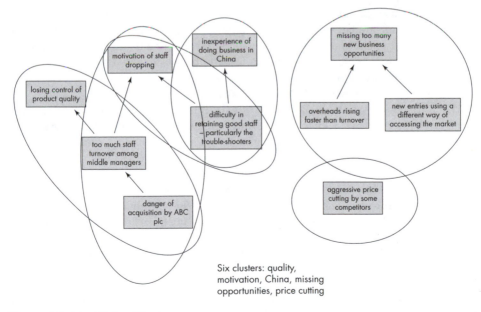

Six clusters: quality, motivation, China, missing opportunities, price cutting

Figure 4.5 Identifying Clusters

Most importantly this process ensures that the strategy-making efforts do not come to nothing. Working with issues as the starting point for strategy making is designed to avoid taking an unrealistic and idealized view of the organization and what it can achieve. Urgent strategic issues engage senior managers; their time is largely devoted to seeking to avoid possible future disasters, managing their own ambitions, protecting their own reputations, and ensuring projects keep on track. Some issues are urgent, some are interesting, some are strategic, and some are tedious but require immediate attention. If strategy making does not at least pay some attention to these dominant drivers of the organization then it will be seen by the power brokers as not connecting with the real world – strategic planning becomes an 'annual rain dance' of no practical import – it is an idealized notion.

The process implicitly respects the history of the organization. It under-stands the organization's ways of thinking and acting in practice rather than those espoused through written statements or by addressing well-versed organizational goals and objectives as if they are the drivers of how issues are defined and addressed. Dealing with live strategic issues is what drives the strategic future of the organization. Issue surfacing gets closer to understanding the embedded strategic future than any other equivalent approach (other than cognitive mapping, if time is available – see chapter 3).

Notes

[1] See Eden and Ackermann (2003) for a discussion about the use of mapping for the analysis of policy documents.

[2] The term is used because oval-shaped cards have been shown to work best in creating cause maps for strategy making. Other shapes, such as hexagons and rectangles, tend to encourage a display or map that is too organized around the regular and restricted shape used. See Eden and Ackermann (1998) pp. 304 for the history of the development of the use of oval shapes.

[3] See Ackermann and Eden (2001a) pp. 47–66.

[4] When discussing strategic planning systems, Johnson and Scholes (2002) p. 61–5 highlight the need to ensure that many views are taken into account so that the strategy is owned more widely within the organization. They highlight the growth in the use of strategy workshops, saying 'a successful workshop process works through the issues . . . drawing on and surfacing different experiences, assumptions, interests and views' (p. 65). They suggest that this helps to take account of the cultural and political processes in the organizations within the strategy design process.

[5] Concepts: see Eden and Ackermann (1998) pp. 94–100; Eden and Ackermann (2001a) pp. 173–95; Eden and Ackermann (2001b) pp. 21–42.
Practice: see Ackermann and Eden (2001b) pp. 43–60; Eden and Ackermann (1998) pp. 284–302.
Examples: six different organizations' uses of mapping are noted in Eden and Ackermann (1998) pp. 194–5, 202, 227–8, 238–42, 255–6, 267–9. In addition there are examples on OMT use in Bryson et al. (2004a).

6 Johnson and Scholes (2002) pp. 179–80 emphasize the importance of knowledge creation and integration to the development of competitive advantage. They go on to discuss the different processes through which this can be achieved.

7 Johnson and Scholes (2002) pp. 43–9 explore the concept of strategy as experience. They suggest that strategy development can be viewed as 'the outcome of individual and collective experience of individuals' . . . which 'can be explained in terms of the mental (or cognitive) models people build up over time'. They also stress the importance of paying attention to the 'taken-for-granted assumptions and routines' that are embedded in the culture of the organization.

8 Referring to a statement from a planner at Royal Dutch or Shell, Lynch (2003) p. 579 suggests that when strategic issues are explored by a management team or group then the group 'develops assumptions about the company and its environment' which need to be made explicit and shared. He goes on to say that they may need to be changed, depending on the strategy to be adopted.

9 See *www.ovalmap.com*.

10 However, group support software is available to permit each participant to contribute individually to the building map on the screen – Group Explorer, see *www.phrontis. com*. Case studies are available in Eden and Ackermann (1998) and Bryson et al. (2004b).

11 Ackermann and Eden (1994) pp. 381–90.

12 Eden and Ackermann (1998) pp. 305 (wall space), 305–6 (pens, stock of oval), 306 (wording of focus question). See also Huxham (1990) and Hickling (1990).

13 When working with large numbers of participants (over 100) it is important to obtain a very powerful projector and a very large screen. We have used a hotel ballroom with a floor-to-ceiling screen and worked with over 20 small groups of five participants at each table with one computer for each group.

Further Reading

Eden, C. and Ackermann, F. (1998) *Making Strategy: the Journey of Strategic Management*, London: Sage, chapter 2.

Ackermann, F. and Eden, C. (2001) 'SODA – Journey Making and Mapping in Practice' in J. Rosenhead and J. Mingers (eds) *Rational Analysis for a Problematic World Revisited*, London: Wiley, pp. 43–60.

Bryson, J. M., Ackermann, F., Eden, C. and Finn, C. (1995) 'Using the "Oval Mapping Process" to Identify Strategic Issues and Formulate Effective Strategies', in J. Bryson (ed.) *Strategic Planning for Public and Nonprofit Organisations* (2nd edn), San Francisco: Jossey-Bass, pp. 257–75.

Case Study 4.1

Understanding the Issues: Seeking to Make a Major Services Contract Successful! (part one)

Phil had just been appointed to run a services contract in a large traditional engineering company, which among other business interests, undertook a considerable amount of work in oil and gas field operations. Phil wanted to know what the major issues facing the contract were, how they impacted upon one another, and what were the really important issues?

The contract focused on one of their major customers. As with many other companies working in the oil and gas industry, Phil's company dealt with a small number of customers. Therefore a great deal of care had to be taken to ensure that they provided effective and efficient services. As such, Phil was keen to surface and manage the various concerns his staff might have, as well as capitalizing on any business opportunities they might see.

In addition, he was very keen to build his team. As there had been a large number of personnel movements over the past year, staff weren't used to working with one another and weren't sure who knew what. Therefore, he wanted to ensure that the process involved as much participation as possible. Phil believed that if he could involve all the managers in the process then they would be able to increase the level of shared understanding of the contract/project and its objectives. He wanted the process to be designed so that through learning about what each participant did in the organization, they would each be able to take more responsibility and act more opportunistically.

As a final consideration Phil also wanted, at some stage, to involve a few members from the customer organization to ensure that the direction taken would be in alignment with their significant customers. He therefore got in touch with Fran (with whom he had worked before) to determine how they might proceed.

As Phil began to provide Fran with the background, he stated early on that the organization's culture was a little conservative. Therefore, rather than starting with computer-based approaches – Phil had already seen the software Decision Explorer® – he asked whether the process could start by using manual techniques and then move on to using the computer-based approaches. This way the staff participating would be able to start with a technique that looked similar to brainstorming – something they were familiar with.

Fran agreed with Phil's request and suggested they spend the morning surfacing the issues, their interrelationships and context, using the oval mapping technique (OMT). They could then spend the afternoon working on the issues they had prioritized at the end of the morning (possibly using a computer-based version of the resultant OMT map). This way the benefits of both modes of working could be capitalized upon. She did, however, have one concern with this design. If they were to work on the computer model in the afternoon or late morning for prioritizing, they would need to have someone entering all of the contributions, noted on the ovals, into the computer. Phil did not see this as a problem. A recent recruit, who already knew the software, would be available to enter the material.

Fran and Phil continued working on the issue surfacing workshop design together. They would need five more similar workshops to ensure everyone who should attend could attend.

The final design called for the morning of each workshop to be spent working with the oval mapping technique. Fran would facilitate the surfacing and the subsequent clustering and structuring, and Barry (the recruit) would capture it all in the Decision Explorer® model. To help Barry, Fran would number the ovals as they were posted up on the wall – this way he would be able to easily determine which of the contributions he had already captured and which were still to be entered into the software. Following this initial elicitation stage, the entire oval map would be reviewed and extended to capture linkages and additional elaboration. The group would then break for lunch. Fran hoped that the break would give her and Barry time to ensure that all was safely captured in the computer (that is, the statements, the links and the clusters). They would also reflect on what had emerged so as to best prepare for the afternoon session. Working in this fashion would enable the link between the computerized model and the wall picture to be transparent.

Time was also spent discussing what was needed for the workshops and who would come to each of them (see chapter 2 for a discussion on choosing participants). Fran was also keen to ensure that they had the right pens, lots of ovals for the participants (at least 30 for each) and that the room they were to use would allow her to put up 16 sheets of flipchart paper (organized as 8x2). Phil assured her that there was an appropriate conference room in the building, which while not taking staff away from the office, was sufficiently distant from their offices to deter participants from continually returning to the day-to-day business. He would also arrange a sandwich lunch. Finally, they considered the time horizon for which issues would be requested and together drafted the focus question to be used to prompt the issues.

The workshops unfolded much as designed. Phil produced an initial introduction with Fran providing more details regarding the technique. Ideas came thick and fast and Fran found herself learning more about the business of oil platforms than she had ever expected. Barry (who was entering the statements into the computer model as fast as he could) asked Fran how she was managing to get them into clusters so quickly. Her reply was that she was not too concerned about getting each cluster absolutely right (the group would help with that), and that she was prepared to change them as new clusters emerged. In addition once a cluster became quite large – 30 or more ovals – she examined it to see if there were subclusters. Finally, asking the participants to put their contributions into the relevant cluster cut down her work. Although, she noted, they did need some encouragement to do this.

At last the group began to slow down – after 40 minutes into the session and with around 130 statements on the wall. As a means of re-energizing them, and extending their thinking, Fran suggested that they a) identify ways of achieving some of the outcomes expressed by the statements on the wall, b) consider some of the constraints and difficulties they faced, and c) put up more arguments about why particular issues seemed to be important. This last request was aimed at beginning the process of laddering up and down the chains of argument and hopefully getting beyond the scripts many of them had. She also encouraged them to consider more positive as well as negative issues – what were some of the opportunities facing them? Having surfaced their concerns, the group were prepared for her asking for opportunities.

Following this burst of activity Fran reviewed the extensive amount of material that the group had surfaced. After a quick overview of the clusters the group was able to gain an understanding of each of the different areas (clusters) as well as see the big picture. These areas or themes included, among others, clusters on safety, communications, information systems, business development, marketing and managing costs. Fran then suggested that the participants take a coffee break during which she and Barry could further work on the clusters, so that each discrete cluster was more easily distinguishable and their contents were hierarchically positioned (that is, those ovals whose content seemed very broad were positioned at the top of the cluster and those that were more detailed were at the bottom). Having lots of wall space available helped, as each cluster could be positioned so that there was clear space between the clusters.

Coffee completed, Fran carried out a review of the clusters to remind participants of their content before beginning to work on each cluster in more detail, particularly with the intention of beginning to tease out the interrelationships between the statements. The structure of each cluster was examined, and the group encouraged to review and confirm Fran's rough hierarchical positioning. In doing so, participants found themselves suggesting that one statement was subordinate to another because it provided support for it – links were beginning to emerge. At times there was disagreement about which cluster a statement should be in as it contributed to more than one. When this occurred Fran suggested that both consequences be captured. Here the numbering on the ovals helped as rather than drawing very long lines across the wall, Fran was able to draw in a small link with the appropriate statement number at the head. Through this process the clusters began to develop the teardrop shape.

Throughout the process of linking the statements with arrows (to show influences, presumed causality and implications) more material surfaced. This occurred as the participants began to notice that they had different interpretations of a particular statement and therefore new material was needed so as to reflect these different chains of arguments. Participants began to realize that they had some quite different perceptions of the issues and that rather than having to decide which one was right, they were able to capture them all before evaluation. As a result they began to get quite excited at how it could all be captured and fitted together and to understand why various difficulties had arisen back at the office.

As the process of reviewing each cluster and determining how its contents related both to the other material within that cluster as well as statements in other clusters, the group also saw the shape of clusters change. For example, two clusters which initially had appeared to be relatively small and apparently peripheral to the overall structure changed their status considerably when considered by the group. This was due to the debate giving rise to additional information both in terms of content (increasing the size of each of the clusters) and relationships, as connections with other clusters were identified and reflected in the overall structure (resulting in both the clusters impacting upon virtually every other cluster theme).

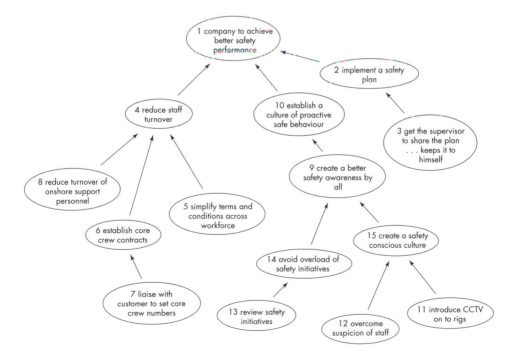

Figure CS4.1 An Example of a Cluster

To help this process of structuring and developing meaning Fran regularly asked challenging or 'obvious' questions about what specific phrases meant. This was particularly the case when one of the participants was looking confused or uncertain about the material. Often participants don't understand the material but don't dare ask in case they lose face. As none of the group expected Fran to have a detailed understanding she was able to question statements and clarify points for others in the group. The questioning also enabled the group to consider and refine the wording of statements, often changing many to an action-oriented statement.

The morning finished with Fran providing the participants with two sets of self-adhesive spots and asking them to allocate them to the clusters (themes) they considered most important if they were to be successful in the long term. Participants could place all of the preferences on one cluster theme if they thought it the most important issue or could scatter them around the clusters according to relative importance. Recognizing the limited amount of time available for the group, the two different coloured sets of eight spots allowed participants to differentiate between long term and short term. This ensured that those which were most urgent could be addressed during the afternoon while highlighting other areas for future development.

To be continued in case study 5.1.

Task 2 Issue Management

a   Decide the relevant time horizon for your strategy (this is typically two to five years).

Task 2 Issue Management

a   Decide the relevant time horizon for your strategy (this is typically two to five years).

b   Each member of the group offers at least four strategic issues facing the organization over the next two to five years, for which the strategy is to be developed. Initially collect these on to a Decision Explorer® view or on to flipchart sheets using a 'round robin'.

Task 2 Issue Management

a   Decide the relevant time horizon for your strategy (this is typically two to five years).

b   Each member of the group offers at least four strategic issues facing the organization over the next two to five years, for which the strategy is to be developed. Initially collect these on to a Decision Explorer® view or on to flipchart sheets using a 'round robin'.

c   **Map out the interrelationships between these issues – as you imagine your team might see them – what influences or drives what?**

Task 2 Issue Management

a   Decide the relevant time horizon for your strategy (this is typically two to five years).

b   Each member of the group offers at least four strategic issues facing the organization over the next two to five years, for which the strategy is to be developed. Initially collect these on to a Decision Explorer® view or on to flipchart sheets using a 'round robin'.

c   Map out the interrelationships between these issues – as you imagine your team might see them – what influences or drives what?

d   **Agree and circle each cluster of linked material.**

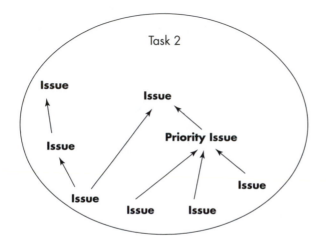

Task 2 Issue Management

a   Decide the relevant time horizon for your strategy (this is typically two to five years).

b   Each member of the group offers at least four strategic issues facing the organization over the next two to five years, for which the strategy is to be developed. Initially collect these on to a Decision Explorer® view or on to flipchart sheets using a 'round robin'.

c   Map out the interrelationships between these issues – as you imagine your team might see them – what influences or drives what?

d   Agree and circle each cluster of linked material.

e   **Identify strategic priorities.**

5 Building Up a Distinctive and Realistic Goals System

Introduction

So far our strategic management journey has been geared to establishing a strategy-making group and facilitating this team to discover what the individuals in the group (chapter 3) and the collective (chapter 4) consider to be the strategic issues they face. As we noted earlier, these issues may encompass members' concerns about possible threats to the organization as well as the realization of potential opportunities. Regardless of which complexion they take, these issues are the focus of the group members' attention and therefore the appropriate place to start. The discovery of these issues involved learning to use sophisticated communications and analysis techniques (mapping) and required the deployment of leadership skills by the consultant/facilitator responsible.

The overall emphasis, therefore, has been on enabling issues to emerge with the intention of building a strategic future based on these realities rather than some abstraction of the future. This is different from many strategy processes advocated in the literature that start with determining the mission first. However, as noted in the introduction and chapter 4, we believe that 'grounding' the strategic future in the context of the issues facing managers not only will ensure that organizational members are able to determine how the strategic intent supports the concerns they are currently wrestling with, but will also ensure a more robust strategic future.

The OMT workshop rolled out in chapter 4 represents the beginnings of a process of not only surfacing but also structuring the information obtained. This structuring process is designed to enable the thinking of the whole group to cohere around a set of strategic issues and their interrelationships, giving rise to an understanding of their impact and therefore priority.

The stage is now set for reviewing the various strategic issues collected in the interviewing and OMT exercises. It is likely that these issues have, by now, been collated, possibly analyzed (see support 1), fed back to, confirmed and clarified by the group members. In this chapter we will work further on the strategic issues in order to develop strategic goals from them. This process, similar to the OMT process, will also be workshop-based involving mapping and review. A substantial number of goals will probably be identified in the first instance. The consultant/facilitator's task will then be to lead the strategy-making group to refine and prioritize this system of interconnected goals. This will involve, among other things, deciding which of the goals identified are largely personal, and which will be crucially relevant to the organization (or the part of it being examined).

A key differentiation of this stage will be deciding which statements truly represent goals – desirable ends for the organization – and which are really elements of strategy aimed to reach these goals – means rather than ends.[1] At this point in the process, the total number of goals will not be an issue: whittling them down will come later. But it will be useful now to remove goals that are 'improper' or inappropriate for various reasons, and to remove any major areas of overlap. Those that remain should be examined carefully for their relevance, robustness and comprehensibility.[2] A further step may then be to bring in whatever externally established goals need be part of the picture – ensuring that the strategic intent of the unit being considered fits within the organizational whole (a form of political feasibility).

The outcome of this process will again be a map – this time of goals, with links, showing how the goals relate to one another, and in particular how they support and feed into one another. This map will be building upon the issues map and therefore it extends the strategic thinking of the group. For a more detailed understanding of what this might look like in practice, see case study 5.2 at the end of this chapter –Strathclyde Poverty Alliance were working to clarify and agree their goals system – along with case study 5.1, the continuation of case study 4.1.

Strategy-making Outcomes

It is often useful to break down this stage into three sub-tasks – to ensure that all three are addressed thoroughly:

- Surface possible goals or aspirations or negative goals based on real concerns and opportunities for your part of the organization (rather than those currently espoused by the organization's strategy rhetoric). Later on, checks with the organization's espoused strategy can be made.
- Identify further issues relevant to your part of the organization.

These outcomes relate to task 3a.

- Explore how these goals and negative goals link together to support themselves and produce a distinctive goals system.
- Identify **particular patterns** emerging from this structuring – particularly feedback loops.

- Consider how the negative goals (or outcomes), which have been identified in the previous sub-task, might be converted into expressions of a desirable future – positive goals.
- Further ladder up the chains of issues or goals to determine the taken-for-granted goals of 'increasing shareholder value or profit' or 'attaining or exceeding mandate'.

These outcomes relate to task 3b.

- Check 'comfort levels' about the content and structure of the emergent goals system.
- Add in any missing goals that are needed, and review the reasons why they did not emerge from the issues.
- Delete any goals that are inappropriate for the future of the organization, after reviewing why they emerged.
- Categorize goals according to their impact on the business versus nature of the organization (**core goals** versus **facilitative goals**) and whether they are directly related to your part of the business or attending to the organization as a whole.

These outcomes relate to task 3c.

The Role of Developing a Goals System

The process of identifying and structuring the goals system that is emerging from an exploration of strategic issues helps clarify what the strategic direction of the organization will be if no deliberate actions are taken to change it. Through understanding the potential impact of the issues and opportunities facing the organization, steps can be taken to position the organization in such a way as to resolve or capitalize upon these. As such, it provides a valuable benchmark against which to consider the strategic future. Thus, the process involves identifying the goals and understanding how they impact on one another. We will discuss briefly in this chapter what we mean by a goal by providing an explanation and some examples. However, we usually find that a developing understanding of the nature of a goal comes from working on your own material.

Although not being absolutely dependent on the previous activities of issue surfacing, or interviewing using cognitive maps, this goal surfacing activity powerfully extends both the initial activities and takes the strategic thinking process one step further towards realizing a strategic intent and direction. An alternative means of surfacing goals can be achieved through starting with a blank wall (or computer screen if using the computer-supported mode of working[3]). However, this form of the process does not recognize the role of

Figure 5.1 Determining Strategic Direction (based on Eden and Ackerman, 1998)

existing problem identification (surfacing the issues) in suggesting what the real goals of the organization are and can be distracted from, through discussing those that are espoused. Starting with a description of apparent goals can miss the reality of the organization and provides an idealistic view of what the organization can and will achieve.[4]

Figure 5.1 illustrates this link between issues and goals. The rationale for identifying the goals or aspiration system in this manner derives from the assertion that problems or issues can only be seen as such, by an individual or an organization, if a situation described by the issue statement attacks a desirable outcome, or creates an undesirable outcome (what we call a negative goal). These envisaged outcomes are seen as seriously good or seriously bad.

Building the Goals System

Goals – What Are They?

What do we mean by a 'goal'?[5] The interpretation we are using here is that a goal is something that is 'good in its own right'.[6] For example, in the academic world a goal might be 'to be seen as research excellent' for some members of faculty. The faculty would regard this outcome as something that is not optional, not a means to an end but an end in itself. For an organization working with social and economic regeneration, it might be 'to improve the living and working environment of the area'. However, it is normally the case that we aspire towards more than one goal and that these goals are interconnected – each goal is supported by others and in turn each goal supports other goals – hence a goals **system**. For the academic world, the goal regarding research might contribute to a superordinate goal relating to 'sustaining an excellent reputation as scholars'. For the regeneration group they might 'regenerate the local economy' to support the goal of 'improving the environment'.[7] In this case, the group would discuss whether regenerating the local economy is just a strategic means to the end of improving the environment, or whether regeneration is in its own right an end – a desirable outcome on its own which in turn is one means to the end of improving the environment.

The relationships between goals are usually what make the goals of one organization distinctive from those of another (although some of the goals statements themselves might also be distinctive). For example, many organizations might state 'better motivation of staff' as one of their goals. However, the distinctiveness of this goal derives from the particular goals supported by 'better motivation', and the particular goals that support the attainment of 'better motivation'. Usually we expect any organization to show distinctiveness in its goals system, as well as distinctiveness in the ways in which it achieves its goals (the business model (chapter 6) that links distinctive competences to the aspirations – goals system – of the organization).

Surfacing Goals

As depicted in Figure 5.1, goals are surfaced through laddering up from the issues surfaced (see chapter 3) – or in our case study from the results of the OMT exercise (chapter 4). In this way we are able to determine exactly what the goals are in practice. Strategic issues and their perceived ramifications reveal a far more realistic picture of our real goals and aspirations – what is driving us in practice rather than that prescribed? Through their examination we can discover the emergent system of goals – those that are actually driving the direction of the organization (which may or may not be consciously known). By laddering up, we can begin to explore how the goals in practice differ from those that are espoused by the organization[8] (often expressed in official strategy statements or motivational literature). Later on we can consider whether this picture (map) paints a sufficiently aspirational view.

Go to task 3a

Choose a particular issue and begin to consider what might be the consequences if this issue is not dealt with. In addition, consider and capture the outcomes if it is managed.

Commentary and Issues

■ Starting from the issues facing the organization and laddering up will not only surface goals, but also will provide a means of determining which issues appear to be most important in relation to those goals.

■ Typically through laddering up, new issues are surfaced that have not been identified before. At a later stage, particularly if these new issues appear to be important, they may need to be considered in more depth and possible options and explanations explored as a basis for developing a strategic programme to deal with them (see chapter 4).

- Not all of the consequences of an issue, arising from laddering up, are good outcomes. In many cases the ramifications have negative outcomes (called **negative goals**[9]). For example, one issue for a cosmetics company might be 'not enough new products' but as a result of that (laddering up) 'loss of research and development requirements' occurs. This in turn may be seen to cause 'closure of the R&D unit' which itself causes 'loss of creative input to the organization'. It is highly unlikely that an organization would articulate as a goal '[NOT] loss of creative input to organization' – nevertheless the laddering has revealed an important negative goal, in the first instance. A negative goal may not be the direct opposite of a goal; rather, it is a dangerous ramification that would benefit from scrutiny and management.
- Added value – task 3 should now begin to show strategic differentiation in goals and their relationships between your organization and a competitor. The issues you have chosen to surface and their subsequent consequences reveal the particular nature of your organization compared with that of another.

Hints and Tips

- Choose which issue to start with: begin with either the 'busy' statements (lots of links in and out) or the 'heads' (no arrows linking out). Taking 'heads' that encapsulate a number of chains of argument (a teardrop, as illustrated in Figure 4.3) can often provide a good starting point.
- Consider creating styles to differentiate issues from the emerging goals. Regardless of whether you are doing this exercise manually or with Decision Explorer® software, using different colours and fonts can help manage the complexity. For example, have a particular style for issues (say, purple italic) and another for goals (say, black and bold) and negative goals (say, red and bold). If existing material (ovals) is used, then the issues might be marked with a purple blob and goals with an asterisk.
- Be careful you don't duplicate efforts when considering the two different questions set in the tasks. For example, if 'customers are no longer turning to us as a first call', results in 'regular customers are getting lost as they are introduced to others' (a negative goal), then don't add the positive goal 'customers stay with us' (see Figure 5.2) as this will not add anything substantial and will complicate the picture.
- Make sure that you consider the positive as well as the negative ramifications – it is sometimes easy to focus too much on the negative issues because these will have inevitably dominated issue surfacing.
- Frequently issues have more than one ramification (laddering up) and capturing this breadth will enrich the resultant outcome (see Figure 5.2 where the issue is shown with three legitimate and one redundant consequence). Don't worry about the growth in material captured. As you work

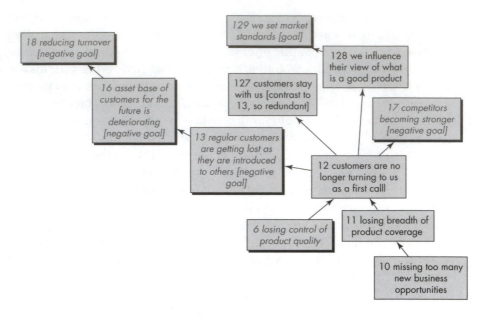

Figure 5.2 Working to Avoid Duplication When Laddering Up

through other issues many of them will link into existing material – the process follows a Pareto-type pattern. Therefore, the first two or three issues will take up the majority of the time with subsequent issues being linked in, in a relatively quick period of time.

■ When the emerging picture begins to look very busy, consider copying some of the issues on to Post-it® notes and placing them on another flipchart (or transfer them to another 'view' in the software) before laddering up. This way the amount of material on one map can be reduced to a more manageable size. However, watch for links between the emerging goals and negative goals on each of the different flipchart sheets – otherwise a coherent view will not be attained.

■ Avoid where possible adding requirements or constraints as if they were goals, for example, needing a piece of equipment or a skills base. These are options or actions for the achievement of outcomes rather than goals or negative goals.

Elaborating the Goals System and Managing Negative Goals

Once the process of laddering up has taken place, it is worth reviewing the emergent goals system. By focusing only on the goals and negative goals (on a separate flipchart or 'view' in Decision Explorer®) a more detailed examination can take place. Here checks can be made regarding the system's comprehensive coverage (both in terms of goals surfaced and their associated links). One means of doing this is through checking whether the laddering up process has been completed as far as possible – that is, are there any further goals to be gained by asking, 'why do we want to do this?' This enables the emergent goals system to be considered in the light of wider organizational goals (the wider context, if you are considering a departmental strategy) ensuring that a fit is made.[10] This is critical for acceptance by a powerful stakeholder.

Go to task 3b

Review the negative goals where appropriate to make them more aspirational and ladder up to wider organizational goals (if, for example, a departmental strategy is being developed).

Commentary and Issues

As the goals make up a system rather than appear as a list of discrete items, developing a hierarchy of goals where one goal supports another and is, in turn, supported by others provides a coherent basis upon which to focus the strategic direction.[11] For example, the hierarchy provides a means for illustrating how all of the different parts of the organization (or unit) fit together (and additionally perhaps through the integration into the wider organizational goals).[12] In case study 5.2, the Strathclyde Poverty Alliance (SPA) aspired towards goals relating to 'gaining funding', 'gaining credibility with those in poverty' and 'developing working partnerships between organizations to tackle poverty', all under the umbrella of 'continued survival of the Alliance' and 'empowering people in poverty to combat poverty on their own behalf'. The structure that this provided gave them a very important insight into the duality of their role as they saw it: attending to those in poverty and influencing decision makers (see Figure CS 5.2). The goals system showed powerfully this duality and also pointed out how central was the goal of 'communicating the work we do and the ethos behind it' – this has five arrows out of it and hits both aspects. While this particular statement could have been seen as an issue by some organizations, for SPA it was considered a goal – due to the nature of their organization.

- Establishing whether the resultant **system** is unique is important. Even if the individual goals are the same as a rival organization's, it may be the linkages that provide the organization's distinctiveness.
- Working to convert negative goals into positive, more aspirational, statements that are subsequently linked with other positive goals ensures that the resultant system can be a description of a positive strategic future.[13]

■ When working in multi-organizational settings, often **meta-goals** emerge that show how it is only by collaboration that some goals can be achieved. These goals belong to all of the organizations, not just one, whereas subordinate goals might be the outcomes from one organization that support the **meta-goals**.[14]

Hints and Tips

■ Try to avoid linking goals to issues. However, there may be circumstances where this is difficult. This often occurs where there is a feedback loop: that is, a dynamic pattern of behaviour that either stabilizes or reinforces (viciously or virtuously) the behaviour. An alternative is where the group is insistent that, for example, 'losing control of product quality' leads to a situation where 'customers are no longer turning to us as a first call' – the first statement being a negative goal linking to an issue.

■ When linking goals together, sometimes it is useful to provide additional linking commentary or argumentation. Where this happens it is helpful to use a different style to illustrate its different status.

■ When converting negative goals to a more positive aspirational phrasing, try out different options. For example, if you had as a negative goal 'lose market share' one rewording option might be 'maintain current market share', another might be 'gradually increase market share', or 'substantially increase market share'. Each of these has different strategic implications and may be differently realizable.

■ Make sure you don't forget to include all of the inter-goal links – often there is a temptation to focus only on the chains of argument up from the issues without considering in detail how the goals might support one another.

■ Check that the language used to describe the goals is aspirational **and** that the goals are clearly goals (that is 'good in their own right' as far as your group members are concerned).

Refining the goals system

Having developed a draft goals or aspirations system, it is often helpful to explore the structure of the goals system and consider the character of the goals. There are a number of different ways for doing this.

> **Go to task 3c**
>
> Check for missing goals, categorize goals, revisit issues and reconsider priorities.

Commentary and Issues

One useful check is to consider whether any of the goals apply to a different 'level' of the organization: are any too personal, are any departmental as compared with organizational (if the strategy is being developed for the whole organization)? Goals that are of a personal nature tend to appear if interviews have been the basis for drafting the goals system (see chapter 3). Their appearance raises issues about who the developing strategy belongs to.

Earlier, in chapter 2, we asked you to decide which part of your organization was to be the subject of the analysis and would benefit from the strategy that was to be developed. Here a check should be made about who wishes to be held accountable for the delivery of the goals. If they are the responsibility of the organizational unit you defined early in this handbook then those goals may be supporting strategies, or strategies for the organization as a whole.

Another form of helpful categorization is to examine the goals to determine whether they are core goals or facilitative goals. Core goals focus on the *raison d'être* of the organization – for example, for an organization dealing with prisons a goal might be 'to provide a humane and yet secure environment'. Whereas facilitative goals focus on the internal support functions of the organization – for example, the computer services department might be seen as crucial to facilitating core goals, and so a facilitative goal may be 'to create a service-oriented and cutting-edge computer services group'.

Hints and Tips

■ Consider whether there are any goals not currently present that should be. This provides the opportunity for more aspirational goals to emerge, thus enabling the organization to frame itself as a place that is attractive to work in (often one of the key reasons for carrying out a strategy in the first place, as this helps retain existing staff and attract new staff). Add in any missing goals that are needed, but only after reviewing the reasons why they did not emerge from laddering up from the issues. If new goals are included then it is important to ladder down to issues that arise in the realization of the new goals and to understand how these issues were not surfaced.

- Check whether any of the goals that are present provide a sense of dis-comfort – both in terms of antagonizing those further up the organization (if doing the strategy-making exercise for a department or division) or outside of the organization, for example, shareholders. Delete any goals that are inappropriate for the future of the organization, but only after reviewing why they emerged from the laddering process. If the issues are still regarded as important, and the laddering correctly captures why they are issues, then they should not be removed.
- Categorize goals according to their impact on the business versus the nature of the organization (core goals versus facilitative goals – see above), and whether they are directly related to your part of the business or attend to the organization as a whole.
- This process of establishing a first draft of the goals system also highlights the priorities for dealing with strategic issues – that is, it reveals what strategies and/or actions need to be developed in order for the goals to be realized.

  - By exploring the emergent system of issues and goals, it becomes pos-sible to identify the centrality and potency of the issues and goals. (Recall the centrality of 'communicate the work we do and the ethos behind it' for the Strathclyde Poverty Alliance in case study 5.2). This gives clues as to where effort might most effectively be placed. Those issues that are central to the structure are those that have many links in and out of them and, if the issue or goal were to be removed from the structure, it would make a significant impact. A **potent issue** is one that impacts many of the goals. Thus, resolving the potent issue (which makes resolving the issue a strategy) will have a larger amount of leverage than resolving issues that support only one or two goals.

- If draft priorities of issues were not established during the OMT task then consider categorizing issues according to their priorities in order to focus effort on goals and/or issues. Simple forms such as a ***, **, * scheme work well, where an issue that impacts upon a large number of goals is allocated ***.

Carrying Out a Final Review of the Goals System

The steps below are useful when tidying up and reviewing the goals system.

Review the number of goals that appear in the system. Most organizations feel uncomfortable with a goals system encompassing more than about 15 goals. However, a first draft often encompasses in excess of 25 goals.[15] At this stage it is not important to reduce the size of the system – this can be done later. Nevertheless, it is useful to get rid of redundancy, and obviously 'improper' goals.

To do this:

■ Check the draft goals are goals rather than potential strategies – consider whether is good in its own right rather than an optional means to an end.[16]

■ Reconsider the time horizon.[16] For example, goals will change depending on whether you are taking a two-year view or a five-year view. The goals system should remain relatively constant over the time period under consideration and should be phrased accordingly. If a goal can be delivered quickly, in relation to the time horizon, then it may be better categorized as a strategy.

■ Where two goals appear to be similar consider merging them. Here, similarity means they have the same supporting and consequential goals. If they are of similar wording but have different support and consequences then their meaning is different and the wording should be changed.

■ For public organizations, review any mandates that might exist (this is particularly important for public sector organizations). While the government dictates these, how they are actuated is the choice of the organization. Check that the goals system and the mandate support one another. Sometimes the mandate acts as a goal and sometimes as a constraint, depending on the point of view of the managers. If it is a constraint then it will be at the bottom of the strategy map as it is preventing or enforcing some particular outcome.

■ Check for cryptic wording. Often those goals that seem to be clear and straightforward to the group working on them will be too cryptic to others.

Agreeing a draft goals system is an appropriate place to start moving towards agreeing the strategic direction. However, remember that we are introducing a cyclical process. Also, the goals system must still be seen as a draft until the validity of the business model or livelihood scheme has been explored. However, as we note in chapter 8, closure may be required at this stage, in which case the goals and priority issues converted to strategies become the statement of strategic intent.

An additional step that might be considered is to try drafting a traditional text-based (rather than map) mission statement from the goals system. By ensuring that the mission statement encapsulates the language from the goals system as well as the relationships, a clear link between the goals system and mission statement is possible, rendering the mission statement more believable. Following this, develop the mission statement to ensure it will get at the hearts and minds of staff. A good mission statement should reflect the uniqueness of the organization and its aspirations and therefore may be as long as 250 words. (Drafting of mission statements is covered further in chapter 8.)

Figure 5.3 shows an example of Scottish Natural Heritage's management strategy goals system. This example shows:

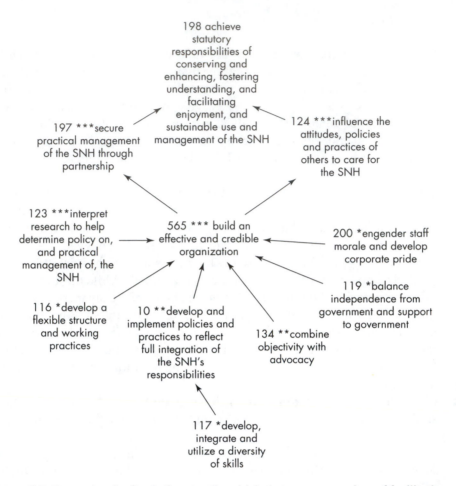

Figure 5.3 Example of a Goals System (in which there are a number of facilitative goals)

- The mandate as the superordinate goal.
- Two core goals (statements 197 and 124) but a system predominated by facilitative goals.
- A prioritization scheme being used. Those goals with three asterisks were seen as more important than those with two and so on.

Summary and Review

Building up a goals system provides an effective way of beginning to formulate the strategic direction by:

- Surfacing goals (and negative goals) suggested by the issues faced by the organization.

- Capturing and understanding how these goals are both supported by and supporting of one another – thus creating a system which helps to clarify the integration of different elements of the organization.
- Providing the means for differentiation.
- Producing the means for writing a mission statement.

Notes

[1] There is confusion in the literature between different definitions of goals. Johnson and Scholes (2002) p. 241 and Lynch (2003) pp. 440–1 differentiate goals from objectives, with objectives being more of a means to assess how you are doing against a goal – i.e. they are very macro forms of goals and can be used for performance management. Chakovarthy and Lorange (in De Wit and Meyer (1998) p. 92) argue the opposite, stating that 'objectives refer to the strategic intent of the firm in the long run' while 'goals . . . are more specific statements of the achievements targeted for certain deadlines'. Wheelen and Hunger (in De Wit and Meyer (1998) p. 49) contradict this, stating that 'in contrast to an objective, a goal is an open-ended statement of what one wishes to accomplish with no quantification of what is to be achieved and no time criteria for completion'.

[2] Lynch (2003) p. 442 discusses the need for objectives to be challenging but achievable. We believe that a level of appropriateness needs to be arrived at when developing goals.

[3] See Eden and Ackermann (1998) pp. 321–40 regarding computer supported workshops and Ackermann and Eden (2001a) pp. 47–66.

[4] Eden and Ackermann (1998) refer to the process recommended here as 'detecting emergent strategizing' and by using it hope to enable the team to reflect on what 'really goes on around here' as the starting point for discovering a goals system – see chapter 5 of Eden and Ackermann (1998).

[5] Johnson and Scholes (2002) p. 13 provide a definition of the difference between goals and objectives. They define a goal as a 'general statement of aim or purpose' while an objective is a 'more precise statement of the goal'. However, even these definitions demonstrate flexibility of language, i.e. aim, purpose, goal. We believe that it does not matter what you call it, so long as it is aspirational.

[6] For additional definitions see Johnson and Scholes (2002) pp. 12–13.

[7] See Eden and Ackermann (1998) p. 433 for more detail on laddering up from issues and developing a goals system.

[8] See Eden and Ackermann (1998) pp. 88 and 89.

[9] See Eden and Ackermann (1998) pp. 90 and 98.

[10] Chakovarthy and Lorange (in De Wit and Meyer (1998) pp. 94–5) discuss the need to negotiate goals for each division and business unit within the organization that are consistent with the corporate objectives and can be supported by the resources available. They also suggest that some goals may need to be modified in order to bring them into alignment with the corporate goals.

[11] Lynch (2003) p. 441 discuss as the potential conflict between growth objectives and the short term requirement to provide returns to shareholders. This reinforces our view that it is important to have coherence of goals. Where there is a conflict of goals,

they need to be adapted accordingly. Understanding the interrelationships between short-term actions and long-term goals can help to manage the conflicts. Johnson and Scholes (2002) include an extract from Drucker on p. 451, which discusses this issue further.

[12] Lynch (2003) pp. 644–5 discusses the concept of the hierarchy of objectives in the context of the organization.

[13] Eden and Ackermann discuss the often required outcome of strategy making being that of gaining emotional commitment to a positive strategic vision – see Eden and Ackermann (1998) p. 15.

[14] See Huxham (1996) and Huxham and Eden (2001) pp. 373–91 for a discussion of the nature of meta-goals and their significance in multi-organizational collaboration.

[15] Eden and Ackermann (1998) p. 428.

[16] Hax (in De Wit and Meyer (1998) pp. 9–10) discusses the development of long-term objectives and the need for them to be stable.

Further Reading

Eden, C. and Ackermann, F. (1998) *Making Strategy: the Journey of Strategic Management*, London: Sage, chapter 2, pp. 314–16.

Eden, C. and Ackermann, F. (2002) 'Emergent Strategizing' in A. Huff and M. Jenkins (eds), *Mapping Strategic Thinking*, London: Sage, 2002.

Case Study 5.1

Understanding the Issues:
Seeking to Make a Major Services
Contract Successful! (part two)

The story from case study 4.1 continues (based on material presented in chapter 5).

While the participants were enjoying lunch, Fran and Barry worked hard to ensure all of the material from the oval mapping session was captured in the Decision Explorer® model. Once completed, Fran set up a number of mini maps (views depicting the clusters) on the computer so that the material for each issue/cluster was presented in an identical pattern to that on the wall. This was designed to help participants transfer attention from the wall to the model and trust in the computer-based version of the work they had done in the morning. She particularly concentrated on the clusters that had emerged from the results of participants expressing their preferences for relative importance.

In addition, she brought on to a new view in Decision Explorer® the most superordinate ovals (potentially a label for a key issue) from each cluster (as the software works on the basis of a relational database, a statement can appear on more than one screen view on the computer). This view would provide an ideal starting point for the process of laddering up to goals. Each statement could be examined, with the group determining whether it was an issue (and therefore categorized as such), and subsequently considering what would follow from it occurring or not. This process of reflecting upon the consequences of each issue – and the consequences of consequence (that is, following up the chain of argument) – gently teased out both the goals and negative goals. Attention was focused on ensuring that where there were multiple consequences these too were captured as well as any links that existed between emergent chains.

The group quickly understood what was expected of them and before long had surfaced a number of goals (see figure CS 5.1). They noted, with some surprise and interest, that these did not completely correspond to those espoused by the organization. However, they did agree that the system reflected what was currently actually driving the organization. After some debate about whether the picture was sufficiently comprehensive, that is, depicting a view of the

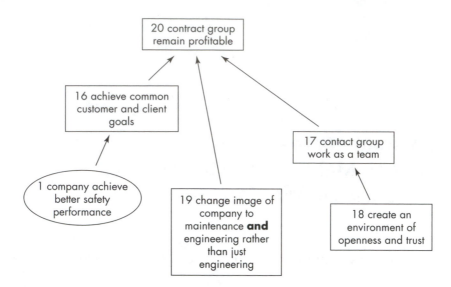

Figure CS5.1 An Early Version of the Goals System

future that they felt reflected both their own and the customer's values, energy was focused on the means of achieving these goals. And so, they began the process of detecting distinctive competences . . .

Postscript

The strategy that developed from the issues surfaced remained in place for the next two years – until it was time to review the direction due to changes in the marketplace. In addition, as a result of involving a number of other directors in the division's journey, the managing director promoted the approach to the next level of the organization to develop a company-wide strategy and an IT strategy.

Case Study 5.2

In Pursuit of a Direction: Clarifying Our Goals

Damian, the chief executive of Strathclyde Poverty Alliance (SPA), was concerned about how he could develop a coherent set of goals for the organization. He wanted the goals to reasonably reflect the multiple interests of all the organizations which were represented on the board of directors of the Alliance. These representatives came from large charities such as Barnardo's (focusing on children), small charities living on a shoe-string, and local government officers representing funding agencies.

For some time he had been reflecting whether the approach that Colin and Fran had written about might help his group. If he sought to address the aims of the organization as an **interlinked system of goals** (developing a distinctive goals system) as suggested by them, might that be the basis for the successful negotiation of a set of goals for the SPA? Furthermore, if this was possible then it might generate some excitement and energy from each member of the board, which went beyond them acting as representatives of their own organizations. The SPA is a multi-organization company limited by guarantee, funded from many sources and set up to deal with poverty in the largest region of the UK. (The organization is now called the Poverty Alliance following the reorganization of local government in the UK.)

This case study reviews how the Alliance went about the process of developing a coherent system of goals. The work on the goals system took place over the space of half a day (with other activities such as issue surfacing (see chapter 4) and the development of a statement of strategic intent (see chapter 7) also being generated).

Damian arranged to meet Colin and Fran. He explained he wanted to develop a goals system and some associated strategies but mentioned that at previous meetings when they had talked about goals they usually became bogged down. Long lists of wonderful sounding aims were discussed during these meetings but, he continued, the results were mostly unrealistic and did not represent the real interests of the people at the meeting or their organizations. To provide some context, Colin began to explain his and Fran's orientation – that of relating, as a starting point, to what people actually did rather than what they say they do. As he spoke, Damian's interest increased. He was attracted to the idea of working up the goals from the reality of the sorts of issues the representatives sought to address. Colin's suggestion of using interviews or the oval mapping technique to surface issues and thus an emergent goals system seemed to make particular sense for a multi-organizational setting.

Damian also commented to Colin that the SPA had always had difficulty in getting all of the members of the board of directors together for more than a couple of hours at a time. This was because they each had other jobs and responsibilities. However, he was hopeful that if they could be persuaded of the usefulness of the outcome and, more importantly, the likelihood of achieving it, then they might attend for a full day workshop off-site. He promised Colin he would try to get their commitment and then get back to him. Damian was successful. When he floated the idea of a workshop there seemed to be enthusiasm for having another go at something they all thought was important. He and Colin then began to design the workshop. One day became two days, and expanded into a bigger task – to put issues on the table, get at goals and attempt to resolve some of the most important strategic issues.

However, as the design unfolded, Damian noted to Colin that if this wider remit was now to be the aim then others should be involved. Colin could see the size of the group increasing! Damian explained that he managed a relatively small organization of full-time staff (at that time 13 project workers and administrative support staff). He wanted to include them as well as the directors. He soon persuaded Colin that it would make sense to include all 22 key actors. After all, involving all of these actors would increase the likelihood of ownership of the outcomes by all who were expected to deliver agreed strategies. Colin, agreeing, warned him that this would mean two facilitators working, for some of the time, with two subgroups. Damian did not feel that was a problem. By now he was warming to the idea of mixing the two groups for two days. In his and Colin's opinion there were a number of benefits from this social mixing, one benefit coming from working off-site and participants being able to pay more attention to each other's views, the other from the strategic issues being surfaced from two, sometimes competing, perspectives (those involved every day and those who were part-time). A more comprehensive set of issues could be accessed and, based upon these, a more wide-ranging goals system developed.

As with many of the public sector bodies that Colin and Fran had worked with, accommodation for the workshop was an issue. The organization was about resolving poverty, so it was clear that it could not spend any more money than absolutely necessary on meeting facilities or accommodation. After some debate Damian and Colin agreed on a location. The workshop was to be held at a mediocre quality hotel. However, it was 100 miles from the offices of participants, and accessible by cheap public transport. When Colin arrived at the hotel he was dismayed by the workshop rooms, which were far from ideal. Not only were they unattractive, but they also had uncomfortable seats and no decent daylight. Working in them was not going to be easy! Nevertheless the rooms did have the main requirement of decent wall space for oval mapping.

Colin and Damian had agreed that the first day should start after lunch with issue surfacing using the oval mapping technique (see chapter 4) undertaken by two equal sized subgroups. Each subgroup would have a mix of staff and directors and would be asked to suggest 'the major strategic issues that the SPA should address in the next few years'. To facilitate this, Colin and a colleague he had asked to help followed the standard approach for issue surfacing in groups. They worked on getting participants to dump ideas on to ovals before moving on to clustering, cluster labelling and capturing some of the links both within and across clusters. As usual, each group changed rooms at the break and began to work on the material of the other group. Exchanging rooms began to help the process of convergence between the members of each group.

Their new task was to build a goals system by trying to work out what goals were implicit in the material in each cluster representing a strategic issue defined by the other group. This not only meant that both groups had to read the other's material but also that a degree of negotiated convergence would occur. Each group therefore examined the clusters by reviewing the structure and beginning to consider the implications. This process of laddering up not only helped surface goals but also gave rise to further issues (widening the growing map further and suggesting that greater consideration of these new issues might be useful in terms of developing strategies). Those statements that the participants felt were goals (following the guideline of 'good in its own right') were allocated a specific style (in this case using asterisks added to the oval) so as to distinguish them from the other material generated. Particular attention was given to capturing not only the positive goals implied by the issues but also the negative ramifications (negative goals) – as usual these negative implications came thick and fast. Moreover, both facilitators made sure that where there were multiple consequences from the issues these were captured on new ovals, rather than lost by just following up a single chain of argument.

As the goals were produced they were placed into one of three categories. The first category comprised **facilitative goals** – goals which did not express the main aspirations of the organization but were seen as fundamental to facilitating their achievement. The second category was the **core goals** of the SPA, which were also goals of member organizations. The third category was **meta-goals** – goals that could only be achieved by successful multi-organizational collaboration. Damian was keen to separate those goals that could represent **collaborative advantage** from those which meant the SPA was only supporting the activities of member organizations rather than achieving something special. 'After all', he commented, 'if we are an alliance and we can't identify some meta-goals, do we have a right to exist?'

The afternoon session finished with the whole group together, packed tightly into one of the rooms. Colin had picked the goals off from the oval maps in each room (helped by having the different styles to distinguish them) and set them out separately on one wall, in a very rough hierarchy – the beginnings of a system with those most superordinate at the top and those most subordinate at the bottom. With his encouragement, the group made some attempts to organize the structure of the top of the hierarchy. New goals were added, as original goals needed more explanation. The new goals provided valuable elaboration to the sometimes cryptic chains of argument generated by the subgroup laddering up or as the group realized they had missed one or two important aspirations. By the time the workshop stopped for dinner, 37 goals had been noted and about half had been roughly linked.

Linking goals

After dinner the work started with a vengeance for the facilitators, with inter-mittent help from Damian. Damian's part attendance was the result of a conflict between his wanting to engage with the important after-dinner socializing and also to gain a better feel for where the group had got to in terms of progress. He reported that most people seemed pleased with their work and what they had achieved. The participants, according to him, felt that the structuring of issues to encompass the views of staff and directors seemed to have been informative and constructive. They also believed that the explication of goals from issues seemed to have got closer to real, and realistic, aspirations – something that paid attention to the complexities they were forced to manage.

Before they could finish up for the evening, the facilitators had six tasks ahead of them. The first task was to move all the issue ovals into one room and merge similar issues generated by each group into a single map (paying strict attention to the meaning underlying each statement – see support 1). One facilitator would focus on this task. Concurrently Colin worked at using his most careful handwriting to rewrite each of the draft goals so that it could be more easily read. This process often involved lengthening the goal statement to make it less cryptic. Second, he reviewed the negative goals and, with Damian's help, sought to rework these (where possible) into a more positive wording. Finally, the rewording process also involved ensuring that the action orientation mapping guideline was adhered to as this would not only help clarify meaning but also help when later considering strategies.

Following this both facilitators cross-checked each of the goals with each of the issue clusters so that each goal could be related to at least one issue theme and vice versa. The combined issue clusters were laid out on the biggest wall.

Both of the facilitators then tried some draft merging of goals to reduce the number to something more workable. They hoped to reduce the total number of goals from 37 to about 15. However, they were keen to pay attention to the material around each goal in order to try to ensure that the meaning was not lost by the merging process. Finally, with their remaining energy they attempted a draft summary goals system (figure CS 5.2), and from this initial system drafted

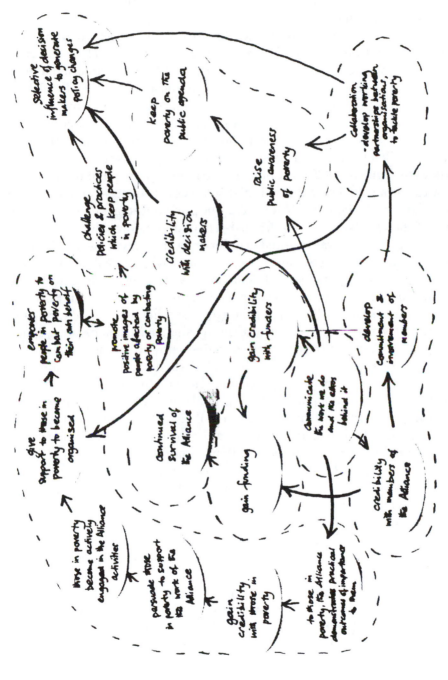

Figure CS5.2 A Photograph Showing the Goals Roughly Clustered into Bundles – the Dotted Lines – to Match the Issue Material

a **mission statement**. Just as they broke up for the evening Damian dropped by and reminded Colin that SPA members did not like the idea of having a mission statement. He and his team felt 'they are for big business'. A quick change of terms and the mission statement became a statement of strategic intent, although its content would be the same.

The first task for the next morning was to ratify the tidied goal map with the participant group. Colin started off by asking participants to check the merging that had taken place and the rewording of the goals. Rather than use the time allotted for the changes expected to be proposed, the group carefully checked each goal in turn and agreed to each of them with no changes! However, as they considered the structure of the goals as a system of linked aspirations several important discussions got going. First, the goal of 'continued survival of the SPA' had been left hanging as a 'head' during the last group session on the previous day (see figure CS 5.2). As Colin and Damian had hoped, it did not take long for the group to demand that it had some consequences, and so it was linked up the goal hierarchy. They were not prepared to acknowledge that survival of the SPA was a high order goal – an end in its own right – but they were clear that survival was required in order to meet other core goals. Second, it was interesting that all noted, and were fascinated by, the apparent two-sided nature of the goals system – one side showing the goals related to influencing policy and the other showing the goals relating directly to those in poverty. This was an important realization for the group and helped them understand why there had been so much difficulty in the debates about their organizational purpose. Third, they were also interested in the centrality of the goal 'to communicate the work we do and the ethos behind it' – five consequences followed, and it hit both sides of the goals system. On reflection it seemed obvious, but they had, nevertheless, not previously identified how crucial it was. There was much debate about whether this was truly a goal (an outcome worth striving for in its own right, rather than as a means to an end). Some argued that it was a powerful strategy and some argued that they should do it regardless of other consequences. In the end there was agreement that even if it was really a strategy it was so important that it didn't matter if they kept it as a goal and forced themselves to take it as seriously as that would imply.

Before finishing with the goals system, Colin encouraged participants to check all of the goals to make sure that they were 'good in their own right' and not potential strategies. Once this had been completed the group reviewed the whole structure once again – they were pleased not only that it was very distinctive (no other poverty charity that they could think of had anything similar) but also that it would demonstrate to their stakeholders, particularly governmental ones, that the Alliance had a clear and coherent statement about what they were about – their way forward.

Three years after the workshop the resultant goals system was still a driving framework for the organization.

Workshop 1 (comprising task 3): Strategic Issues and Emergent Goals

The Value Added: the first draft of a revised, distinctive and realistic goals system (including articulated draft strategies resulting from prioritized issues)

Task 3a   Building the Goals System

■ **Agree on the most important cluster and then identify the highest level issue within it or, alternatively, take the highest priority issue and ask:**

  ■ **'What might happen that is undesirable if we don't address it?' or alter-natively:**
  ■ **'What might we achieve if we were to find an effective way of addressing the issue?'**

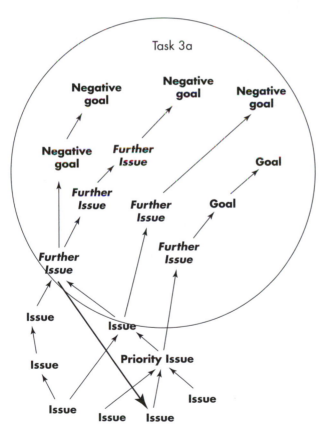

Task 3a   Building the Goals System

■ Agree on the most important cluster and then identify the highest level issue within it or, alternatively, take the highest priority issue and ask:

    ■ 'What might happen that is undesirable if we don't address it?' or alternatively:

    ■ 'What might we achieve if we were to find an effective way of addressing the issue?'

■ Ask the same questions of that answer, and so on, until the answer given is a goal or negative goal (an obviously bad achievement/outcome for the organization).

Task 3b   Elaborating the Goals System

■ Copy all of the goals and negative goals on to Post-its® and place on a separate flipchart sheet (or view in the software) drawing in the identified links.

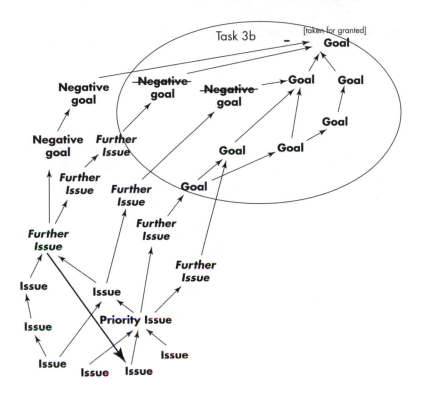

Task 3b Elaborating the Goals System

■ Copy all of the goals and negative goals on to Post-its® and place on a separate flipchart sheet (or view in the software) drawing in the identified links.

■ **Examine each of the negative goals in order to make them more aspirational.**

■ **Try putting NOT in front of the statement as a starting point.**

Task 3b Elaborating the Goals System

■ Copy all of the goals and negative goals on to Post-its® and place on a separate flipchart sheet (or view in the software) drawing in the identified links.

■ Examine each of the negative goals in order to make them more aspirational.

  ■ Try putting NOT in front of the statement as a starting point.

■ Ladder up further where possible.

  ■ Capture the wider organizational goals, e.g. 'increase shareholder value/ profit' (private sector) OR 'attain/exceed mandate' (public/not for profit sector).

Task 3b Elaborating the Goals System

■ Copy all of the goals and negative goals on to Post-its® and place on a separate flipchart sheet (or view in the software) drawing in the identified links.

■ Examine each of the negative goals in order to make them more aspirational.

  ■ Try putting NOT in front of the statement as a starting point.

■ Ladder up further where necessary.

  ■ Capture the wider organizational goals, e.g. 'increase shareholder value/ profit' (private sector) OR 'attain/exceed mandate' (public/not for profit sector).

■ **Check whether there are any further links between goals and whether the goals are worded in a suitably aspirational manner.**

Task 3c Refining the Goals System

■ **Check for missing goals.**

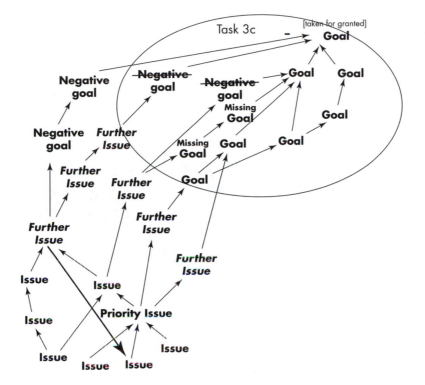

Task 3c Refining the Goals System

■ Check for missing goals.

■ **Delete goals that are discomforting for the future of the organization.**

Task 3c   Refining the Goals System

- ■ Check for missing goals.
- ■ Delete goals that are discomforting for the future of the organization.
- ■ **Categorize goals according to:**

  - ■ **Whether they are core or facilitative.**
  - ■ **Whether they are directly related to the business/division/department being considered or are part of a wider system (the organization as a whole etc.).**

Task 3c Refining the Goals System

- Check for missing goals.
- Delete goals that are discomforting for the future of the organization.
- Categorize goals according to:

    - Whether they are core or facilitative.
    - Whether they are directly related to the business/division/department being considered or are part of a wider system (the organization as a whole etc.).

- **Revisit issues and reconsider priorities.**

6 Developing a Business Model or Livelihood Scheme: Identifying Distinctiveness and Core Distinctive Competences

Introduction

In the last chapter we tackled the tasks of surfacing and categorizing the strategy-making group's strategic goals based on the issues surfaced. A considerable number of goals may have surfaced – 25 or so being common in this kind of exercise. Some of these goals will have been detailed elaboration of others, and there may have been some redundancy, so the number may have been reduced on these accounts. You should now be able to draw up a map of the goals and the issues, showing how these relate, and distinguishing between those that are core goals and those that are facilitative goals, and those that relate to the wider organizational context. The final stage in this process will have been to prioritize the goals.

To summarize, your strategy making has now provided you with a strategy-making team, a map of strategic issues indicating those that are most central, a draft distinctive goals system, and a revised map of strategic priorities for your organization based on the prioritization of the goals. We now take a major step forward by building the business model – the test of whether the strategy that is unfolding is realizable.

In this chapter we tackle the issue of competences – the assets and characteristics that make the organization distinctive. These are the basis for a sustainable strategic future – the explanations of strategic success. It is, of course, possible for organizations to continue muddling through without any distinctive competences (DCs) and so no clearly realizable business model – but they cannot be assured of a sound strategic future.

This chapter thus concentrates on identifying the distinctive competences of your organization, in order to relate them to your draft goals system. This may involve modifying your goals, or even adding new ones, as this critical information is brought to bear. Likewise it may suggest the need for new competences. The outcome should be a coherent business model (or livelihood scheme) in which strategic issues, the goals system and the business's distinctive competences are dynamically but robustly linked. Following this process you will be able to identify the **core distinctive competences** of the organization.[1] It is worth noting that core competences arise from understanding those distinctive competences that are at the core of the business model, and so until the business model has been fully explored and developed it is not possible to know what the core competences of the business are.

So what are distinctive competences? In one sense they are conventional, but distinctive, strengths. Within a market for, say, construction contracts, all the big players will be expected to possess certain basic strengths – a skilled workforce, management expertise, technical equipment, capital, service standards – in order to even enter the game.[2] Here we are looking for something more: competences that make a difference, those things that make your organization stand out from the field, and which all customers will perceive as adding special value to the products and services that you provide. Distinctive competences may range from material strengths, such as the ability to develop unique technology, or having the ability to locate a large number of outlets in places that cannot be replicated by others, to intangibles such as having earned a high level of trust among clients, or a strongly positive public image. In practice, once we begin to analyze these distinctive competences, we will probably find a mixture of factors. A technological lead, for example, may be due to heavy commitments to R&D, or to effective partnerships with universities or with overseas firms. Thus, as with other parts of strategy making, the network or **pattern of competences** enables the group to reach a greater understanding of not only the competences themselves but also how they support one another.

An analysis of distinctive competences, however, will not necessarily be a comfortable experience. The things an organization thinks it is good at, and on which it has traditionally lavished resources, may turn out to be marginal, or even negative factors. They may prove to be of little significance to the strategic future that you have been developing.

Strategy-making Outcomes

The stage can usefully be separated into two substage sets of outcomes:

■ Surface the particular distinctive competences of your part of the organization for which you are developing a strategy.
■ Understand how these competences relate to each other and so create **distinctive patterns**, as well as possibly being distinctive in their own right.

These outcomes relate to task 4.

■ Test how the distinctive competences support (or not) the intended goals and so explore the business model or livelihood scheme and determine the feasibility of the goals and the effective use of resources.

■ Search for the way in which the DCs can be exploited more effectively to support goals.

■ Revise goals to account for the DCs.

■ Consider developing new strategies to reinforce weak DCs (these will be determined as a part of agreeing strategies – chapter 7).

■ Revisit the DCs to establish those that are core or central to the business model and reduce emphasis on those which do not play a role.

■ Revise the business model or livelihood scheme to refine the linkage between core distinctive competences and goals.

These outcomes relate to tasks 5 and 6.

The Role of Developing the Business Model

Developing and testing the business model (or livelihood scheme)[3] is the most crucial stage in making strategy. The aim is to capitalize on the work carried out in the last three chapters. Briefly, this was the identification of strategic issues, through either cognitive mapping (chapter 3) or OMT (chapter 4), and the development of a draft goals system (chapter 5). This is done by pulling the results from these activities together in a way that increases the robustness of their outcomes and ensures that the strategy being considered is both **distinctive** (gaining and sustaining competitive advantage[4]) and **achievable**. Although the logic of starting with strategic issues, moving to drafting a goals system, and then considering distinctive competences is powerful, when time is tight, it is possible to start with distinctive competences and use them to elaborate goals.

To benefit fully from the process of the development of the business model needs to be seen as a cycle (see Figure 6.1 below). This figure shows how, by starting with the surfacing of strategic issues, a draft goals system is developed, and subsequently distinctive competences are surfaced, based on the needs expressed by the draft goals system. By trying to link each distinctive competence (or pattern of competences that are distinctive) to each goal, a first draft of the business model or livelihood scheme is then developed. Where the distinctiveness does not serve goals, then new goals might be added or the distinctiveness is taken as redundant[5] (thus potentially freeing up the resources devoted to sustaining it). Alternatively, where goals are not served by distinctiveness then the goals need to be modified, or strategies drafted that will support the development of distinctiveness. Thus, the *process* is cyclical until a robust business model or livelihood scheme is developed and the goals system becomes stable. The development of the business model can be seen as one way of proving the validity of the business idea.[6]

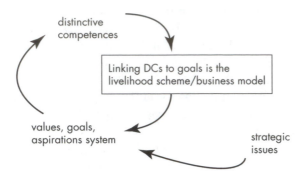

distinctive
competences

Linking DCs to goals is the
livelihood scheme/business model

values, goals,
aspirations system

strategic
issues

Figure 6.1 The Process of Coherence Between Distinctive Competences, Goals and Development of the Business Model/Livelihood Scheme

Eliciting Distinctive Competences

As we noted above, most management teams find this exercise to be the most difficult of all those undertaken as a part of strategy making. Teams find it difficult to surface competences that they see as distinctive (and yet they have a 'gut feel' that there are particular or unique characteristics of their organization that do help differentiate them from their competitors).[7] Consequently, this exercise, when undertaken for the first time, often requires a number of sequential and developmental attempts with the group, first to identify distinctive competences, and second to arrive at a business model or livelihood scheme they feel comfortable with.

Beware:

> All organizations have the weaknesses of their strengths and all organizations have the strengths of their weaknesses, if they are recognized.
>
> Pugh's Paradox, Derek Pugh

What is a Distinctive Competence?

Distinctiveness is a relative concept – an organization is distinctive with respect to a benchmark established with reference to aspirations (the goals system). For example, an organization may aspire to become the largest organization of its type in the southwest region. Thus, one aspect of distinctiveness will be related to other organizations within the southwest region, as this is their benchmark – not elsewhere in the world. However, the benchmark for distinctiveness may change as the business model or livelihood scheme is explored – aspirations may become more ambitious as the group discovers that its distinctive competences are more distinctive than they had thought. Alternatively, sometimes a group realizes that they are not exploiting their distinctiveness as fully as they might, because they have not appreciated fully the nature of their distinctiveness.

The opposite may also occur. Here, a group discovers that much of what is distinctive is also useless in relation to their current aspirations! As noted above, many distinctive competences of an organization grow over time and the organization becomes so proud of them that they forget why they needed them. Distinctiveness is, therefore, relative to a benchmark, usually with respect to other organizations, existing or potential, as defined by the aspirations and goals system, rather than to any absolute criterion. This means that aspirations can subsequently be changed to become less demanding if increasing distinctiveness is difficult to come by. Exploring distinctive competences and goals systems must therefore be done together (see Figure 6.1).

The Nature of Distinctiveness[8]

One means of surfacing distinctiveness is to ask: 'What do we do, or can we do, exceptionally well so that our customers perceive we add more value than alternative providers?'[9] An organization stays alive by providing value to a stakeholder base. These stakeholders are most often customers for private and public organizations, public sector divisions which gain services as public goods, as well as those stakeholders who directly fund or provide a mandate for the provision of the service. This value is derived from a combination of stakeholder demands and the distinctive competences of the supplying organization. Distinctiveness means some measure of difference, of being able to offer to the customers something that no other competitor can. For an organization to be able to claim a position of sustainable profitability it has to be able to satisfy a customer market in a manner that resists easy emulation.[10] Thus, distinctiveness may derive from:

■ Difficulty of emulation.

This may mean that:

■ It cannot be easily bought, or
■ There is a very high cost of entry.

And this may derive from:

■ It taking a very long time to attain the competence (for example, trust and loyalty of employees or customers).

In addition, distinctiveness is often about processes rather than infrastructure. For example, the complex harmonization of technology and production skills, the ability to organize work to deliver value, or even the ability to exploit competences effectively, could be considered.[11] Where the competence surrounds a particular piece of equipment (regardless of how expensive or new) there is always the danger that the distinctiveness could soon be eroded as competitors find ways of accessing this equipment.

Distinctiveness therefore is 'definitionally' related to uniqueness (where it is difficult to substitute), rare among a firm's competition, imperfectly inimitable, and valuable (through being able to exploit opportunities or neutralize threats). An example might be 'potent access to a wide variety of markets' possibly through a unique distribution network and the ability to present the product as being valuable.

As a result of this uniqueness it is possible to encounter a type of distinctiveness that is seen to be important, but is extremely difficult to make explicit. Here it can be given a label but one that everyone is aware does not fully recognize the competence. Competences that are uncodified are likely to be distinctive – you don't know how it works or how you developed it, thus others can't work out how it works either![12]

Some of the items often proudly presented as distinctive competences include – large-scale production, high market share, successful diversification, or being the sole organization in the marketplace. These are not distinctive competences but rather are usually the consequences or outcomes of the exploitation, either deliberate or emergent, of distinctive competences. Indeed they are most often the successful exploitation of a **system of interlocking competences** (only some of which might be distinctive). Thus, it is important, in any discussion about competences, to separate outcomes from the competences that drive the outcomes. The outcomes may, or may not, be desirable in relation to aspirations and goals but must be distinguished from characteristics that are exploitable (that is manageable) emergent properties. The distinction is often difficult to make, but discussion aimed at drawing out the distinction is usually helpful in good strategy making, as a better understanding of the organization's perceived competences are surfaced and refined.

When carrying out this process, it might also be worth considering the difference between competitive strategy at the level of a business and at the level of the entire company.[13] How can synergies be best exploited – the $2+2=5$ objective (where the interaction between the two competences have more than an additive effect). What often happens is that distinctions between strategic business units (SBUs) are seen only as sources of profit rather than as part of a coherent system and thus the potential to leverage further benefits is missed. This issue is even more significant when considering, for example, the business model of a corporate head office, where their contribution to corporate goals depends very much on bringing together competences that derive from the full range of SBUs.[14]

Go to task 4a

Decide what your reference point for distinctiveness is – related to your draft aspirations or goals system.

Commentary and Issues

The draft goals system may not, at this stage, benchmark your aspirations against those of your competitors. If so, now may be a good time to review and redraft.

The relative nature of distinctiveness of competences may be very loosely defined by the draft goals system, even after it has been modified. It is not helpful to become too precise at this stage; the benchmarking is expected to provide guidance only and, in practice, is to ensure that the demands of distinctiveness are not treated as if they were absolute.

It is often difficult for public or not-for-profit organizations to establish a benchmark because they often do not believe themselves to be in competition. In these circumstances it helps to think of what would happen if competitive tendering were invited, or in the case of charities, which organization might be considered better able to deliver the mandate or goals.

Comment 6.1

- If the goals system states: 'we shall deliver exceptional quality products to our chosen market', this could be changed to 'we shall deliver products that represent exceptional quality relative to any others'. Here the change implies that the reference point for distinctiveness of products is probably global and encompasses all other competitors.
- If the goals system states: 'an increase in staff motivation', then we need to know more about the structure of the goals system in order to establish how this general goal reflects a distinctive goals system where motivation in this organization is for a distinctive purpose. When we know more about the links in and out of motivation then we may know more about its role in determining a reference for distinctive competences.

Go to task 4b

Write down (on Post-it® notes or using Decision Explorer®) your distinctive competences, and spread them around the flipchart covered wall or computer screen.

Commentary and Issues

Many DCs listed will be distinctive **outcomes** not distinctive **competences**. For example, high levels of customer loyalty may be displayed as a distinctive competence. This is clearly an important characteristic of your business which may be distinctive – not available to use by competitors – but it is the outcome of *competences* within the organization. It is probably related to the way in which you do business that is different from that of competitors. This distinctiveness must be displayed but, ultimately, must be elaborated so that the competences that drive this outcome are identified – it is only competences that can be managed strategically, not outcomes of them.

Do not worry about a focus on distinctive outcomes at the start of the task. This can come later.

Distinctive competences usually come from the **interrelationships** between competences rather than one single factor. Therefore, there are two ways of thinking about distinctiveness:

1   Single characteristics that in their own right are distinctive.
2   Competences linking together to create a unique pattern, and this means that we shall, at a secondary stage of surfacing distinctive competences, relax the constraints and consider important competences.

Thus, as so-called distinctive competences are displayed, a debate may occur about whether those displayed are indeed distinctive. Avoid too much debate at this stage, because important distinctiveness will gradually appear as interrelationships emerge. Wait until later to evaluate.

Once again, do not worry about finding this task difficult, most groups do! Public and not-for-profit organizations usually find this very depressing. They will have rarely considered these aspects of their role, rather presuming they simply have the right to earn a livelihood from delivering a service (which is why we refer to their equivalent of the business model as the livelihood scheme, as in this type of organization it expresses the right to a livelihood as compared to others delivering the service).

Hints and Tips

■ Start identifying competences:

  ■ Think about what you believe you do better than anyone else. What are you proud of? What makes you special?
  ■ Think about how you are different from the competition – what makes you stand out (gives you competitive advantage[15])?
  ■ Think about customers – what distinctive 'added value' do they see you offering?[16]

■ Make sure the competences are worded as a **competence**. As with writing out the issues and goals, avoiding single or two word phrases will help.
■ DCs cannot usually be 'lower costs' unless you have distinctive competences that result in lower costs as a distinctive outcome. So do not accept 'lower costs' as a distinctive competence but as a distinctive outcome.
■ Watch that competences and DCs don't duplicate issues. Sometimes it is possible to see contradictions here. For example, say an issue highlighted notes a concern about 'damage to reputation', but when identifying DCs, reputation is considered as a distinctive outcome. If this is the case then add a negative link from 'damage' to the DC to show that it is under attack.
■ Keeping the group moving.

  ■ Relax the requirement for displaying DCs, and encourage the displaying of **important competences**: competences that you're good at, that are crucial to your past success, competences you're proud of. Try something like **unusual competences**.
  ■ One aspect that helps in surfacing distinctive and important competences is to look from the 'outside in'. It is often easy to disregard something special as it is an organizational norm or practice and therefore taken for granted. Try to imagine doing the exercise as a customer or competitor or some other stakeholder. Additionally, trying different means of viewing distinctiveness helps in surfacing new competences.

■ Examine all of the competences – is it clear exactly what they are referring to? Would others in the organization agree with the competence? Would those outside? Asking these questions will help with identifying what particular aspect is unique and special to the organization.
■ At first, concentrate of the emergence of DCs rather than identifying links. This means that as the group runs out of material there might not be many links, and so this is the time to encourage attaching links where appropriate. Here the link shows which competence sustains or supports another. (Remember the potential for too many links that was discussed in the earlier

mapping chapters: A>B>C and A>C, where A>C is simply a summary of A>B>C.)

Go to task 4c

Ladder down at least three levels from distinctive **outcomes**. Ladder down at least two levels from distinctive **competences** by asking 'what is it that really sustains this DC?'

Commentary and Issues

Usually, when in the early stages of building a distinctive competences map, groups work at too abstract a level, and do not address actionable competences – competences that can be sustained, improved or dropped. The technique of laddering down (see chapter 3) is designed to address this issue.

The first attempts at developing a map of distinctiveness tend to be dominated by too many vague statements – statements that are not precise enough about exactly which competences make the organization distinct (although, as noted above, this is important for getting started). Later on in the process, getting the wording of the distinctive competence right can help define what is distinctive. Often the description is simply too short (eight to ten words are usually needed).

Laddering down not only seeks to discover the processes and characteristics that sustain a distinctive outcome or competence, it also can elaborate their meaning by identifying a range of characteristics that typify the competence (see Figure 6.2), as well as giving prompts to surface further distinctive competences.

Hints and Tips

■ Ladder down the competences by asking: 'What is it that really sustains this distinctive competence or important competence?' For example, if the competence is 'we have a culture of innovation', ask how the organization achieves this. One answer might be that a subordinate competence, namely 'staff have no fear of failure', exists. Therefore, check whether each competence is a competence or an outcome of a competence. Indeed, no fear of failure also begs the question as to how this was attained.

■ Although we recommend laddering down two or three levels, the objective is to ladder down until **competences that are actionable** are identified. Ask

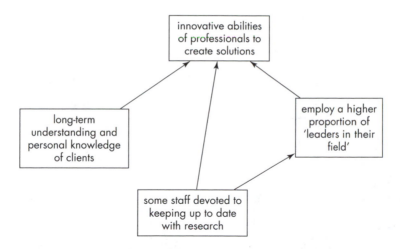

Figure 6.2 An Early Stage of Competency Identification: "innovative abilities" as a distinctive outcome is examined to determine what is meant by this assertion

the group to think as managers and to consider whether they would know what to do if they were asked to be responsible for ensuring that the competence was sustained or strengthened. In this way, a competence displayed as 'high reliability' would beg the question 'reliability for what?' and require both better explication and laddering down.

■ This process will add more important competences to your emerging map.

Go to task 4d

Add all linkages between competences and distinctive competences.

Commentary and Issues

Our key objective in linking competences and distinctive competences is that of looking for patterns in the map. In Figure 6.3 the linkages inserted at this stage show that the competence to 'be more assertive' is a crucial part of a self-sustaining feedback loop involving two distinctive competences. The loop itself is a distinctive competence. However, less obviously there are two other feedback loops involving 'staff have confidence in dealing with people – no fear of failure'. Each of these feedback loops may be a distinctive pattern, and 'confidence' is likely to be a very significant distinctive competence. 'Confidence' is likely, but not certain, to be a candidate for core distinctive competence.

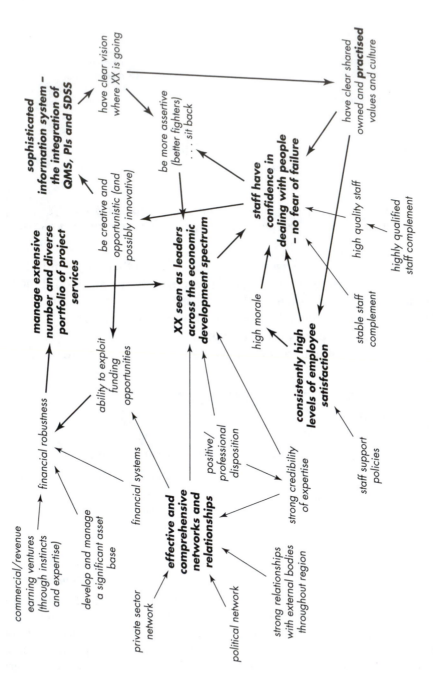

Figure 6.3 Emerging Patterns of Competences and Distinctive Competences (bold statements are regarded as distinctive competences or outcomes)

Watch out for:

■ A positive feedback loop of competences (see Figure 6.4) might make the loop a distinctive competence[17] (see the discussion of feedback noted in support 1 of this book and comment 6.2 below).

■ A **positive feedback loop with at least one distinctive competence in it** is important because the behaviour of the loop sustains the distinctive competence.

■ A particular and **distinctive patterning of competences** that might be particularly important (in other words the pattern is the DC because nobody else could achieve the pattern even if they could get the competences)[18] – this in essence is the **portfolio effect**.

■ A **positive feedback loop with the ability to support and sustain a distinctive competence** (Figure 6.5) where one of the statements in the loop ladders up to a DC – this makes the DC more powerful.

Comment 6.2

What is a feedback loop? What is a positive feedback loop?

The arrows that link statements of distinctive competence reflect the notion that the arrow represents the belief that the competence at the tail of the arrow supports the existence of the competence at the head of the arrow. A feedback loop exists when it is possible to follow a chain of arrows that feed back to the starting point. For example, competence A helps support competence J, which in turn helps support competence P, which in turn helps support competence D, which in turn is believed to support competence A. Starting the trail arrows from any of A, J, P or D will lead back to itself.

See also support 1 on the analysis of cause maps.

Feedback loops[19] of distinctive competences are particularly important because they illustrate the self-sustaining nature of all the competences encompassed within the feedback loop. Thus, an outstanding distinctive competence incorporates the sustaining **relationships** as well as the distinctive competence itself. Furthermore, if these feedback loops of distinctiveness support the organization's aspirations then they must be prime candidates to become a core distinctive competence – simply because of their power to self-sustain a desired strategic future.

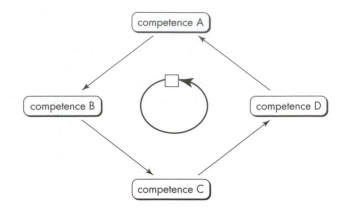

Figure 6.4 A Distinctive Competence Arising from a Feedback Loop of Competences

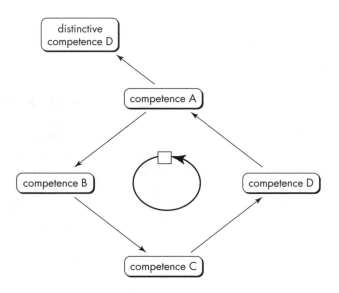

Figure 6.5 A Loop that Supports and Sustains a Distinctive Competence

■ If there are no virtuous circles (positive feedback loops working in your favour), then look out for the possibility of creating loops by developing a potential strategy to create new links and thus exploit the competences further.

Linking distinctive competences or competences can often reveal that some attack rather than support one another – they are in competition with one another – possibly for resources. For example, one competence might lead negatively to another revealing a potential conflict. Some means of managing or resolving this conflict will need to be found.

Hints and Tips

■ Developing a *system* of interrelated competences encourages the group and can further trigger the emergence of new competences.

■ Often when seeking to surface distinctive competences with senior staff, the distinctive competences surfaced by them are not considered to be either distinctive or a competence by others further down the organization. Those at the top of an organization often see the world through 'rose-tinted glasses'! Therefore, at some later stage, it might be worth testing the surfaced system with others in the organization to see if it is recognizable, or getting another group to surface distinctiveness from scratch and then to make comparisons.

Exploring the Business Model or Livelihood Scheme

The business model or livelihood scheme expresses the links between distinctive competences and goals, and the goals system expresses the distinctive aspirations of the organization that will deliver shareholder value or the mandate (for public organizations) – see Figure 6.6.

Distinctiveness, as noted earlier, was considered in relation to the aspirations or goals of the organization – that is, the goals system was the benchmark against which distinctiveness was judged.[20] As examined in the early part of this chapter, distinctive competences were identified as individual properties or as patterns (task 4 – delivering the first substage outcomes). Here, we consider them in relation to the goals they support and how they can be exploited, grown and sustained. Task 5 explores how the distinctive competences provide support to achieve the goals, and so create the business model.

profit/profitability/shareholder value or mandate

↑

distinctive system of goals/aspirations

↑

core distinctive competences

↑

distinctive competences

Figure 6.6 Summarizing the Business Model/Livelihood Scheme

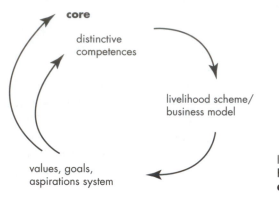

Figure 6.7 Conceptualizing the Process of the Identification of **core** Distinctive Competences

Figure 6.7 replays the diagram presented at the start of this chapter. In presenting that diagram we suggested that the process of developing the business model or livelihood scheme is cyclical. In this figure we reinforce the point, by showing how the process gradually allows core distinctive competences to emerge. Here we use the term 'core' in a commonsense way. It means that some distinctive competences will be central or potent to the attainment of goals. In creating the links between competences, patterns of competences that are distinctive, distinctive competences and the goals, it will usually become obvious which are at the core of the business model or livelihood scheme. Those distinctive competences that 'hit' many goals, that is, provide the greatest leverage towards attainment of the goals, are usually at the 'core' and will

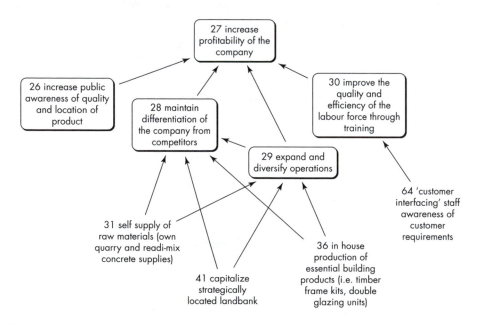

Figure 6.8 An Example of Linking DCs to Goals

be core distinctive competences. (More formal analysis of the map that is the business model is possible using some of the analytical tools presented in support 1.) The important point here is that contrary to many views of core competences, they are not a simple category of competences, rather the model's structure determines what they are – **core distinctive competences are discovered**.

Go to task 5a

Exploiting distinctive competences to realize goals.

Commentary and Issues

Developing a coherent system of goals and distinctive competences is important because we wish to **harness our competences effectively** – that is, link them to our aspirations and make sure that the energies of the organization are focused on the future leverage of competences to attain the goals of the organization, rather than on their past use.

A strong business model will show at least one distinctive competence supporting each goal, and each goal supported by at least one distinctive competence.

■ For goals without DCs supporting them, strategies will need to be put into place to develop new competences. These competences should be distinctive whenever possible, although it is very difficult, by definition, to develop new DCs. It is, however, possible to develop new patterns which can be distinctive, particularly where new virtuous feedback loops of competences can be developed.

■ If some goals do not seem to have any competences supporting them, then it begs the question of whether the goal is achievable. It may be achieved by the support of other subordinate goals that do have the support of DCs. Or, alternatively, DCs may need to be developed to ensure the viability of the goal (however, see the comments above about the difficulty of developing new DCs).

■ Where possible these new foci of energy (new competences or competence links) are designed to support not only a single goal but also other goals. Looking for the **greatest leverage** extends the potency of new developments.

Some distinctive competences will appear to support no goals. This circumstance raises two questions. Are some goals missing from the system that might be advantageously delivered using the distinctive competence? Perhaps the competence is no longer something to expend energy upon because it is not supporting a goal (as elaborated below)?

As noted at the beginning of this chapter, organizations typically expend a considerable amount of energy sustaining competences and distinctive competences that have been an important part of the history of the organization. Sometimes there is significant pride in them, and yet they are no longer important to a sound strategic future. There is always a need to balance the sustenance of old competences against the need to provide resources to develop new competences. By stopping or reducing effort on the old competences that no longer support the aspirations system, energy can then be released to be expended on developing the new competences.

So, a distinctive competence may not always be a good thing! As noted above, one of the important outcomes from considering distinctive competences and their role in the business model or livelihood scheme will be the discovery that the organization is wasting energy and costs in sustaining competences and patterns of competences that are of no help in the creation of a strategic future for the organization.[21]

Hints and Tips

■ Use a new flipchart sheet, or make a new view in Decision Explorer,® comprising only the patterns of DCs and goals system – otherwise the material can become too busy and unhelpful. (Although when DCs are importantly made up of linked competences then these will need to show on the new map also.)

■ Remember DCs may be defined by clusters or feedback loops, and so it is the links between key statements within the cluster or loop that are inserted. Thus it is the system of competences that can often supply the competitive advantage and provide the basis for the business model or livelihood scheme.

■ Sometimes goals seem to link upwards to DCs – when this occurs it may be that you are discovering a DC that is a goal (see case study 6.1). Alternatively the linking is incorrect and needs to be reviewed or the goal is a strategic option and needs to be reviewed.

■ DCs for start-ups often appear to be related to one person (the entrepreneur) – in this case it should be made clear that the strategic future of the company lies with this one person[22] (and, by definition, it cannot really be a DC unless there is a 'mechanism for stopping that person leaving'!).[23]

■ For some types of organization, it is difficult to ignore people as being an important competence or even a DC. Professional services organizations are a good example where the professional people (for example, lawyers, accountants) are at the heart of both the service delivery and the service provision. In these circumstances, you should consider what competences are in place to support those people and, if necessary, what competences will help to retain them.

■ Keep asking whether there are other **chains** or **routes** between a DC and goals to ensure that the full impact of each DC or competence has been considered (competences often support more than one goal or further competence).

■ Consider whether you need to develop any existing DCs or competences to support the goals. If you do, explore whether you can develop new feedback loops of existing competences.

■ Ask the following questions:

   ■ Which DCs or competences are no longer central to your strategic future?

   ■ Are there **new links** between competences that could:

      ■ Form a feedback loop to give sustainable advantage, because they feed off each other?
      ■ Support more goals?

   In these circumstances a potential strategy arises: that of developing the link.

Go to task 5b

Find the core distinctive competences.

Commentary and Issues

As discussed in the introduction, understanding which distinctive competences are core to the business model is crucial because these must be protected at all costs – they are at the core of achieving our aims. Core distinctive competences are core only in relation to the goals system.

Within the context of developing strategic vision, core distinctive competences are those that primarily drive the aspirations system. Thus there are direct and powerful links between the competence and many of the goals.

Competences that are not distinctive may be candidates for outsourcing, although it is often the case that apparently peripheral competences are absolutely essential to the sustenance of core competences, and so need to be maintained through internal control. When a core distinctive competence is derived from the existence of a self-sustaining feedback loop of non-distinctive competences then these competences, when taken together, are crucial and so considering outsourcing of any one of them can be a recipe for failure. (Eden and Ackermann, 1998)

Hints and Tips

■ When a distinctive competence is a loop then it will inevitably show up as core because the probability of links to many goals or many links to a single goal will be higher – this is the potency of a competence. Each node on the loop can be tracked to at least one goal or aspiration in its own right but also through every other node on the loop.
■ Ask: 'Is there anything we should or should not be outsourcing?'[24]

■ Be careful of the danger of losing competence links that are important if you outsource.
■ Is too much energy being used on things that are not crucial?
■ Figure 6.9 illustrates some of the considerations in evaluating appropriate strategies for outsourcing.

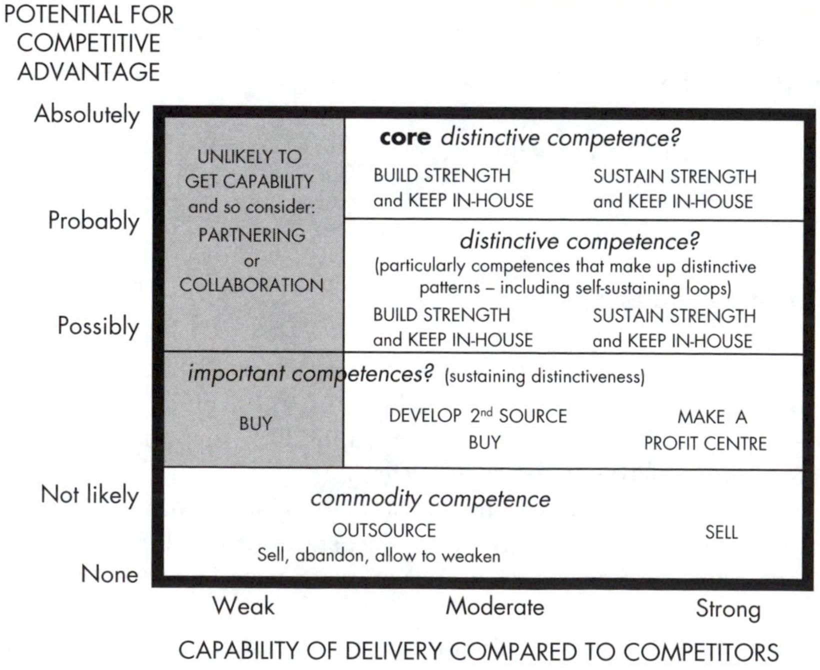

POTENTIAL FOR
COMPETITIVE
ADVANTAGE

		core *distinctive competence?*	
Absolutely	UNLIKELY TO GET CAPABILITY and so consider:	BUILD STRENGTH and KEEP IN-HOUSE	SUSTAIN STRENGTH and KEEP IN-HOUSE
Probably	PARTNERING or COLLABORATION	*distinctive competence?* (particularly competences that make up distinctive patterns – including self-sustaining loops)	
Possibly		BUILD STRENGTH and KEEP IN-HOUSE	SUSTAIN STRENGTH and KEEP IN-HOUSE
		important competences? (sustaining distinctiveness)	
	BUY	DEVELOP 2nd SOURCE BUY	MAKE A PROFIT CENTRE
Not likely		*commodity competence*	
None		OUTSOURCE Sell, abandon, allow to weaken	SELL
	Weak	Moderate	Strong

CAPABILITY OF DELIVERY COMPARED TO COMPETITORS

Figure 6.9 Outsourcing Strategies (based on ideas from Insinga and Werle, 2000)

> ## Go to task 6
>
> **Make the goals system realistic and powerful.**

Commentary and Issues

The development of the business model or livelihood scheme will have suggested that some goals are less realistic because they do not have the sustenance of at least one distinctive competence. Similarly, some distinctive competences that are core might attain goal status (see for example in case study 6.1).

Our objective in this task is to make the goals system more realistic while also keeping it aspirational.

Hints and Tips

Where a goal is not supported by a DC (including a DC which is a pattern, particularly a feedback loop) then it may become:

■ A reworded goal, making it more realistic.
■ Reduced in status to a low level goal or redefined as a possible strategy.
■ Dropped altogether from the goals system (but look out for the impact of dropping it on superordinate and subordinate goals).

Summary and Review

Exploring distinctive competences and developing the business model or livelihood scheme are powerful as they mean:

■ Explicating and exploring the relationship between possible competences and DCs to discover *patterns*, which are distinctive.
■ Extending the model to determine the causality between distinctive patterns of competences **and** the system of goals or aspirations.
■ Modifying aspirations so that they become realistic over time, and/or modifying distinctive competences. This may mean:

  ■ Identifying strategies for the development of new competences and making distinctive competences more powerful.
  ■ Dropping the wasted sustenance of unnecessary competences.

- Creating a business model or livelihood scheme:

  - That is distinctive in relation to the distinctive aspirations or goals of the organization.
  - That enables the identification of core distinctive competences as those which are central or core to the attainment of a realistic goals system.

- Enabling us to outsource appropriately.

Being clear about what makes us distinctive (goals, competences and so the business model) and what we are aiming to achieve allows us to:

- Be clear about the added value we are able to create and sustain.
- Have a coherent and well-understood direction based on realistic goals and the ability to be able to deliver them.
- Have a sustained strategic future.

Notes

1 Johnson and Scholes (2002) pp. 149, 156–9 discuss competences and core competences in some detail, which helps to add more meaning and context to the topic. They place emphasis on linking competences to customers, although they also make reference to linking them to 'critical success factors'.
2 Johnson and Scholes (2002) pp. 156 and 169 discuss the concept of 'threshold' resources and competences, which are those that every company in the industry or sector will need to achieve.
3 Eden and Ackermann (1998) pp. 102–5 use the term 'livelihood scheme' to describe the equivalent of a business model as applied to the public sector or not-for-profit organizations. In these instances the role of mandates and the source of funding play major roles. Johnson and Scholes (2002) pp. 94–5 and 253–62 refer to the 'business idea', which is not always the same as business model or livelihood scheme – the business idea is generally a less formal and less analytically sound version of the business model. Nonetheless, the way that Johnson and Scholes describe it suggests that it is closer to our thinking than many writers in this field.
4 Johnson and Scholes (2002) pp. 324 and 336 discuss how core competences can lead to sustainable competitive advantage which others find difficult to imitate.
5 Johnson and Scholes (2002) pp. 169 and 495 discuss how competences can diminish with time and core competences can become threshold competences as others match them.
6 Van der Heijden (1996) pp. 59–81 discusses the business idea of an organization in some depth.
7 Lynch (2003) p. 495 proposes a ten-point list of guidelines that explore resource-based competences and capabilities, which could help with the identification of competences and DCs. Schoemaker (in De Wit and Meyer (1998) pp. 254–8) discusses what he refers to as 'capabilities', which we believe are essentially the same as

competences. He suggests a number of ways in which an organization's capabilities can be identified.

8   Eden and Ackermann (1998) chapter 6 provide an extended discussion of competence possibilities. Johnson and Scholes (2002) pp. 174–9 discuss in some detail the robustness of competences in relation to sustaining competitive advantage.

9   Van der Heijden (1996) pp. 64–5 gives a number of examples of distinctive competences which he groups into five categories – institutional knowledge, embedded processes, reputation and trust, legal protection and activity-specific assets.

10 Johnson and Scholes (2002) pp. 336–7 consider how differentiation-based competitive advantage can be sustained by leveraging competences.

11 Stalk, Evans and Shulman (in De Wit and Meyer (1998)) discuss the four basic principals of capabilities-based competition in order to 'identify and develop the hard-to-imitate organizational capabilities that distinguish a company from its competitors in the eyes of customers' (pp. 232–3). They identify four basic principals in which processes play an important role.

12 Johnson and Scholes (2002) (pp. 177–9) discuss complexity and causal ambiguity in relation to competences.

13 Prahalad and Hamel (in De Wit and Meyer (1998) pp. 296–301) discuss the issues surrounding core competences and SBUs.

14 Van der Heijden (1996) pp. 75–8 discusses the business idea in relation to SBUs, considering ways in which synergy between business units and corporate units can be exploited. He suggests that distinctive competences play a key role in this process.

15 Lynch (2003) pp. 125–30 provides a useful discussion about sustainable competitive advantage. He also discusses (pp. 200–47) the resource-based view of sustainable competitive advantage. It is our view that in discussing resources, Lynch is effectively discussing competences.

16 See perceived user value analysis in Johnson and Scholes (2002) pp. 130–2.

17 When discussing the systemic structure of the business idea, Van der Heijden (1996) pp. 68–9 highlights the importance of feedback loops that strengthen the competences of the organization. He also stresses the need to keep the loop positive.

18 Van der Heijden (1996) notes that 'the strongest business ideas derive from a set of competences that are unique because of the way that they are combined systematically' (p. 65).

19 As Figure 6.3 illustrates, finding all loops can be difficult. In Figure 6.3 there are many loops and these are only successfully identified using computer software such as Decision Explorer®, where the command 'loop' finds all loops.

20 Referring to work by Hamel and Prahalad, Lynch (2003) pp. 235–6 links the development of core competences to the provision of benefits to customers. This is different from our view that competences should be linked to goals – which may include goals relating to customers but will also include other goals.

21 Johnson and Scholes (2002) pp. 150 and 169.

22 Van der Heijden (1996) p. 63 argues that if a company relies on an individual expert for its business success then that person will eventually appropriate the profits. He goes on to suggest that in these circumstances, it is important to identify the strengths of the organization that support the strengths of the individual.

23 Lynch (2003) p. 494 discusses competences in the context of strategy development. He proposes a hierarchy of competences. Interestingly, this is based on the individual and group skills of people, suggesting that people can be a core competence. This is

in contrast with our view that people cannot be viewed as a DC because they can move.

[24] Johnson and Scholes (2002) pp. 176 and 450 discuss the need to take care when making decisions as to which activities should be outsourced and which should not. They stress the importance that core competences should be owned by the organization. Prahalad and Hamel (in De Wit and Meyer (1998) pp. 294–5) discuss the dangers of outsourcing core competences.

Case Study 6.1

A Question of Turning Around

Neil was new to the company, but not to the industry. He had recently been appointed as chief executive with responsibility to turn around the company over the next three years. The company was extremely short of cash and so was finding it difficult to invest in a sound strategic future. The organization was relatively small, with just over 200 employees, and was privately owned. Neil had bought into the company to the extent that he had a small shareholding, as did the other members of the senior management team.

This case study reviews how the management team set about developing a strategy for the organization. The part of the strategy-making process reported here considers the first day of a two-day workshop that used group mapping as the core technique.

Neil was keen to take a completely fresh look at the strategy of the organization but, given the precarious position of the organization, could not afford to spend too much time or money on doing so. A meeting with Neil led to an agreement that only the senior management team would be engaged in a strategy-making workshop. There was some conversation about involving other key players beyond the management team because of the significant role they would be expected to play in the implementation of any new strategy. However, it was decided to restrict the workshop to only the most senior managers who were also shareholders (task 1 – see chapter 2). This would mean that all those attending would have the same focus on a three-year time horizon. The business operated against a continuous a set of deadlines – at that time they were involved in the publication of magazines, the running of conferences and the organization of exhibitions. This meant that, even given the importance of a strategy-making workshop, senior managers could not take any time out of the normal working week. The workshop was planned to take place in a local hotel over a weekend.

Most senior managers, in many organizations, spend a great deal of their time fire-fighting and dealing with the issues rather than the opportunities. Consequently, strategic thinking tends to be set within the context of burning issues. In this particular case it was even more so – the everyday operations of the organization clearly were not running efficiently and stress levels were high.

In addition, the imposition of a new chief executive was stressful for other senior managers in the organization – there were likely to be tensions within the management team. Therefore, the strategy-making workshop needed to be about team building as well as making strategy. The thinking of the senior management team certainly mattered for the future of the organization.

The objective for the workshop was to develop a sound strategy for the organization, tested through the creation of a business model. The business model needed to show with some degree of confidence that the fortunes of the company could be turned around within the three-year time horizon. Doing this over a weekend was not going to be an easy task. In addition, it was essential that at least half of Sunday be spent discussing the immediate plans for the delivery of the strategy and what was to be said to all of the other employees of the company. As planning for the workshop continued, all of the other staff became aware that the strategy workshop was taking place and that it was significant for the future of the company. They were, therefore, keen to hear about outcomes first thing on the Monday following the workshop.

Testing out the strategy through developing a rough business model was likely to take at least half a day and given that there would be some cycling between a statement of strategic intent and its implications for cash flow and profits, this meant that the equivalent of one long day remained for the strategic thinking.

Colin and Fran, who had been asked to facilitate the strategy making, had worked with Neil ten years before when he was in a different organization. Neil had experienced the oval mapping technique and Decision Explorer® at that time. He was keen that a mapping approach be used on this occasion and, anyway, knew that Colin and Fran would expect to use some variety of mapping as part of their approach to strategy making.

Ordinarily Colin and Fran would have been inclined to use oval mapping in the first instance and then move to a more detailed strategy map through the use of Decision Explorer® interactively with the group. This would have enabled the group to become accustomed to a 'simple' hand-mapping process before being faced with computer technology. However, given the time constraints they persuaded Neil that it would be necessary to use a more efficient method for capturing the maps in real time by using a system of networked laptop computers linked directly to the public Decision Explorer® display.

The system (Group Explorer) would improve the productivity of the group while replicating the principles of the oval mapping technique. Participants would be able to type the text that they would have otherwise written on to an oval directly into a laptop computer. After hitting carriage return, the text is sent to the Decision Explorer® public display, which all members of the group can see. Figure CS 6.1 shows the type of arrangement that would be expected. Each statement appears on the screen within an oval shape and the leader of the group, or facilitator, is able to use their computer (which is running Decision

Figure CS6.1 A Group Working Through Networked Computers (Group Explorer)

Explorer®) to move the statements to different positions on the screen in the same way that ovals are moved around a wall surface. However, by using Decision Explorer® directly instead of wall space, each participant can also use their own laptop to instruct the display to show arrows to link statements and to produce a cause map.

Usually such workshops would require only one leader or facilitator. However, in this case it was important to ensure that there was one facilitator available to work directly with the group and another to think quite carefully, as an outsider, about the material coming forward. In this way, some short cuts could be taken, but with the risk that the workshop might move too fast for members of the group. Experienced facilitators can sometimes use their experience to move a workshop along quickly, but may risk losing participants for whom the process begins to become opaque.

Thinking Through the Workshop

How to Get at the Different Views About What Is Important for the Future of the Organization

As mentioned above, this was a senior management team under some significant pressure. Consequently, the first part of the workshop had to pay due attention to the urgent strategic issues facing the team in order to ensure that these would not become a continual background of niggles as other tasks were attempted. The workshop was therefore planned to start with an **explication of the strategic issues** facing the organization with respect to an impact three years into the future. With the networked computer system to help, and only five members in the group, it seemed likely that half an hour would be enough time to get these issues on to the public screen and to do some rough structuring of the statements into a map.

It is usual for managers to have some **important and urgent items** they wish to air early on in a meeting. Unless these get aired the participants are then more concerned about finding the space to 'grind their own axes' than in listening to others or extending their own contributions. This timescale was considered to be enough to get urgent issues 'out on the table' early in the workshop and to make sure there was clear acknowledgement of their having been stated: their presence on the public screen was planned to give comfort to those wishing to ensure that their concerns were not 'glossed over'. This would be followed by the need for the group to make sure they understood all the material surfaced.

Unlike the traditional oval mapping session, the contributions made using the networked system are completely anonymous. This has both disadvantages and advantages: it can provide a licence for blunt and honest comments, which can helpfully surface embedded frustrations; participants are able to disagree with statements without disagreeing with the person connected to the statement; and participants can more easily and deliberately seed a discussion topic. However, participants have no responsibility, at this time, for defending or elaborating their views. Full anonymity (as compared to the partial anonymity of oval mapping) can help break down the tendency of a group to suppress important views in order to maintain the social wellbeing of the group – a phenomenon known as **group think**.

Embedding full anonymity, at this stage, was a balance between the positive outcome of getting honest statements surfaced and the risk of irresponsible statements arising that would not need to be explained. A facilitator must take care to watch for scurrilous contributions, and when they arise, to carefully manage their impact on the group. Sometimes humorous statements, and deliberate typing errors, can help the group's progress, while making a serious statement at the same time.

As with traditional oval mapping, clustering similar topics or themes was likely to be helpful as a starting structure to the map. However, given the action orientation of a serious strategy workshop the more important clusters would come from a consideration of the causal links between statements. The next stage, following queries about potential misunderstandings, was planned to involve each of the participants adding causal arrows to introduce links across all of the material (not just between statements they had contributed).

Given that the group members were inexperienced in mapping, it seemed likely that, at least to start off with, the linking process would be less than perfect. While the facilitator working with the group would be attending to the positioning of material on the screen, the second facilitator would be able to monitor potential problems with links. For strategy making it is crucial that causal links are believed to be accurate by all members of the group since these linkages might have a profound impact upon strategy implementation at a later stage. It seemed likely that this stage could take up to an hour.

It is rare that a group will ever have mapped out the interaction between all of the issues faced by the organization. In this case it seemed likely that the anonymity feature would be particularly helpful, and that the issue map would reveal something new to every member of the group. It was expected that 50 to 70 issues would be surfaced during this stage. It was therefore going to be important to establish some draft priorities – both as a consequence of the statements themselves, but more importantly from simple analysis of the structure of the map on the screen facing the group. Half an hour was set aside for this task, which should provide the group with an important milestone. The milestone was expected to be an identification of central issues; of those issues that were significant drivers of many other issues; and of those bundles of issues (clusters) that were relatively separated from one another.

How to Gain an Understanding of the Implicit Strategic Direction of the Organization

With many strategy-making groups, this process of surfacing issues of importance to the group is used to provide clues about implicit, taken-for-granted, purposes or goals of the organization. When an issue is identified, it is put forward as an issue for the organization because it is implicitly, or sometimes explicitly, presumed to be attacking something that it is important for the organization – a goal. In this instance, some of the goals were sacred – they were set targets established by the major shareholders of the organization. The senior management team, who were also shareholders, needed to show how a resolution of what they regarded as important issues would drive through to these targets via some business outcomes or goals.

The issues or problems that managers actually deal with give a good indication of what goals are really driving the organization forward. Seeking to understand what outcomes are expected from dealing with issues begins to identify these goals. These goals should be the link between issues and ultimate outcomes, such as shareholder value (in the private sector), or meeting the mandate of a public sector organization.

At this stage participants were to be asked: 'What is achieved if an effective way is found of addressing the issue?' or 'What might happen, that is undesirable, if the issue is not addressed?' The answers to the questions about each issue would ladder one level up the causal map (see chapter 4). Asking the same question of the answers would continue the laddering up towards outcomes that are good or bad in their own right – goals.

How to Surface and Agree a Draft Strategic Direction

The next task for the group was expected to be a ratification, or otherwise, of why the issues were important for the future of the company. The group would be asked to identify the outcomes and goals that would be attained by addressing the important issues suggested by the previous task of issue identification and structuring. In doing so, there would be an expectation that the process of laddering up towards increasingly higher order outcomes would show a linkage between the resolution of the issues and the inviolable goals. The objective of the task would be to articulate some draft goals expected to drive the organization towards the delivery of shareholder needs. In addition, there was an expectation that some of the important issues may be re-evaluated because they do not deliver these needs in a clearly articulated manner. It was expected that this process could take up to an hour and a half.

The completion of this task should also represent a significant milestone for the group. They should have a much clearer view of a **distinctive (possibly) set of goals for their organization**. The goals should be represented as a network with each goal helping to sustain other goals and, in turn, being sustained by the resolution of an issue or a goal. It should be possible for the group to construct a **draft statement of strategic aims** for the organization. The statement should be a narrative that fully expresses the network of goals. It is likely that the statement would exclude the needs of the shareholders, and moreover, be an expression of what should be driving the operational activities of the managers of the organization in meeting the needs of shareholders.

A statement of strategic aims is powerful when it represents the interaction between all of the goals: the goals are seen as a system where each goal helps deliver other superordinate goals and may in turn be helped by the delivery of subordinate goals.

The power of the emerging goals is tested by the extent to which they are different from those of competitors. If they are the same then the group is facing head-on competition where the winner will be determined only by the different quality of the competences of the organization. Delivering shareholder value through a distinctive system of goals is, therefore, likely to be more sustainable over a long period of time.

How to Explore What the Organization Was Really Good At

To some extent, the company had been plodding along in the same business, and with the same products, presented in the same way, for many years. There was an implicit assumption that the delivery of these products was the best exploitation of the competences and particularly the distinctive competences of the company, and its staff. However, in order to deliver the shareholder needs, it seemed likely that the company would need a tighter focus on exploiting its distinctive competences, and that where distinctive competences were being sustained and yet did not significantly support the required strategic future reorganization, then effort on sustaining them should be reduced. Therefore, the next planned task for the workshop was to be the **explication of distinctive competences** within the context of the draft goals. Once again, these could have been surfaced using the oval mapping technique, to ensure that the interrelationship between competences and distinctive competences could be identified through a map. By using the networked computer system the map of competences could be created faster, anonymously, and with the ability to continuously create a computer-based record.

How to Test Whether There Was a Viable Business

When taken together, the previous tasks allow the development of a **qualitative business model**. This process seeks to: a) test the distinctiveness of the draft distinctive competences, and b) demonstrate that an exploitation of the distinctive competences can resolve the important strategic issues, and address the realization of each of the goals within the draft goals system.

Typically this task can be difficult and testing for the group. With a management team of eight to ten people, usually a two-day workshop would be required to reach the stage of a well-constructed qualitative business model. With five people it might be possible to complete this task in three hours.

Neil mentioned that while the members of this group knew the language of core competences, they were not clear about what a core competence was. Consequently, it was going to be necessary to ensure that they knew the difference between a distinctive competence and a core competence: that core competences only emerge after the link between all distinctive competences and the goals of the organization have been established. Core competences are those that are 'at the core' of the business model (delivering a successful and realistic strategic future).

In thinking through this workshop, we were hoping to get to this stage by the end of the first day. It seemed just possible . . .

The Plan

The planned timetable for the workshop at this stage looked something like this:

■ 0.900–10.30 – Issue surfacing and mapping. Issue prioritization (milestone).

- 11.00–12.30 – Explication of outcomes and goals that are linked issues to shareholder needs. Drafting of a distinctive network of goals and draft mission statement (milestone).
- 13.30–15.00 – Explication of and network of competences and distinctive competences.
- 15.30–17.00 – Drafting the business model. Linking the exploitation of distinctive competences to the goals system, and the development of strategies for the resolution of issues.

While it is rarely possible to stick to a planned timetable precisely, it will give form to the workshop and permit contingencies to be dealt with in the full knowledge of the consequences of changes to the plan. The participants must also be told that the plan may be adjusted to account for important considerations that will arise from what actually unfolds as the workshop progresses.

This timetable, therefore, left the following tasks to be undertaken during Sunday:

- Reviewing issue prioritization and goals system.
- Quantitatively testing the business model against shareholder needs.
- Drafting a statement of strategic intent.
- Considering immediate implications for strategic action priorities.
- Agreeing the way forward.
- Agreeing what to tell staff on returning to the office.

Given the amount of work that had to be completed on the first day, it was felt that the detailed planning for Sunday should be left until the end of Saturday. Nevertheless, it was important to establish that it was just about possible to manage all of these tasks on Sunday, or at least establish the rough proportional break down of time to be allocated to each of them.

The final plan suggested: three-quarters of an hour on reviewing issue prioritization and goals; an hour and a half on quantitative testing; half an hour on drafting a statement; an hour and a half on immediate implications; two hours on agreeing the way forward; and half an hour agreeing what to tell staff. This suggested about seven hours of work on Sunday, which was agreed to be just possible.

The Workshop

Arrivals

Neil, Colin and Fran arrived on Friday evening to ensure that the hotel room was adequate, and to set up the networked computer system. The hotel room was disappointing, and so stage management was going to be difficult – the standard hotel boardroom style was wholly inappropriate for a team-building/ strategy-making workshop. The room was cluttered with too much furniture, pictures and wall lights. Two hours later, most of the furniture had been removed, pictures taken off the walls and the room layout completely changed. The process facilitator was to be seated at the front-side so that they could be an integral part of the group. A small table and chair were set up at the back of the room for the content facilitator. Colin and Fran planned to exchange these roles after each task. The remaining furniture was set up as a semi-circle of small tables, each having a laptop computer.

The five participants arrived on time on Saturday morning to an inadequate supply of coffee and stale biscuits! Other than Neil, no participants had taken part in a serious strategy-making workshop, and none had experienced an approach to group work using a high productivity computer-based Group Support System. Personal introductions to Colin and Fran took place over coffee. As expected, it became clear that while some of the group were able to work together on operational issues of mutual interest, their conversations and thinking about the nature of the organization and its future differed markedly.

Colin started the workshop by introducing the objectives, the rough pro- gramme and timings for the day. Colin took care to ensure the explanation used no jargon, and made it clear why each of the tasks were important and how they fitted in to the whole programme for the workshop. Fran went on to introduce the processes that would be used, including the way the computer system would work. As none of the group, other than Neil, had experienced mapping, their introduction to it would have to be exceedingly transparent and incremental. The intention was to provide the group with realistic expec- tations about objectives and timing of the workshop and to indicate some clear milestones.

Fran explained some of the reasons why it was helpful for a group to get the issues they felt were important for the strategic future of the organization out on the table.

The 'Issue Dump' (task 2)

Fran introduced the standard oval mapping conventions (see chapter 4) – as conventions not rules:

- It does not matter whether the issues stated are set out in detail or are more ambiguous.
- Issues may be those that relate to your own responsibilities or to other parts of the organization.
- They do not have to represent issues that have been regarded as important in the past.

- Each statement should represent one issue – issues that are linked to one another can be established during the next stage.
- If possible, try to characterize the issue in six to eight words – more than eight words usually means that there is more than one issue and it will help to decouple them.
- Just agreeing or disagreeing with issues already on the screen is not permitted – however, alternative views and additional commentaries are encouraged.
- An issue is something about which somebody needs to do something – if nothing is done then the successful future the organization is at risk.
- The quality of typing and spelling is absolutely unimportant, as long as everyone understands what is meant.

There was no hesitation among any participant about contributing issues. Sometimes, there are some participants who are unhappy about their computer skills, or their competence in selecting good issues. However, full anonymity reduces some of these risks.

After about 20 minutes the group had produced the work output shown in Figure CS6.2. Fifty-two issue statements are shown. Fran had been moving the issues around the public screen so that they appeared to her to be in rough clusters according to themes/topics (see chapters 3 and 4). These topics provided a useful way for Fran to summarize this first stage. As she did so, she checked her impressions of the emerging themes with the group.

Interesting features of the issue dump are that: a) it was dominated by internal issues; b) there were many issues about the working and effectiveness of the senior management team (implying that they are more of a group than a team) – it was encouraging that they were prepared to acknowledge this so explicitly; c) there were many issues about staff – keeping the best, getting the best, locking them in; d) at this stage there was very little material about specific products or the marketplace.

Issue Structuring

The group added more material as they queried and elaborated the first issue dump and then moved on to explore linkages across the material. The display on the screen was now changed to show reference numbers against each statement – this makes linking easy since each participant can add a link by typing two numbers linked by a '+' sign, for example, typing 23+46 places an arrow from statement number 23 to statement 46.

The linked map is shown in Figure CS6.3. After (not during) the linking, the statements were moved around the screen to try and make the picture clearer. As always, the rough clustering (which was undertaken without attention to causality) changed as the links appeared. Linking focuses attention on action,

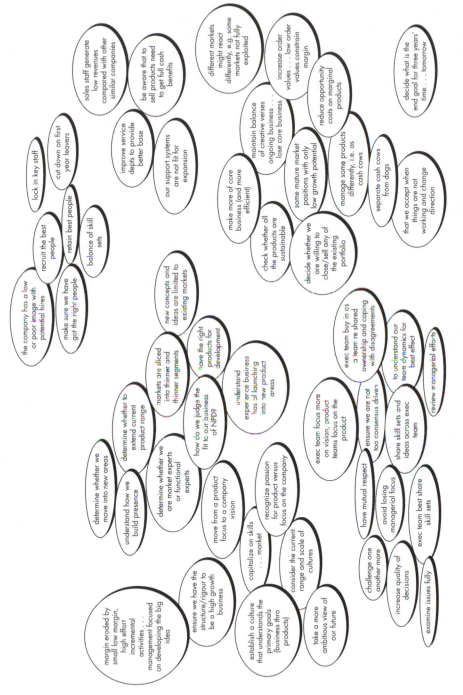

Figure CS6.2 In 20 minutes the group produced 52 issue statements. Fran moved them into rough topic clusters. In the next stage, topic labels would be attached to the clusters – a useful way of summarizing this first stage.

rather than the topic: why things are done and what things need to be done to make other things happen. This means that links will be across clusters and themes as much as they will be within them.

After the group felt confident in their **issue structuring** (see chapters 3 and 4) they found it easy to suggest some initial ideas about how the large number of issues could be reduced into a set of priorities. These initial ideas emerged from considering the new clusters that appeared after links were made. For example, looking around the screen it seemed possible that 44, 13, 29, 60, 74 and 68 were likely to be important since they each seemed to be at the centre of a cluster.

It had taken over an hour and a half to set a good issue structure, which means that the schedule was already running slightly late and developing a consensus about priorities was still required.

Prioritizing Strategic Issues

To help the group establish how much consensus there was, the group software was used to allow anonymity in identifying these priorities. The first task was for the facilitator to work with the group to identify no more than about 12 statements that captured clusters of strategic arenas. The analysis of the map gave the group some clues: some statements were very busy (they had lots of causes and consequences – for example, obvious candidates were statements 44, 68, 13, 25 and 29), others were drivers of many consequences (such as statements 26, 37, 40, 56 and 123, each of which connect through to three end points). However, the group, while acknowledging this rational approach, also wanted to add some other statements that represented arenas they thought important. This resulted in a total of 13 potential strategic arenas.

The group was invited to prioritize the statements by allocating **resources** to each. In addition, they were allowed to allocate some **negative resources** to indicate that they would be very disappointed to see a particular strategic arena prioritized – a sort of veto. In effect, each participant is given a restricted number of resources that could be used to implement whatever actions are required to resolve the issue. This allocation was done anonymously, so each of the five participants was invited to be very blunt in expressing their views. With the help of the computer system, the exercise took about 12 minutes. The outcome shown on the public screen indicated the total resources devoted to each statement and the degree of veto, and the facilitator's computer showed the degree of consensus.

There was, in fact, little disagreement in the group and only a couple of vetoes. The priority list is shown. The scores are in square brackets where the 'P' indicates that these are the results of a preferencing exercise (calling it preferencing rather than voting is deliberate), the number indicates the allocated resources, the letter 'G' for positive resources (which were coloured green), and the letter 'R' for negative resources – the veto (which were coloured red).

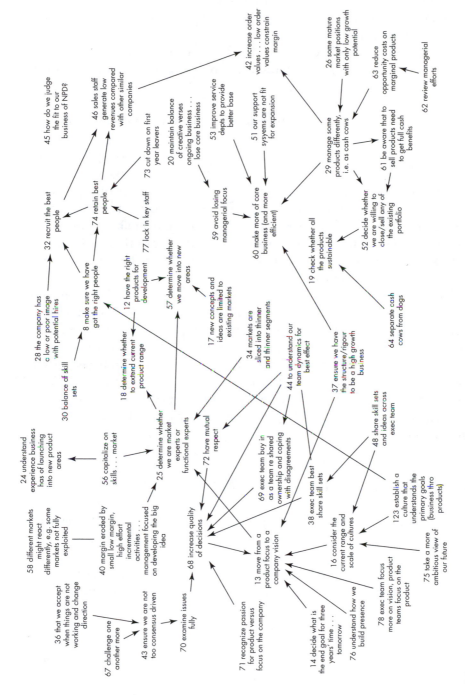

Figure CS6.3 The group added more material to their first attempts, and added linkages across the material.

25 Determine whether we are market experts or functional experts [P 7G]

16 Consider the current range & scale of cultures [P 4G]

44 To understand our team dynamics for best effect [P 4G]

77 Lock in key staff [P 2G]

32 Recruit the best people [P 1G]

29 Manage some products differently i.e. as cash cows [P 1R]

46 Sales staff generate low revenues compared with other similar companies [P 2G 2R]

Figure CS6.4 illustrates how the **preferencing** process is managed within Group Explorer.

There was consensus about the importance of the top priority, with everyone allocating at least one resource of the four they were each able to allocate. There was, however, disagreement about dealing with the issue of 'sales staff generating low revenues'. Discussion revealed, importantly, that this disagreement was the consequence of a disagreement about the assertion rather than about its importance. Notably the strategic priorities at this stage of the workshop were largely related to internal issues: cultures, team dynamics, and recruiting and keeping the best people.

At this stage the priorities can often be misleading because they are neither set within the context of agreed goals or the viability of the business model (whether the goals can realistically be delivered). Nevertheless the exercise provides an initial closure to working with strategic issues – the first milestone. This stage of the workshop is typically cathartic for participants because they are able to get out in the open the worries, niggles and concerns that would otherwise get in the way of making more analytical progress.

To recognize this progress the group took a break at 11.10 (40 minutes later than the planned schedule).

Finding the Emergent Goals System (task 3)

They returned from the break to explore why these high priority issues had been allocated high priority. Why was resolving them so important to their future success? Answering this question would explicate emergent goals that were actually driving the organization. This involved them laddering up from each of these priorities while recognizing their full context of related statements.

The group was invited to ask: 'What do we achieve if we were to find an effective way of addressing the issue?' or alternatively: 'What might happen, that's undesirable, if we don't address it?' When answered they were then asked the same question of that answer, and so on, until the answer given was a goal or negative goal (an obviously bad achievement for the organization).

Figure CS6.5 shows an example of how the group started laddering up from the prioritized 'range and scale of cultures' issue. Thus, the two important, and

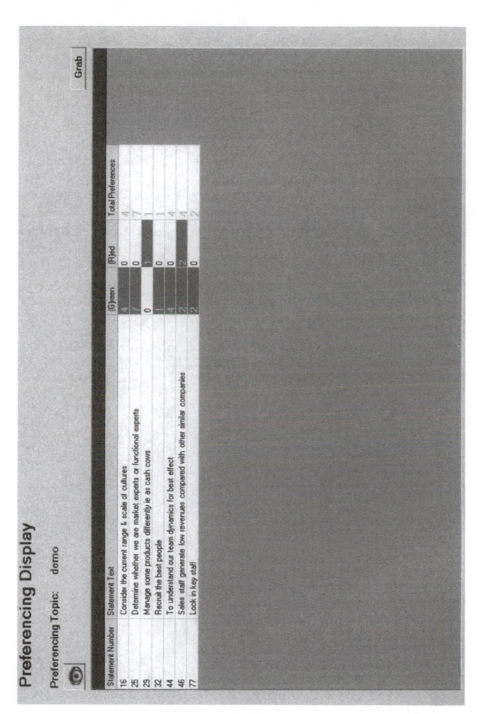

Figure CS6.4 The Summary Public Screen Showing the Results of Preferencing

related, outcomes of reconsidering cultures were that they felt this would 'move the organization out of its comfort zone', which would, in turn, 'lift the lid on the scale of ambition for the business'. Both of these outcomes were considered to be important future goals of the organization (in Figure CS6.5 they are shown boxed and in a different font in order to identify them as likely goals). Later in the workshop, 'lift the lid on the scale of ambition' was taken to be one important goal that would contribute to the goal 'aim for high growth/turnover potential' (in Figure CS6.5, the same font is used for both goals, but the latter is not surrounded by a box, to indicate that this was a financial goal for the organization). For Neil it was important to distinguish financial goals (and the sacred goals) from other goals. Similarly, at a later stage, high growth potential was linked to the financial goal 'a fast profit growth'.

Using the networked computer system, the group considered each of the prioritized issues in turn and laddered up in each case. Typically there were several different outcomes from addressing each issue. Often, the initial outcomes were not goals of the organization; rather, they were the further consequences of these outcomes. As each prioritized issue was discussed there were fewer new goals that were presented by the group. This is not untypical, as the goals become increasingly interlinked and gradually lead towards fewer and fewer outcomes at the top of the map.

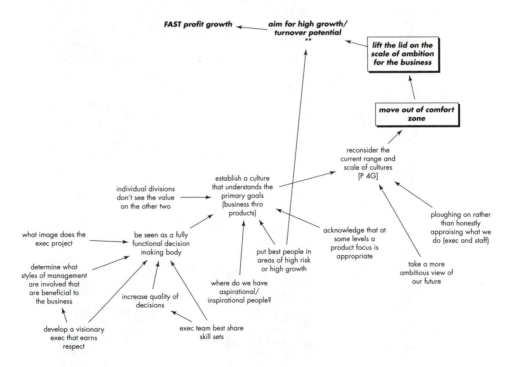

Figure CS6.5 Laddering Up: this shows how the group started laddering up from the prioritized "range and scale of cultutres" issue. (Boxed bold are possible goals, and unboxed bold are possible financial goals.)

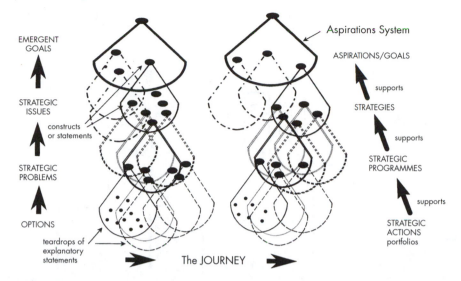

Figure CS6.6 The Strategy-Making Structure (from Eden and Ackermann 1998, p. 164)

The general structure of the developing map is illustrated in Figure CS6.6. At this stage of the workshop the group had been concentrating on the top part of Figure CS6.6 – the surfacing of strategic issues and goals. As this figure shows, the general structure of a strategy map is a linked series of teardrops. Figure CS 6.7 shows the goals system teardrop drafted at this early stage of the workshop. This draft goals system was established by 13.15 – in time for a late lunch!

Neil was reasonably buoyant at this stage because his senior management group were beginning to behave like a team – they appeared to have listened to one another and were being constructive in their responses.

Discovering Patterns of Distinctive Competences to Deliver Goals (see task 4)

The most crucial part of a strategy workshop of this type tends to be the work that is undertaken in trying to establish the distinctive competences of the organization. If organizations have nothing distinctive to offer to the marketplace then other organizations can jump in and make equivalent profits. If a competitor is able to do this easily then neither organization is able to make a profit! All organizations must have something distinctive about them in order to survive in the long term.

However, understanding the nature of distinctive competences is not straightforward. For many years businesses have referred to their **core** competences, but core competences are different from distinctive competences. For Neil, it was important to discover the nature of their **distinctive** competences, and to subsequently understand how these could be significant in driving the

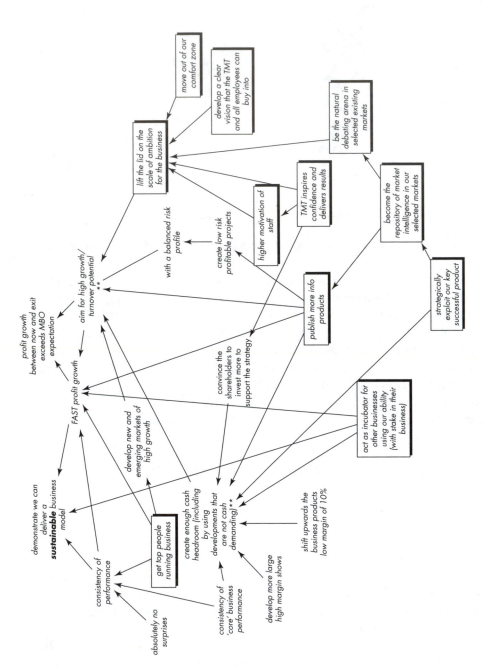

Figure CS6.7 The Goals System teardrop Developing: this goals system is in draft from an early stage in the workshop (without boxes are financial goals, with boxes are other goals)

business forward. Only when this question could be answered satisfactorily was it possible to determine core competences. Core competences are, naturally, those distinctive competences that are at the core of future business success – they are discovered following an analysis of the relationship between distinctive competences and goals (establishing the business model).

As noted above, the exercise of exploring competences and distinctive competences is often difficult for a group. In public sector organizations it is not unusual for 15 to 20 minutes to pass before some material starts emerging. When helping a group discover their distinctive competences it is important for participants to realize that some of the most significant distinctive competences arise from the existence of a very particular **network of competences**. It is often the case that no competence within the network is distinctive on its own but that **the network itself is distinctive**. As we shall see, this was the case for Neil's organization.

After lunch, the group got together to start this exercise, with Colin leading the group and Fran in the support role. At this stage, the group members were feeling reasonably pleased with themselves – they had mastered the use of the computer technology, they felt they had got most of the important issues facing the organization on the table and understood their impact on each other. Each of them expressed the view that they had been able to participate fully in the morning's activities, and they felt that the draft goals system was not a bad starting statement.

To start the session, the group was presented with some ideas about the type of competences to think about. Figure CS6.8 shows the slide used for this purpose. Colin and Fran gave a few examples of each type and also provided examples of some of the difficulties in thinking about competences. In particular

Distinctive Competences:

■ *Distinctive in relation to . . .*

    ■ *as defined by the goals of your organization*

■ *difficult to emulate*
■ *cannot be bought easily*
■ *very high* **cost of entry**
■ *very* **long time to attain**
■ *a competence is not usually the product, rather it is the process:*

    ■ *ability to* **organize** *work to deliver value*

■ *ability to* **exploit** *competences*
■ *potent access to a* **wide** *variety of markets*

Figure CS6.8 Ideas About the Type of Competences to Consider (from Eden and Ackermann, 1998)

they alerted the group to the likelihood that they would start by thinking of distinctive *outcomes* rather than competences. For example, customer loyalty, successful brands and a strong reputation are often given as distinctive competences. These must be surfaced, but there is a danger in not digging deeper to discover the competences that provide these distinctive outcomes.

The group started suggesting distinctive competences with great confidence – they were beginning to enjoy themselves! Over 30 competences were surfaced and argued to be distinctive. Many of these were, as expected, distinctive outcomes, but nevertheless important to have been stated and mapped. If they were to prove to be significant in the business model, the group was reminded that they must be laddered down to explore the competences that supported the outcomes.

After discussion, the map was focused on those competences that at least one member of the team argued was definitely distinctive (even if others disagreed). Colin pushed them all very hard during this stage, asking them to argue for (not against) each item on the screen which they had identified as distinctive. This was done without any expectation that an individual should defend their own contribution, rather that they should, in turn, address each suggested distinctive competence. The final map is shown in Figure CS6.9: it contains 16 potential distinctive competences (in boxes) and three other items that are linking explanations and possible important supporting competences.

To test the view of the group of the relative distinctiveness of each of the 16 items on the map each participant was invited to rate every item. Using the computer system, they were asked to decide on the least distinctive item and the most distinctive item and rate these at 0 and 10 respectively (thus forming 'anchor points'). Every other item was then rated relative to these two anchor points on the 0–10 scale. The computer system then calculated the average score and the measure of variability in the assessments made.

The ratings given by the group show that 'ability to build very extensive community products around core brands beyond any other company's focus [R8, 6   1, 2]' was the most distinctive competence (with an average rating of 8.6 and a standard deviation of 1.2). The distinctive outcomes of 'trusted brands [R7, 8   0, 98]' and 'events are a hot ticket [R7, 2   1, 72]' were highly rated, but there was less consensus about events being a hot ticket.

Since **patterns of competences** are often the most important characteristic of distinctiveness, the feedback loops were marked on the map (and the arrows that were part of feedback were shown in bold). There were two feedback loops, and both of them were self-sustaining (positive feedback loops: vicious or virtuous circles). Providing one or more of the items within these loops support goals (that is they make up a part of the business model) then the loops are likely to be core distinctive competences because they are self-sustaining. It was important to note that all of the items were linked with the exception of having a 'wider range of products than other media businesses of similar size [R7,4   1,02]', which was rated highly. The network was of importance.

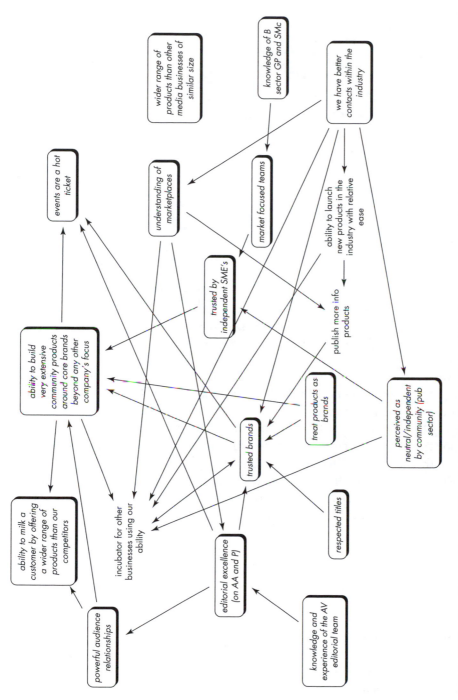

Figure CS6.9 Distinctive Competences: this map emerged from discussion about any **potential** distinctive competences (DCs). There are 16 DCs here (in boxes) and 3 other linking explanations or supporting competences. (Figures in brackets indicate the results of their judgements about the degree of distinctiveness. The first number is a rating and the second the degree of variance of view among the team.)

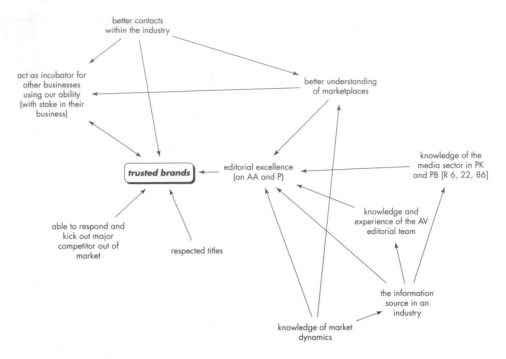

Figure CS6.10 Supporting Competences: added here are the links to the characteristics of the business that sustain the "trusted brands" outcome

Also, given that some of the most distinctive items were outcomes, rather than competences, then exploring the network of links to the outcomes would be a first stage of understanding how these outcomes could be managed through levering competences within the organization. Figure CS6.10 shows these supporting competences or characteristics of the business/organization that sustain the outcome of 'trusted brands'.

Having completed this exercise, it was time for a break. The exploration of distinctive competences had taken longer than planned, partly because of the discussion time. However, discussion about distinctiveness must be allowed to be completed because of the absolute importance of distinctive competences in developing confidence in a sound strategic future for the organization. Often the distinctive competences the organization has are of no future use to the organization, even though the managers are very proud of their existence.

The Business Model (task 5)

The next stage of the workshop was to test out the role of distinctive competences (as patterns or single items) in delivering the future goals of the organization.

In the case of Neil's organization this was easier than is often the case. All of the distinctive competences supported the goals they had earlier identified.

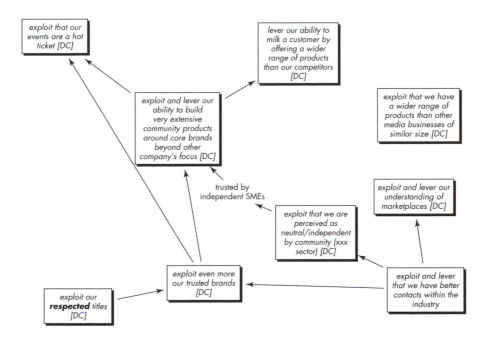

Figure CS6.11 The distinctive competences have now been redefined and rephrased as goals (in boxes). (Thick arrows indicate the links are part of a feedback loop.)

Indeed the feedback loop became so significant that the distinctive competences in the loop became goals in their own right. Figure CS6.11 shows that many of the distinctive competences became redefined as goals and the wording of most of them was changed so that they were re-expressed as goals. In many other cases the wording was changed so that they were expressed as strategies.

As the total map of the links between distinctive competences and goals emerged it became clear that one particular pattern was absolutely core to the business future of the organization – this was the core distinctive competence.

Ending the First Day of the Workshop

Following the creation of the business model, and the strong appreciation of the strategic future they had created, the group returned to the strategic issues. The whole issue map was revisited to establish a new set of possible priorities in the light of the new map structure (after the laddering to goals process) (**tasks 6 and 7**). All of the previous priorities were included. The group then went on to re-establish priorities using the same process as before. However, after priorities had been established, the facilitator required the group to articulate the reasons for the final priorities. This process forces the group to express verbally reasons for the importance of the strategies. In doing so the group will usually use the causality shown on the map, but add the extra wording that brings the strategy alive; or alternatively, add new reasoning that has not been fully explicated before – when this happens the map is elaborated.

The workshop ran on late into the evening (stopping for dinner at 20.00). However, when the group finished for the day, they had convinced themselves that they had created a robust business model. The first item on the agenda for Sunday was to convert the business model into a spreadsheet model and test out its quantitative implication for the next three years.

While the team had dinner, Fran and Colin translated the map of the business model and reprioritized strategies (now re-evaluated after the business model work) into a narrative **statement of strategic intent for the organization (task 8)**. In doing so they literally translated the maps into a bullet point format (**outliner**) and then converted the outlined text into sentences and paragraphs (see chapter 7). They did not seek to make the statement journalistic or attractive but rather wrote out the logic of the business model: goals, core distinctive competences to deliver the goals, strategic issues that needed to be resolved to make it happen, and strategies to be delivered in order to exploit and sustain the competences. Their purpose was to allow the team to test whether they were persuaded by the logic of the more traditional narrative statement, not whether it could, at this stage, persuade others.

Postscript

After a couple of years had passed Neil reported that the strategy was still in place. There was satisfaction in having delivered much of the strategy but disappointment that other aspects were taking too long. The organization had resolved its cash crisis and was building confidence with its shareholders.

As Neil said: 'We have loads of cash in the bank – we've created clear cash headroom and profits are up on last year and we still have a chance of making budget this year; margins have started to grow on business magazines, and much more . . . In short we are grinding our way through the strategy actions and the team remains really committed to the programme. What the strategy has done is to give us all a common language to use and has removed a lot of the "fire" from argument and debate as we all have to push towards the same set of objectives.'

Workshop 2 (comprising tasks 4 to 6)
Distinctive Competences, the Business Model/
Livelihood Scheme and Core Distinctive Competences

The Value Added: the second draft of the goals system and the first vision/mission/
statement of strategic intent (including articulated draft strategies resulting from
prioritized issues, and strategies to develop the business model/livelihood scheme)

Task 4 Map of Distinctive Competences

a   Decide what your reference point for distinctiveness is – related to your draft
     aspirations/goals system.

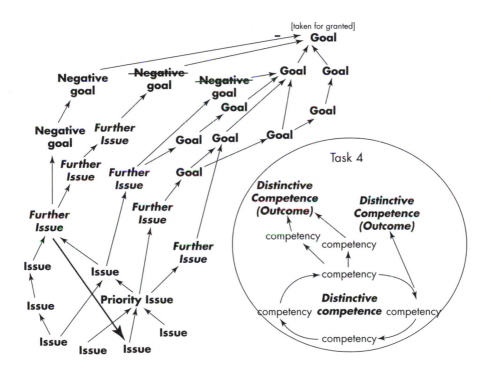

Task 4 Map of Distinctive Competences

a   Decide what your reference point for distinctiveness is – related to your draft
    aspirations/goals system.

b   **Note down (on Post-it® notes or using Decision Explorer®) your distinctive
    competences, and spread them around the flipchart covered wall or computer
    screen.**

Task 4 Map of Distinctive Competences

a   Decide what your reference point for distinctiveness is – related to your draft aspirations/goals system.

b   Note down (on Post-it® notes or using Decision Explorer®) your distinctive competences, and spread them around the flipchart covered wall or computer screen.

c   **Ladder down at least three levels from distinctive outcomes. Ladder down at least two levels from DCs by asking 'what is it that really sustains this DC?'**

Task 4 Map of Distinctive Competences

a   Decide what your reference point for distinctiveness is – related to your draft aspirations/goals system.

b   Note down (on Post-it® notes or using Decision Explorer®) your distinctive competences, and spread them around the flipchart covered wall or computer screen.

c   Ladder down at least three levels from distinctive outcomes. Ladder down at least two levels from DCs by asking 'what is it that really sustains this DC?

d   **Add all linkages between competences and distinctive competences.**

Task 5 Developing the Business Model

a **Exploit distinctive competences to realize goals.**

- ■ **Test how distinctive competences, as individual statements or patterns, support (or not) the intended goals: map the links (arrows between DCs and goals).**
- ■ **Search for the way in which the distinctive competences can be exploited more effectively to support goals.**
- ■ **Revise goals to account for the DCs.**
- ■ **Develop new strategies to reinforce weak or developing DCs.**

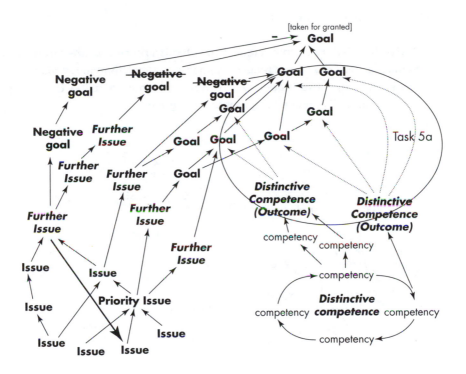

Task 5 Developing the Business Model

a   Exploit distinctive competences to realize goals.

- ■ Test how distinctive competences, as individual statements or patterns, support (or not) the intended goals: map the links (arrows between DCs and goals).
- ■ Search for the way in which the distinctive competences can be exploited more effectively to support goals.
- ■ Revise goals to account for the DCs.
- ■ Develop new strategies to reinforce weak or developing DCs.

b   Find core distinctive competences

- ■ Revisit the distinctive competences to establish those that are core/central to the business model and reduce emphasis on those that do not play a role.
- ■ Revise the business model or livelihood scheme to refine the linkage between core distinctive competences and goals.

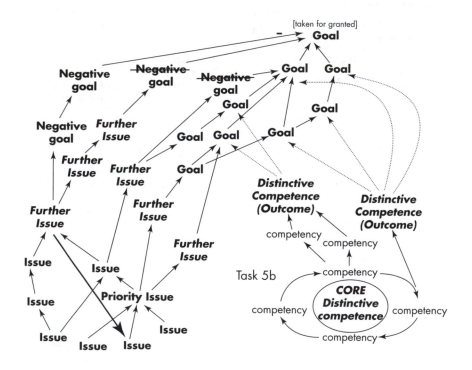

Task 6 Revise the Goals System If Necessary

■ **Make the goals system realistic and powerful.**
■ **In the light of the business model/livelihood scheme development identify:**

    ■ **Goals that are less realistic because they do not have the sustenance of at least one distinctive competence.**

    ■ **Distinctive competences that are core and might become of goal status.**

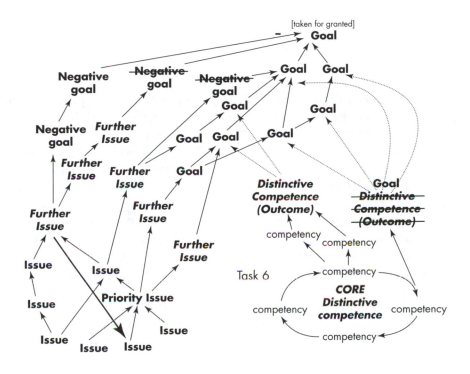

7 Agreeing Strategies: Sustaining the Business Model or Livelihood Scheme and Resolving Key Strategic Issues

Introduction

This chapter closes the strategy-making process (although in practice many organizations would decide to keep the cycle rolling forward). In a nutshell, the purpose of closure is to put a halt to discussion (at this stage) and start the process of more formally delivering the strategy.[1] By the end of this stage you should be in possession of a strategy that matches the organization's competences, that meets its needs as perceived by key groups within it, and whose core content and key priorities are clearly identified. You have probably developed a draft mission statement that encapsulates the business model or livelihood scheme (and which can be further developed in chapter 8). In fact, it is probable that delivery of the strategy has already started, as the members of the strategy-making group, through discussion, begin to take into account their new thinking about the strategic direction proposed.

Thus, having developed a business model or livelihood scheme and identified those competences that are distinctive and core, it is worth returning to the issues identified in task 2 (chapter 4). They reflected the concerns of those involved in the strategy-making process and almost inevitably will have an impact on the proposed strategic future. As you will remember in task 2 we did some prioritization of the issues – in accordance with their systemic properties. However, this prioritization usually changes as new priorities emerge, based on the goals system and the business model or livelihood scheme identified (task 7a).

In addition to this review of prioritization, it is usually helpful to focus some attention upon developing strategies for protecting and ensuring the business model or livelihood system (task 7b). This might encompass putting in place strategies for making weak distinctive competences stronger. Alternatively it might focus upon growing new competences. An easier route to developing the distinctive nature of the organization and its future is to consider strategies that build new links between competences to create distinctive competences. These links may create new patterns between competences and distinctive competences, which themselves generate distinctive competences. One particular and powerful example of this ability focuses upon the production of virtuous circles whereby competences and distinctive competences support one another, building a positive feedback loop and thus supporting the future direction.

Finally, recognizing strategies for protecting and sustaining core distinctive competences will provide a focus against which energy and resources can be assessed and appropriately channelled. Consideration can be given to the means of concentrating effort away from competences that don't support the business model or livelihood scheme towards those that do – that is freeing up resources to support the new strategies enabling the strategic future to be realized. Appropriate outsourcing may, therefore, become a serious issue for consideration (task 7c).

Strategy-making Outcomes

■ Identification of a system of strategies that reinforce one another and allow the issues and concerns of those participating to be managed and the new strategic future to be realized.
■ Production of a set of strategies that protect the identified core distinctive competences.
■ Renewal/development of new patterns of competences and distinctive competences.
■ Agreed plans for diminishing, arresting or outsourcing activities that enable resources to be made available for other activities.

Reviewing the Issues

As noted above, once the business model or livelihood scheme has been developed, it is important to review the original set of issues. This is partly to ensure that those issues which group members feel important are being considered but also to review their prioritization (and therefore where management attention and resources should be focused). Developing the business model or livelihood scheme will almost certainly have suggested a rethink of the importance of managing the issues.

Go to task 7a

Return to the issues map (task 2) and explore how these now impact upon the goals system and business model or livelihood scheme. Reprioritize the issues and consider possible strategies for managing these repriortized issues.

Commentary and Issues

The goals system was initially developed laddering up from the issues, and subsequently augmented with goals reflecting the group's desire for a more aspirational future. In addition, where you have also paid attention to the wider environment of the organization as a whole (should you be focusing on a particular unit or department) new connections, further goals or changes to their meaning or language are likely to have taken place. In all cases, these changes will have changed the structure and yielded new insights into the centrality of the originally identified issues.

Furthermore, the process of developing the distinctive competency map has, to date, not attended to the links to issues. It is now worth considering whether there are any impacts between the issues and competences or distinctive competences. Where there are, capture these (using either the software or Post-its®) so that the resulting impact can be reviewed. This will inform the reprioritization.

■ Consider strategies that will enable the issues to be managed (impacts avoided, reduced or capitalized upon).
■ Reprioritize, based on the new structure of the whole map.
■ Review how this prioritization compares with the initial prioritization. Are there any useful insights to be gained from this?

Hints and Tips

■ Make sure that the competences surfaced don't contradict the issues! A common trap is to have as an issue 'diminishing reputation' and yet surface 'good reputation' as a distinctive competence.
■ At all times remember that resource demands of strategies have to be considered.[2] Therefore try not to have more than five top priority strategies.
■ Make sure that the strategies for resolving one issue don't impact or compound the effects of another or have negative ramifications for other areas – remember you are building a coherent system of goals, competences and strategies.

Sustaining the Business Model or Livelihood Scheme

Building on the work undertaken to create the business model or livelihood scheme, it is worth considering how this anticipated strategic future can be realized. In many cases, the process of surfacing and structuring the competences and distinctive competences provides the strategy-making group with new insights into where their strengths lie, and often how unappreciated they are. Therefore developing strategies for sustaining those competences that are core or distinctive is important – effort is required to avoid them withering and being lost. In addition, considering whether new competences or distinctive competences can be strengthened may also increase the chances of successfully realizing the strategic intent.

Go to task 7b

Consider the distinctive competences map. Are there any vulnerable distinctive competences that need to be strengthened? Are there any new distinctive competences that need to be developed? Finally are there any possible new linkages that could be made that would create distinctiveness?

Commentary and Issues

- An important part of ensuring that the business model or livelihood scheme is realizable is to examine first the core distinctive competences, and then the remaining distinctive competences, to ensure that they are sufficiently supported in terms of resources (both cash and staff energy).[3] Where they appear to be vulnerable, or further support would increase their effectiveness substantially, develop strategies to do so.
- Developing new distinctive competences is very difficult (as noted in chapter 6), and although some organizations do manage to achieve this, it is usually over a lengthy period of time (and this time lag needs to be taken into account). However, a more achievable means of developing new distinctive competences is to review the competences already surfaced and determine whether any of these can be made distinctive. (This can be done either through linking them to other competences and thus making the combined set of competences distinctive or through allocating sufficient resources, converting the competence itself into something distinctive.)
- How competences and distinctive competences link together may also yield further leverage points. This is particularly the case where a strategy that enables one competence or distinctive competence to support another creates a feedback loop, which sustains all of those comprising the feedback loop structure.

Hints and Tips

- Look for any pattern of competences that supports a number of goals. Is there a means of making it distinctive either through linking other competences to it, or enhancing or extending its capability to make it distinctive?

- Review the competence or distinctive competence structure – where there are chains of competences is there any means of linking those at the top of the chain back to those at the tail (bottom of the chain). This will create a feedback loop.
- Start with those competences identified as core. Consider what resources support them. Are there sufficient resources to ensure that they remain distinctive and viable?

Creating Strategic Slack

In considering strategies for supporting or protecting core distinctive competences and growing new ones, the issue of resource demands has to be considered.[4] One means of releasing resources is to review those distinctive competences that are no longer central to the strategic future. As is often the case in organizations, competences and distinctive competences emerge, and become embedded into the culture/consciousness of the organization. However, as organizations change their strategic direction, the utility of these competences may reduce, sometimes with them becoming completely irrelevant. Identifying these will free up resources – creating strategic slack. Where competences (or the activities supporting these) are to be withdrawn, careful consideration of how this is to be achieved is necessary (who needs to be consulted? what needs to be put into place?) so as to ensure that the resources are freed up rather than covertly protected (see chapter 8 about stakeholder management).

An obvious means of freeing up resources is through outsourcing.[5] Through building the business model, those areas that are considered potential candidates for outsourcing will have been scrutinized. Often organizations outsource units, departments and tasks without considering the overall impact on the business model,[6] or on a distinctive competence.[7] For example, having up-to-date and accurate databases on clients and being able rapidly to update and tailor the information may be a crucial contributor to a distinctive competence and outsourcing IT services would impact on this. Understanding how the particular area or task to be outsourced fits in with the overall model can thus ensure a more sustainable and coherent approach.

Go to task 7c

Review the distinctive competences map, are there any competences (or distinctive competences) that are not supporting the goals? Where these exist consider strategies for phasing out energy and thus freeing up resources. Review the entire set of strategies to ensure coherence and feasibility.

Commentary and Issues

■ In reviewing the resultant strategies it is often worth thinking about whether any 'quick wins' (see Kotter 1996) could be achieved. Are there current initiatives going on that with a little conversion could support the strategies identified? Alternatively, are there actions that could be put in place relatively quickly so as to demonstrate and illustrate commitment to the strategy?

■ It is also important to ensure that the resultant portfolio of strategies is coherent. Do any of the strategies conflict with one another or any of the goals? Are there any links that could be identified between the strategies so as to reinforce them and increase the likelihood of successful implementation?

■ Test whether the resultant portfolio can be delivered with the current resources. Reviewing what competences or actions have been stopped and what resources exist in the organization can help carry out this analysis. It is worth remembering that rarely can you do everything. We have found through experience that around five to seven strategies is a reasonable number, and that focusing on one strategy each year is effective.

Hints and Tips

■ Check each of the strategies to determine whether there are any missing links (to strategies, competences or goals).

■ One of the most important reasons for using mapping in making strategy is that maps show strategies are undertaken for a purpose. The arrows are a critical aspect of delivery. It is no use committing resources for the wrong reasons, and the arrow shows the reason. Check the links – the means to ends.

Summary

The resultant map should now encompass the goals system, supported by both the distinctive competences and strategies. It should reflect the means by which the issues originally surfaced in task 2 are to be managed, the direction the organization aspires to achieve, and the means of achieving this direction (through both the core and distinctive competences and the strategies). It should also reflect the activities to be outsourced or gradually discontinued and how these changes are to be effected. The next step (see chapter 8) will be to convert this into a statement of strategic intent and to consider how this stands up against the structures and systems.

Notes

[1] See Eden and Ackermann (1998) chapter C9 on closure, particularly pp. 167–70, which deal with the consideration of strategies in terms of their resources and political feasibility.

[2] Johnson and Scholes (2002) pp. 147–150 introduce the concept of strategic capability, which includes the need to determine if the organization has the resources and competences required in order to meet customer requirements. They suggest that four characteristics of resources should be assessed: their availability; their threshold level required to support the organization's strategies; their uniqueness to the organization; and their adequacy. Each of these is discussed in more detail on pp. 152–6.

[3] Lynch (2003) pp. 493–503 discusses in some detail the identification of those resources that are important to the delivery of sustainable competitive advantage. He argues that these resources represent an important starting point in the development of strategic options.

[4] Lynch (2003) pp. 200–47 reviews the analysis of resources in some detail. He suggests that in addition to exploring the contribution that resources make to the organization, we need to develop an understanding of how resources add value or deliver profits and we need to identify those resources that enable the organization to compete or provide competitive advantage.

[5] Johnson and Scholes (2002) pp. 450–1 discuss the principals of outsourcing and the implications it has for the organization, including the need to manage suppliers and the additional skills that this may require.

[6] Prahalad and Hamel (in De Wit and Meyer (1998) p. 294) discuss the issue of identifying core competences and losing them. They warn of the potential danger that core competences can be unwittingly surrendered when internal investment is cut in favour of cost outsourcing. They also point out that outsourcing can provide a fast-track to product development but this is at the cost of not developing the competences that will be required to sustain product leadership.

[7] Johnson and Scholes (2002) p. 176 emphasize the importance that core competences are undertaken within the organization (and not outsourced). On p. 334 they highlight the danger that organizations can outsource activities in order to gain a cost advantage but can inadvertently outsource activities that have potential for strategic differentiation.

Task 7a Review the issue map (task 2) according to the strategic direction proposed by the business model/livelihood scheme

■ In the light of your work on developing the final goals system and business model/livelihood scheme reprioritze the issues. Mark those issues that have considerable impact (that is, where there are a number of chains of argument laddering up to the goals and/or competences/distinctive competences).

■ Consider using a scale where *** denotes those issues with the greatest impact, and then ** and * for lower levels).

   ■ Priorities should be based on an analysis of the relationships between issues and the importance of their resolution/management (as strategies) to **sustain DCs and so goals**.

   ■ Make sure that this reprioritization shows changes (in priorities) that take into account the goals system – therefore the resultant map will be different from the original prioritization, which was based only on the issues' structure.

   ■ Consider possible strategies for managing the reprioritized issues but remember to be careful with how many strategies are put in place (no more than five *** strategies is sensible).

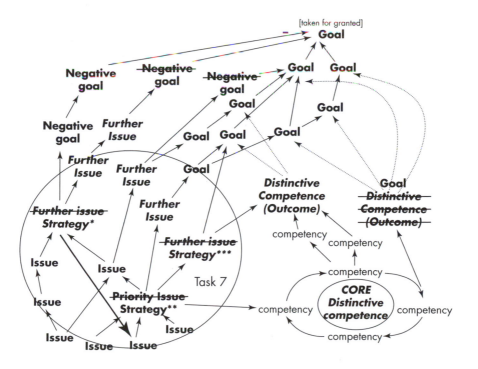

Task 7b Consider Strategies for Ensuring the Feasibility of the Business Model/Livelihood Scheme

■ Identify any DCs that need strengthening – particularly those that appear weak or vulnerable – and develop strategies for reinforcing them.

■ Consider whether it is possible to grow any new competences/distinctive competences – or convert a competence into something distinctive.

    ■ This can often be quite difficult!

■ Build links between competences and distinctive competences considering how new linkages that will create distinctiveness can be put in place.

    ■ Focus particularly on dynamic patterns.

Task 7c Review the Resources Necessary for Implementing Strategies

■ Examine the competences/distinctive competences map for those not sup-porting goals in order to:

   ■ Consider winding down competences no longer supportive to the business model/livelihood scheme.
   ■ Outsource particular tasks or areas that no longer are relevant to the business model.

■ Review the overall picture of strategies to ensure:

   ■ That they don't conflict with one another.
   ■ That they don't have negative impacts on the goals system (or distinctive competences).
   ■ That they are feasible in terms of resources (and political good will).

8 Making a Statement of Strategic Intent and Other Aspects of Making Strategy

Introduction

Chapters 2 to 6 have focused upon a strategy-making approach that involves a group. The strategy-making process used has been designed to exploit the wisdom and experience of each member of the group. However, more importantly, the process has involved group members in a journey of discovery in order that their commitment to the strategy is as high as possible. The process has involved a considerable amount of managed **social and psychological negotiation**.

Causal maps have been used because they focus the attention of the group on strategic action within the context of purpose – the causal arrows indicate means to ends or options to outcomes. While this consideration of the implications of statements along with reviewing options and constraints enhances the group's shared body of understanding, the maps that have been produced, edited and modified will remain somewhat cryptic to anyone other than those who participated in their creation. This is inevitable because the full subtlety of their meaning derives as much from the social negotiation that has been undertaken as it does from the content and shape of the maps. Nevertheless there is greater precision of meaning in maps than in, for example, bullet point lists because every statement is given meaning by the actions that underlie it (in arrows) and the outcomes that indicate purpose (out arrows).

With the social process largely complete there is a requirement to indicate some degree of closure by creating a normal statement of strategic intent (SSI). This statement comprises sentences and paragraphs and provides a powerful summary of the strategy making that has been undertaken. It is what some would describe as a **mission or vision statement**. However, there has been a great deal of debate over the years about what constitutes a mission statement or a vision statement. We find ourselves less concerned about such definitional niceties and more concerned about the functional nature of a summary statement of strategic intent. The strategy-making group therefore can choose whatever label they think appropriate (given the organizational culture, personal preferences, etc.) to describe such a summary statement. Nevertheless, we are persuaded by the useful research that has been undertaken to determine the requirements that such a statement should have, if it is to have an impact upon others in the organization. In particular, the research indicates that a powerful statement would include four linked aspects:

1   A statement of purpose that should be inspirational and emotional and include core goals and the business model or livelihood scheme.
2   A statement expressing the key strategies that will deliver the goals.
3   The values of the organization.
4   The standards and behaviour patterns of staff that will guide how the organization operates.[1]

The work undertaken in chapters 2 to 6 provides the material for the first two of these requirements.

Therefore, in this chapter we discuss this task of writing such a statement of strategic intent. However, in addition we present one final task (9) that acts as a way of testing whether the systems and structures within the organization can (or cannot) deliver the strategic intent. Understanding the role systems and structures play in determining the strategic future of the organization is crucial. They are a fundamental part of detecting emergent strategizing. We will have discovered some of their roles through the processes of a detecting emergent strategizing presented in chapters 3 and 4. Nevertheless because their role is so crucial it is important to go further. In doing so, we expect to discover ways in which these systems and structures should be changed to support the implementation of the strategic intent (or, alternatively, amendments made to the strategic intent). In addition, their current role in emergent strategizing provides us with a reference point for evaluating strategy delivery at some time in the future.

In addition, in most of the work we have undertaken, we found it important to test the business model beyond the important tests identified in chapter 6. In particular, before the strategy-making group completes the tasks we have encouraged members to undertake 'back of the envelope' spreadsheet analyses of the financial costs and revenues embedded in the business model. On some occasions we have gone beyond a spreadsheet analysis to the use of visual interactive simulation modeling in order to capture the dynamics of the business model over the strategy-making horizon.

The robustness of the strategy is perhaps most significantly tested by the extent to which it has **commitment from the power brokers** who drive the strategic future of the organization. The tasks undertaken in chapters 2 to 6 were designed to address this requirement through their participative nature.

Nevertheless, the process has, so far, ignored the external environment, at least to the extent that if it has not been recognized as a part of issue surfacing then no further consideration has been undertaken. Our experience suggests that the group processes presented in this book do identify most of the key aspects of the impact of the environment on the future of the organization. This occurs because the process is intended to drive deeper into the concerns and wisdom of the participants than is normally the case. Many of the issues identified will be driven by considerations of the role of the external environment, providing that we did go deeper into the explanations for issues (laddering down) and so we will inevitably find ourselves addressing the impact of the environment. However, our experience also indicates that it is important to use a designed process for further exploring the impact of, and relationship with, the powerful and interested stakeholders, and for exploring possible alternative futures. In addition, addressing the issue of developing clearly stated qualitative and quantitative performance indicators associated with goals and strategies converts the strategy into a deliverable form. These processes will be introduced in brief in this chapter (see Figure 8.1, based on Figures 1.1–1.4).

Strategy-making Outcomes

- A one-page summary of the outcome of the strategy making which clearly and concisely expresses the goals system, the business model or livelihood scheme, and the key strategies to deliver the goals and sustain the business model.[2]
- An agenda for further strategy-making work to test out and develop the strategy.

  - Assessment of the impact of systems and structures on the proposed strategic intent.
  - Testing the business model using quantitative modeling.
  - Attention to the external environment: powerful stakeholders, and possible external events that may create significant alternative futures.
  - Consideration of performance indicators.

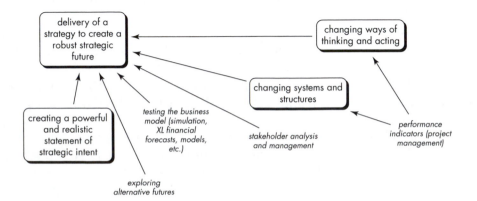

Figure 8.1 Additional Strategy-making Processes

Developing a Statement of Strategic Intent

Very few organizations in the Western world believe that they can get away without a statement which starts 'our mission is . . .'. To some extent this is a pity. The mission statement has become disreputable, and those cynical about organizational strategy will use mission statements as an example of strategy nonsense. Their case is that the statement is meaningless, unrealistic, not related to what the organization is really doing, has no impact on the behaviour of senior management, and so on. They are often absolutely right. There are frequent examples of double messages evident in an organization's strategy, where the management team does not take seriously a statement that is made public. Sometimes there is confusion on the part of all in the organization, senior managers and other staff, about the role of a mission statement for stakeholder management compared with its force as a statement intended to effect strategic change. While the logic of a mission statement for stakeholder management can be sound, the potential confusion about its role within the strategy must be taken seriously. The rhetoric of strategy is to dismiss the confusion by stating that the two purposes are the same – and for a fully coherent strategy they should be. Nevertheless, as we have seen in our discussion about stakeholder management and multiple futures, often there can be a need for different statements internally and externally.

A mission statement, as a 'call to arms' or 'battalion flag', can be a motivator for strategic change.[3] As a consequence we should use this symbol of closure purposefully and take great care over its content. A mission statement can be, at one extreme, a short and pithy statement (a couple of sentences) which must nevertheless differentiate the organizational aspirations from those of other organizations. At the other extreme it can be a full page of material focusing solely on content with no attention to sentence construction or style, clearly setting out a realistic strategic intent and designed for internal consumption. Our own preference is towards the longer version – a version that expresses a full account of strategic intent and encompasses the business idea or livelihood scheme.[4]

Go to task 8a

Construct a first draft statement of strategic intents. If you made an initial attempt during chapter 5, take this into account.

Commentary and Issues

The maps being used to develop the statement have been constructed with care, and they illustrate a distinctive system of goals and a plausible business model or livelihood scheme. In addition, they have been constructed with an action orientation showing means to ends – the purpose of action and ultimate objectives. Thus, the task of this first attempt at constructing the statement of strategic intent is to translate a two-dimensional structure in to a one-dimensional stream of words.

In principle this means working down the hierarchy of goals in stages and indicating supporting goals, particularly central goals, and also ensuring that the structure of the goals system is reflected in the ordering of the material (for example, using an 'outliner' format).

McKinsey has managed to construct a very powerful and simple mission statement, which is, in effect, a very pointed statement of goals – the first part of an SSI:

> To help our clients make distinctive, lasting and substantial improvements in their performance, and to build a great firm that is able to attract, develop, excite and retain exceptional people.[5]

Figure 8.2 shows a reverse engineering of this statement into a map. The power of the statement is illustrated by it being a self-sustaining loop.

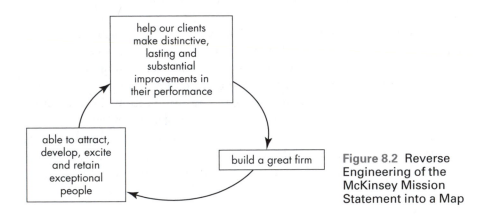

Figure 8.2 Reverse Engineering of the McKinsey Mission Statement into a Map

For case study 6.1, this first part of the SSI (goals) unfolds as:

There is an expectation that:
167 profit growth between now and exit exceeds MBO expectation, with
11 **fast** profit growth, and
21 high growth potential.

These levels of financial return are to be coupled with a clear demonstration of:

(continued)

79 capability to deliver a **sustainable** business model, with
181 consistency of performance, and
161 absolutely no surprises, and
2381 consistency of core business performance

and requiring:
180 a balanced risk profile, with
2431 low risk profitable projects, and
50 development of new and emerging markets of high growth.

Significantly we must:
10 create enough cash headroom (including by using developments that
are not cash demanding).

It recognizes that to achieve these circumstances it will need to:
23 lift the lid on the scale of ambition for the business, and
27 move out of the comfort zone, and

develop higher motivation of our staff, by:
186 a TMT that inspires confidence and delivers results, including
41 developing a clear vision that the TMT and all employees can buy into,
with
188 top people running the business.

*Note: In this case the drafting of the SSI suggested there were probably too
many goals. The team had already categorized their goals into financial
goals (the top part of the above statement) and non-financial goals in order
to simplify the statement. However, they had finished up converting eleven
of their DCs into goals. In the above statement these are not included and
it was decided that they should be expressed as core strategies in the SSI.*

(based on Figure CS6.7)

When using Decision Explorer® to record the maps, the material is easily copied and pasted into a word processor document.

Similarly, the business model – the distinctive competences and their links to the goals – is written in this crude fashion. In this case there may be a self-sustaining feedback loop that represents the core distinctive competence. The nature of the feedback loop needs to be clearly illustrated, and the core distinctive competence highlighted from other important distinctive competences. Thus, for the same case study we have:

The core competences on which the business model depends are that of:
2389 an ability to build community products around core brands, which enables
2415 a role as an incubator for other businesses, enabling
2401 ownership of trusted brands, which also reinforces
2415 a role as an incubator for other businesses.
Thus, these core competences are mutually self-sustaining.

In addition the business model depends upon core strategies to exploit linked distinctive competences which:
2407 lever our ability to 'milk' a customer by offering a wider range of product than our competitors
2389 exploit and lever our ability to build very extensive community products around core brands beyond any other company's focus, by aiming to:

    2401 exploit even more our trusted brands, and
        2419 exploit our respected titles
    2418 develop a distinctive conference business
    2415 exploit 'the organization' events that are a hot ticket
    2386 exploit and lever our understanding of marketplaces
    2420 exploit and lever that we have better contacts within the industry
    2413 exploit that we are perceived as neutral/independent by community.

We will also:
2399 make ideas happen quickly! (not just when under competitive pressure)
32 recruit the best people, and
    74 retain best people
103 develop 'the organization' way of doing things
2433 seek out appropriate businesses going into receivership.

('the organization' has replaced the real name of the business)

Hints and Tips

- For a first draft list the statements in each of the maps.
- Order the list according to the map hierarchy.
- Link the statements with words such as: by, and, with, also, etc.
- Use indent to demonstrate bundles of material.

> ## Go to task 8b
>
> **Construct a revised statement of strategic intent based upon the first draft.**

Commentary and Issues

The first part (paragraph) of the SSI is tantamount to being a mission statement for the organization. Therefore, a good test of the written material is to see whether it can stand on its own, without the material associated with the business model or livelihood scheme and strategies. In particular the first paragraph of the statement of goals should be capable of being presented as a stand-alone brief mission statement.

For case study 6.1, this first part of the SSI (goals) now unfolds as:

> **'The organization' will seek fast profit growth between now and exit. This growth will exceed the MBO expectation, and show high growth potential. These levels of financial return are to be coupled with a clear demonstration of capability to deliver a SUSTAINABLE business model, which has a consistency of performance, and absolutely no surprises.**
>
> We will create a balanced risk profile, through low risk profitable projects, which develop new and emerging markets of high growth. Significantly we aim to create enough cash headroom (including by using developments that are not cash demanding) to ensure satisfactory development of the projects.
>
> We recognize that in order to achieve these circumstances we must lift the lid on the scale of ambition for the business, move out of the comfort zone, and develop higher motivation of our staff. This will involve developing the TMT so that it inspires confidence and delivers results, provides a clear vision that the TMT and all employees can buy into. We need top people running the business.

Note how this statement meets the test presented above, where the first paragraph (in bold) could be used as a brief mission statement. Indeed if this is still too long then the first sentence, or two sentences, could be used.

Remember, this document is for use by the strategy-making team at this stage. It is not intended to be a selling document,[6] other than to be persuasive to those who developed the strategy.[7] Nevertheless, without doing violence to the intentions of the wording of the statements in the maps, it is sensible at this stage to adapt the wording so that sentences are as powerful as possible. If drama and rhetoric can enhance the power of the SSI then adjust sentence construction accordingly.[8]

Hints and Tips

■ Start the writing process by simply connecting the list of statements into sentences, with no elaboration or wording changes.

■ Add more refined sentences, drama and rhetoric as a second stage – too clever copy writing can easily lose the original meanings!

■ Make sure the goals are presented as aspirational.

■ Use bold and capital letters to emphasize key statements and words in the SSI.

■ Clearly break it into three parts: statement of goals, statement of business model or livelihood scheme, strategies to support the business model and goals.

■ Make sure the three parts are identifiable.

■ Test the goals part of the SSI for its adequacy as a mission statement. Test the first paragraph and then the first sentences for similar adequacy.

■ Do not go over one page of A4 (using an 11pt font).

The Impact of Systems and Structures

We usually recommend that one of the first tasks of strategy making is the detection of emergent strategizing.[9] In the approach presented in this book we have, so far, focused on one aspect of emergent strategizing: the role of problem and issue formulation and resolution as it is embedded in the culture of the organization (chapters 2 and 3). The other aspect is the often subtle impact of systems and structures, both formal and informal. Here we consider their role as we move towards closure and so strategy delivery.

Our experience suggests that there are two very significant systems that impact emergent strategizing and thus the reality of strategy delivery: reward systems (both formal and informal), and costing or transfer pricing systems. Others that are often considered are: information systems, architecture (and its influence on social processes), and budgeting procedures.

Reward systems are considered in the next chapter and relate also to the appropriate development of performance indicators (considered later in this chapter).

Go to task 9a

Consider two different approaches to costing products (or transfer pricing), and how each of these approaches might influence the emergent strategizing of the organization.

Commentary and Issues

Costing systems are usually designed by cost accountants and reflect the traditions of their profession or of industry practices (they are often a part of the 'industry recipe'[10]). They are rarely designed to support the delivery of a particular strategy, and yet their role can be profound. In all organizations costs are the result of subjective judgements, not objective analysis. For example, overheads can usually be allocated in many different ways, each of which is seen as 'rational' by the proponents of the method of allocation under consideration. In a consultancy business overhead costs of marketing staff, the salaries office and facilities management can be allocated by: proportion of customer revenue generated, by headcount, by different product types, etc. Each method will show different levels of profit for business units and so significantly influence motivations of staff, and ultimately budgeting, and so strategic futures.

Hints and Tips

- Think of any alternative costing system or transfer pricing system that could be used. It does not have to be a good proposal – be creative: consider different ways of allocating overheads, basing transfer pricing on contribution rather than profit, etc.
- This is done simply to set up a tension between the existing system and an alternative, thus allowing you to consider the way in which the existing system drives managers to act in ways that create one particular strategic future rather than another strategic future from the alternative system.

Go to task 9b

Establish how the two different approaches to costing products might influence the delivery of the strategy explicated in the SSI.

Hints and Tips

■ Be clear about the underlying logic of the alternative system.

■ Think about the way in which a 'rational manager' would act in order to maximize their own success in the organization by their understanding of the costs.

■ Typically investment decisions and effort are organized according to the understanding of costs and so relative profits. Sales staff may put their effort into those products or product types that show the most apparent profit (according to the current costing system). Consider how investment and effort will push the organization in a particular strategic direction, and how this might be different for the alternative costing system.

'Back of the Envelope' Spreadsheet Analysis

Typically the maps that are the basis for linking strategies and distinctive competences to goals also provide the basic structure for a spreadsheet model. Each causal link implies a possible arithmetic relationship. Each node implies a possible revenue or cost. Indeed, one of the earliest forms of spreadsheet software (Javelin) allowed causality – words and arrows – to be the basic structure for building the spreadsheet. It would have been a very useful product to help in the evaluation of a business model, had Microsoft not dominated the marketplace!

Of course, difficulties arise when there are feedback loops. A feedback loop depicts a dynamic outcome, where the nodes are variables that will change over time in an accelerating and exponential manner when there is positive feedback – sometimes this dynamic has an undesirable outcome (vicious circle) and sometimes a desirable outcome (virtuous circle). They may also form a negative feedback loop where the impact is controlling. Without the use of specialist computer software it is difficult to anticipate the behaviour of feedback loops as often there are counter intuitive aspects.[11] For the purposes of a 'back of the envelope' check on the business model then the first step will be to establish whether the first period of analysis can be estimated to show positive results. However, it is worth recalling that often a strategy is expected to trigger the feedback loop, and in doing so, demands a cost before revenue follows. Thus, the strategy is expected to have a long-term positive impact alongside a short-term negative impact. In these circumstances, an evaluation of the best-case and worst-case outcomes, both in terms of time to deliver and revenue, must be undertaken.

The spreadsheet can be constructed interactively in the presence of the strategy-making group (as happened in case study 6.1). Indeed, it is crucial that those who have formulated the strategy provide estimates of revenues and costs as they have intimate knowledge of the possible behaviours of the nodes.

Nevertheless, for many strategy-making group members the construction of a spreadsheet is seen as a back-room activity that is of a specialist nature. In these circumstances there is likely to be resistance to the idea of building a spreadsheet interactively. In this case, the facilitator needs to be skilled in the fast construction of the spreadsheet and to do so in such a manner that the process is seen to be transparent to all group members and at a level of detail that is appropriate. Alternatively, the basic structure of the spreadsheet could be constructed off-line as long as it can be shown to represent faithfully the structure of the maps, and is reviewed with the group.

As noted above, in order to adequately test the robustness of the strategy and in particular the business model it is important to consider best-case and worst-case situations. However, in doing so, it is important to remember that it is extremely unlikely that all worst-case revenues and costs will occur at the same time. Also, each member of the strategy-making group is likely to have differing views about costs and revenues. It is often helpful, therefore, to encourage each member of the group to make independent estimates and then pull these together as a basis for both discussion and final estimation of the expected outcomes and possible variance from these expectations.[12] The process for doing this type of analysis is outlined in Figure 8.3.

Expected = sum (L+4M+H)/6

- M = most likely
- L = low surprise limit
- H = high surprise limit

Variance = average((b–a)/3^2

Figure 8.3 Developing Group Estimates

In our experience it is rare for the spreadsheet analysis to imply that the strategy and business model are unrealizable or incredible. However, it is extremely common for the outcomes of the strategy to be evaluated as overly optimistic. In these circumstances, it is likely that strategies will need to be refined.

Stakeholder Analysis and Management, and Alternative Futures

The approach to strategy making presented in this book is largely focused upon developing a strategy that the power brokers own, and therefore will implement – a **politically feasible strategy**. It has, therefore, focused upon getting the right strategy-making group and then paying attention to the views of the members of that strategy-making group. In doing so it will take in to account the external environment as members consider it: powerful external stakeholders likely to support or sabotage the organization, and external events likely to interfere with success.[13] However, it is not sensible to depend solely upon the concerns and worries of each member of the strategy-making group raised during the group's consideration of the issues. The group will still need to think explicitly 'outside the box' (tapping their creativity and expertise), and to do so in a manner that still provides ownership of the results.

The analysis of stakeholders is undertaken in order to facilitate the strategic management of their power and interests in the organization. The analysis of alternative futures is about understanding the nature of events that are not capable of strategic management by the organization.

Based upon stakeholder theory and years of practical experience of working with management teams, a number of techniques have been developed that facilitate stakeholder analysis and management, and the analysis of alternative futures.[14]

Stakeholder Analysis and Management

Stakeholder analysis is dependent upon the development and use of a **power-interest grid**[15] on to which all possible stakeholders are placed. Those who have both a high level of interest in the future of your organization and the power to influence its outcome are the stakeholders who are most worthy of greater analysis. Those who have a high level of interest but little power are still stakeholders who must be considered because of their ability to form coalitions in order to gain power. Those who have considerable power to influence the strategic outcome and the organization, but little interest in it, are not stakeholders at present but should either be considered as a part of alternative futures and managed accordingly or reviewed with the intent of gaining their interest.

Thus, those stakeholders who have power and interest need to be managed. There are two dimensions to be managed: the nature of their power and the nature of their interests. Understanding these two dimensions provides the basis for strategically managing stakeholders.[16] New strategies will arise from this work and need to be integrated into the strategic intent.

Moreover, as the strategies are being developed (both for realization of the strategic intent and management of stakeholders) it becomes important to test out their viability. This is often best undertaken through the use of a **role-think** workshop. Role-think allows the group to explore the possible responses of each stakeholder to the strategies thus providing insights regarding stakeholder management along with determining which of the strategies these stakeholders will notice and what their possible courses for action will be.[17]

Alternative Futures

> The future cannot be forecast with a high enough degree of certainty for precise strategic plans to be constructed that will not be knocked off course. A management team needs, therefore, to understand the structure and character of possible futures rather than predictions. By understanding the nature of **multiple possible futures**, the team will be in a position to act opportunistically within a strategy framework. More importantly, it will be able to do so faster than its competitors, or fast enough to avert disasters, or fast enough to lever aspirations more efficiently. (Eden and Ackermann (1998) p. 137, our emphasis)

An organization that changes its strategy in response to changes in the environment tends to outperform those that do not (and research supports this view).[18] Thus explicitly and carefully exploring the future is an important part of strategy making.

In recent years the approach to scenario planning (one means of exploring the future), originally developed and implemented by Shell, has gained popularity, albeit often in adapted forms.[19] The approach used is all encompassing and expected to be the driver for strategy development, rather than just an important part of strategy making. The approach is highly qualitative and depends upon extensive interviewing and workshops. It is, therefore, often considered to be too sophisticated and expensive for many organizational settings.

The principles of exploring alternative futures are, nevertheless, the important aspect to scenario planning. There are quicker and less expensive approaches that reflect these principles. Indeed, our experience has shown that a two-hour alternative futures workshop generally provides significant value-added to the strategy-making group. This depends upon their involvement in the generation of the alternative futures and their evaluation of them with respect to their developing strategy.

Performance Indicators (and Project Management)

The development of performance indicators obviously plays a role in the delivery of a strategy. Establishing appropriate performance indicators can take an organization some way towards combating the problems of strategic control outlined in the next chapter. However, the development of performance indicators additionally tends to provide significant value in the development of strategic options and the refining of strategies and goals.

The greatest danger in establishing performance indicators is to overcome the temptation for all of them to be quantitative. The old adage 'what gets measured gets done' is a great danger for strategy delivery. Progress towards most goals can only be established by creating a **portfolio** of qualitative and quantitative performance indicators. The now well-established **balanced scorecard** approach offers some assistance.[20] Through directly considering four dimensions (financial, customer, internal processes, and innovation and learning) the organization is moved away from a focus only on the bottom line (often short term in nature). Moreover, the scorecard recognizes the interactivity of the measures – allowing synergy to take place. This direct acknowledgement of the impact of measures on one another is also carried through, in terms of mapping measures, on to the organization's strategy (the strategy map). As noted in this chapter (when reviewing the goals) and case study 6.1, a large number of the goals were financially based. Here obvious measures could be derived but for them to be fully exploited a set of qualitative as well as quantitative measures were necessary (to ensure the integration of the goals system).

A final consideration, and one that ties in with earlier comments regarding the building of qualitative simulation models, is recognizing that often performance drops as new strategies are put in place (as staff become accustomed to the new ways of working). Frequently there is the temptation to assume that the strategies aren't working and so change direction before any of the benefits can be realized.[21]

Summary

The latter part of this chapter has provided a very brief introduction to aspects of making strategy that go beyond the initial strategy development process which is the main part of this book. We have sought to argue persuasively that these aspects are important additions. It is rare for us to be involved in strategy making that does not encompass at least some work on a quantitative analysis of the viability of the business model, stakeholder management, alternative futures and the development of performance indicators (albeit these activities can be very rough and ready).

Nevertheless there have been many management teams of large organizations who have been extremely satisfied with developing a robust SSI with its clearly articulated strategies and business model. They have determined that they have considered stakeholders and alternative futures adequately enough through working on their own independent views of the future. They have been committed to a mapping outcome that shows clearly why things need to be done and how they are to be done. They have used the causal arrows as the basis for project management of their strategy, and in many cases they have used Decision Explorer® as the basis for that project management. Establishing whether strategies have been implemented is one thing, establishing whether they have been implemented for the right reasons is almost more important!

Notes

1. Lynch (2003) alternatively sees the purpose of an organization shaped by vision, leadership and ethics (chapter 10). He sees a clear process of moving from purpose to mission and objective through stakeholder analysis (see later in this chapter) and organizational culture (chapter 12).

2. As the research mentioned in Campbell and Tawadey (1990) indicated, a mission statement includes statements of values. This goes beyond the statement envisaged here. Campbell and Yeung (in De Wit and Meyer, 1998) reiterate this point when they discuss mission planning. As they argue: 'strategic intent is another concept that overlaps with vision and mission' (pp. 147–56). Prahalad and Doz (in De Wit and Meyer, 1998) argue that we should distinguish the strategic intent from the strategies: 'intent is used . . . to describe long-term goals and aims, rather than detailed plans' (p. 518). Johnson and Scholes (2002) are clear that a mission statement is a 'generalised statement of the overriding purpose of an organisation' (p. 239). Lynch (2003) suggests the 'mission of an organisation outlines the broad directions that it should and will follow and briefly summarises the reasoning and values that lie behind it' (p. 435). In our case the reasons are encompassed in a statement about the working of the business model or livelihood scheme. Lynch presents the process for developing a strategic vision and argues that it is a 'mental image of a possible and desirable future state of the organisation', 'vision is not the same as purpose' (p. 363). In this sense our statement of strategic intent is unlike a vision statement. Wheelan and Hunger (in De Wit and Meyer, 1998) assert that a 'corporate mission is the purpose or reason for the corporation's existence' (p. 48). They discuss the issues in determining the narrowness or breadth of a mission statement. They are also more fussy about the terms used and state that a 'goal is often confused with objective'. We have used the term goal to encompass ideals, values, objectives, aims, etc. and in practice use the term that is effective in working with a strategy-making team, rather than being pedantic. In this book we are less fussy about the terminology used and prefer, when possible, to use the language that the strategy-making group feels comfortable with.

3. William George (2001), in an address to the American Academy of Management, made a compelling case that 'mission-driven companies create long term shareholder value'.

4. See Eisenberg (1984) p. 231; Eden and Ackermann (1998) p. 161.

5. See www.corporatefinance.mckinsey.com/aboutmckinsey/ourdoublemission.htm.

6. As Johnson and Scholes (2002) assert: 'it should not be assumed that the drawing up of some sort of value statement or the publishing of a document explaining a strategic direction will of itself change [the organisation]' (p. 49). As they also remind us, 'the evidence from research is that a values statement is likely to be more effective if its use is judged "locally" for different types of staff' (p. 483).

7. As Lynch (2003) argues: 'the purpose of an organisation can and probably will change over time' (p. 737) and so when drafting the statement of strategic intent it is as well to remember that the language used might take account of future changes.

8. This is close to the Johnson and Scholes (2002) view of strategic intent which 'encapsulates the desired future state or aspiration of an organisation – the sense of discovery and destiny – that motivates managers and employees alike' (p. 239).

9. See chapter 5 in Eden and Ackermann (1998).

[10] See Spender, 1989, where he introduces the term.

[11] See Pettigrew et al. (2003). For a consideration of counterintuitive behaviour see Forrester (1971).

[12] The process involves what is usually called a nominal group technique (Delbecq et al., 1975) and a Delphi technique (Dalkey and Helmer, 1963; Rowe and Wright, 1999).

[13] See Ackermann and Eden (2003) for a discussion of the relationship between stakeholder theory and the techniques developed.

[14] Eden and Ackermann (1998) chapter P4 pp. 341–70 provide practical guidance in the use of these techniques.

[15] The development of the power-interest grid is discussed in greater detail in Eden and Ackermann (1998) pp. 121–5.

[16] This process uses a 'star diagram' which illustrates the bases of power and interest and is discussed in greater detail in Eden and Ackermann (1998) pp. 126–7.

[17] Role-think is discussed in greater detail in Eden and Ackermann (1998) pp. 133–4.

[18] See Haveman (1992) and Smith and Grimm (1987) for the evidence.

[19] For example, Van der Heijden (1996) and Van der Heijden et al. (2002).

[20] Kaplan and Norton (1996) introduce the concept of the balanced scorecard, explaining how it is built and how it can help to align the organization's performance measures to their strategy. Kaplan and Norton (2001) move the balanced scorecard from a performance measurement system to a system which can help an organization become more focused on their strategy. They explain the five key principals for building what they refer to as a 'strategy-focused organisation'.

[21] See note 4 above for further details.

Task 8a Statement of Strategic Intent (SSI)

■ **Construct a draft statement of strategic intent in the form of bullet point statements from the maps, ensuring there are three parts covering:**

> ■ **A statement of purpose that gets across the goals system hierarchy.**
> ■ **The business model.**
> ■ **Draft strategies for sustaining DCs and delivering the goals following from prioritized issues and strategies to develop the business model/livelihood scheme.**

Task 8b Statement of Strategic Intent (SSI)

■ Construct a statement of strategic intent based upon the first draft, by converting the list of statements into sentences and paragraphs, ensuring there are three parts covering:

■ A statement of purpose that gets across the goals system.
■ A punchy statement of the business model.
■ Articulated draft strategies for sustaining DCs and delivering the goals following from prioritized issues and strategies to develop the business model/livelihood scheme.

■ Make the document dramatic and emotionally engaging.
■ This must be a document that is persuasive to your strategy-making group in the first instance, it is **not a selling document!**

Task 9a Impact of Systems and Structures

■ Consider two different approaches to costing products (or transfer pricing).

■ Establish the manner in which each of these approaches might significantly influence the emergent strategizing of the organization.

Task 9b Impact of Systems and Structures

■ Establish the manner in which each of these two different approaches might significantly influence the emergent strategizing of the organization, and so the delivery of the strategy explicated in the SSI.

9 Managing an Incomplete Process to Achieve Strategic Change

Introduction

We now have to recognize that strategy making may involve changes that might not be palatable to everyone. Some much-prized competences thought to be distinctive (and crucial to the organization's livelihood) will have been seen to be unimportant. Others need to be given more resources, and entirely new directions may have emerged. All these things will affect people, sometimes negatively, and therefore the management of implementation moves to the top of the agenda. Central to this will be the establishment of control systems to measure the progress of the new strategies, and a careful review of the reward systems. As you will discover in this chapter, we often reward the wrong actions as well as the wrong people. We need to ensure rewards themselves are effective.

During our strategy making, we have lingered on some highly important phases. Yet we have taken many short cuts, and have skimmed over several important issues. Even the stages which we described in detail are likely to take longer in the real world, and there may be more difficulties to deal with – particularly in the internal dynamics of your organization and your strategy-making group. The demands of the real world might also be greater: it will often be necessary to look at a wider range of strategic options, and evaluate them against each other and against the various risks that the outside world – and your competitors – may present.

However, one thing that should have become apparent from this process is that the effective strategy maker needs to be alert and flexible. There are many contingencies: organizations vary, and also change, the environment certainly changes, and 'shocks' of various kinds are commonplace in a globalized and ever-more complex world. Tomorrow's technologies and market conditions will probably be different: the demands of your customers certainly will be. Strategy will have to change, and change frequently.

Conditions may also prevent you from conducting strategy making in the well-planned linear fashion that we have described here. Sometimes closure will be needed earlier in the process. In fact, you can be confident that every strategy-making exercise that you undertake will be different. In this chapter we discuss how the premature need for closure can still result in a tangible value-added product.

Strategy-making Outcomes

■ An ability to bring a stage in strategy making to a close with your strategy-making team, based on the steps you have undertaken.

Commentary and Issues

This book has introduced you to more details of the practical approach to helping a small team of managers develop a strategic direction for their own part of an organization. In this chapter we discuss the different stages of strategy making at which closure may be achieved based on the steps covered in this handbook.

Closure is a problematic notion because for many organizational groups strategy making and strategy adaptation will be continuous. To some extent strategy making is itself part of a continuous improvement process in organizations, and certainly can be an important part of organizational learning[1] and team building.[2]

> in many respects, shared understanding about strategic intent will make things happen differently – this has been the essence of our case that the most successful strategic change will come from managers construing their world differently and so acting differently. However realistic this approach to organizational change may be, it does not satisfy the need a person and an organization has for an artifact, something concrete, which signifies that the task of strategy development has been completed and, later, that progress in strategic change has been made. (Eden and Ackermann (1998) pp. 159)

This quote suggests that some clear milestone is needed. Usually others need to be informed of the agreed strategic direction, especially as we are working with small groups and some dissemination will probably be required.

Closure will also often imply consideration of the best methods for project managing the delivery of strategy (see chapter 8).

However, the purpose of this final chapter is to discuss a number of different ways in which the use of the processes described in this workbook might lead to a natural point of closure, or what to do about an unnatural closure, and to then discuss issues of control systems and reward systems that follow closure.

The second chapter of this book asked you to consider the make up of your strategy-making team. We argued that the success of strategy making would depend upon your ability to gather together an appropriate group of power brokers. For many of you, as managers, wishing to undertake some serious strategy making, the major difficulty will not be your ability to use strategic management concepts but rather your ability to engage your strategy-making team. It is possible that you will be forced to adopt a form of closure earlier than you would wish because you cannot get the members of your strategy-making team to devote any further time to the activity. There is little point in forcing a team, against their will, to continue the process, even if it would make sense from the point of view of developing a better strategy on paper. Strategy delivery must be politically feasible. However, do not regard this as a statement suggesting that the likelihood of your succeeding in strategy making is small. As we stated in the first chapter, very many MBA students and middle, as well as senior, managers have succeeded in delivering major strategic change in their organizations.

Ideally, the most appropriate point in strategy making to develop closure is when the most appropriate balance between emotional and cognitive commitment and strategic analysis has occurred. For the facilitator, or manager, driving strategy making, it can sometimes be frustrating when the strategy-making team are clear in their own minds that they have a robust strategy and yet they have not undertaken all of the analysis that would seem to the facilitator to be sensible. Remember that it is better to have strategy that is less well thought through but will be delivered, than a strategy that has been fully developed but will not be delivered because there is no commitment to it from those who must deliver it.

We have suggested in this book a series of strategy-making workshops. This series is likely to be undertaken over several weeks. It is not uncommon for one outcome of a successful workshop to be that some members of the team start implementing the consequences of the workshop before the series is complete. This means that strategy delivery will have commenced before the strategic thinking is complete. When this occurs it is more likely to be a cause for satisfaction rather than frustration – it means the team have engaged with the strategy making and have been able to translate it into action.

The strategy-making outcome will always be contingent upon the particular circumstances of your own organization.[3] There is a spectrum running from agreement to a deliberate emergent strategy; through to the development of a statement of strategic intent; through to a published strategy containing some form of mission statement, a clear system of distinctive goals and a set of interacting strategic programmes; through to a detailed strategy involving carefully evaluated budgets, project teams, responsibilities and control systems.[4] Deciding the most appropriate position along this spectrum, for your own organization, will have occurred by default during the process of making strategy. It may be important to make this choice in a more deliberate manner, for example, there is always the risk that you stop strategy making too early, and will never know with certainty that this was the case!

- We introduced above two of the major considerations in determining closure: the social demands of your strategy-making team, and the ideal considerations of the development of an appropriately contingent strategy.
- We have also reminded you that the processes presented in this workbook are potentially incomplete (see chapter 8).

Closure Following Individual Interviews and the Use of Cognitive Mapping (Chapter 3)

Although cognitive mapping is one way of starting the strategy making, it may, unusually, also be a point of closure. A series of good interviews, that are undertaken with the help of live cognitive mapping, may just about provide enough input to the facilitator or analyst for a statement of strategic intent to be constructed. This will only be worthwhile when the key interviewees (power brokers) are prepared to trust the facilitator to take seriously the material presented.

Merging all of the cognitive maps, with the specific identification of the material from each of the key interviewees, can provide the basis for establishing a goals system for the organization and a set of prioritized strategies. The goals system and strategies are established through a careful analysis of the merged maps (see support 1). The analysis leads to the creation of a strategy map that can be the basis for the publication of a draft strategy document which can be circulated to at least all of the key interviewees (likely to be the same people as those identified in chapter 2). Inviting comment from each of the recipients of the draft strategy may enable agreement to be reached after redrafting.

Undoubtedly, such an approach is less likely to develop the higher levels of emotional commitment of the extended stages. However, it may be a better outcome than forcing participants to attend further workshops. (Note that in the MBA case study (support 3), Ian was able to gain considerable ownership from his group for a map constructed several months after the interviews were conducted. If the cognitive mapping exercise has been good then the maps will have captured important and enduring aspects of the thinking of the interviewees.)

Nevertheless, it is unusual for participants involved in a good interview to be lacking in curiosity about what others have expressed about the needs for the strategic future of the organization. This curiosity will be even greater if a first interview is followed up with a second interview where a good (faithful to the interviewee) cognitive map is fed back to the interviewee for comment and collaboration. As participants see their own views reflected in a map, and recognize the potential opportunity for seeing their own views set within the context of the views of others, then their curiosity will increase. Also the process of considering strategic issues in an interview usually raises their consciousness about the desirability for strategic thinking. Under these circumstances it becomes easier to get attendance at the first workshop, so that closure at this stage is not necessary.

If closure is necessary at this stage, then it can be more successful when both avenues of 'detecting emergent strategizing' have been explored. Not only have interviews been conducted in order to explore the emergent belief systems and value systems that guide the approach to dealing with strategic issues, but also the implications of systems and structures on the strategic future of the organization have also been explored (see chapter 8). The analyst is then in a better position to consider the possible disjunction between aspirations and taken-for-granted realities. Recall that systems such as costing, transfer pricing, reward and information are crucial, and usually unintended, determinants of strategic futures.

Probably the most significant analytical disadvantage that derives from closure at this stage is that there has been no consideration of the extent of the distinctiveness of the goals system, and no work on exploring distinctive competences. Thus, there has been no exploration of the practicality of the business model or livelihood scheme.

■ The product of closure: goals system and some significant strategies (expressed at a high level). Taken together these can constitute the first step towards a version of a statement of strategic intent. Increased shared understanding or meaning between participants is also an important outcome.

Closure Following the Development of a Group Strategy Map Using the OMT (Chapter 4)

In this book we have considered the use of the oval mapping technique in a group setting as an alternative to individual interviews using cognitive mapping, or in addition to cognitive mapping of individual interviews. Your own strategy making, experimentation or simulation of strategy making will probably have tried either one or other of these approaches to starting the process of strategy making.

Using cognitive mapping as an initial stage prior to the use of the merged map in a group workshop setting may be appropriate. The group workshop would then be likely to involve, in addition to working on the merged map, use of the oval mapping technique.

When the OMT has been used in a workshop as the first step in exploring potential strategic futures through the identification of strategic issues, then the commentary above about closure following cognitive mapping can apply. However, there is likely to be considerably higher levels of emotional or cognitive commitment because of the contribution from the social processes following good workshop design. The social processes will have enabled some psychological, emotional and social negotiation to have occurred and so created wider ownership of the outcomes of the workshop.

For many organizations an OMT workshop can provide enough of a strategy framework to make a significant difference to the way in which the organization creates its own future (see the Strathclyde Poverty Alliance case study 5.2).

A single workshop can create a workable goals system, mission statement and a number of high priority strategies. In this book we have deliberately suggested a minimalist target of two to three hour workshops. It is just possible to create a rough framework that will guide strategic behaviour within an organization in this short time. This is particularly possible, and probably the only practicable approach, when working with community groups or temporary project teams such as those dealing with a single issue – for example, pressure groups. Here the opportunity to get a group of volunteers together is rare and so a single one-day (or ideally two-day) workshop may be the only opportunity to develop a clear statement of strategic intent that can guide strategic opportunism.

Analytically, the process of closure replicates that undertaken with respect to cognitive mapping. However, analysis will often be conducted in real-time with the strategy-making team during the workshop. A draft one-page mission statement, or even two-thirds of a statement of strategic intent, can be written directly from the goals system and priority strategies developed by the team. The mission statement is typically drafted in real-time, and must follow exactly the systemic properties of the goals system.

■ The product of closure: some degree of emotional commitment to a mission statement, goals system and some significant strategies (expressed at a high level). Taken together these can constitute a version of a statement of strategic intent.

Closure Following Either Cognitive Mapping or an OMT Workshop, with a Goals Workshop (Chapter 5)

This stage of strategy making assumes that strategic issue surfacing has been undertaken by using interviews and cognitive mapping or through the OMT workshop. With an expectation of being able to work explicitly towards the development of a goals system as the final product, the latter stages of a workshop exploring the merged cognitive maps can be openly declared as a focus of goals and aspirations. Similarly, the OMT workshop can have the declared purpose of prioritizing strategic issues and developing a network of goals.

In both cases, closure will involve:

■ Developing an appreciation of the interaction between strategic issues.
■ Understanding the nature of this interaction, as a network, so that issues can

be prioritized based partly upon the extent to which dealing with one issue can resolve many others.

■ Appreciating that identification of strategic issues, by implication, suggests that they will be attacking important emergent goals of the organization.

■ Identifying a system of goals that emerge from the identification of issues.

In doing so, the emergent goals can be evaluated with respect to the view the team have of their aspirations for the future. Strategic issues and thus emergent goals are often based too much upon the past, and so need to be considered with respect to an idealized strategic future. As the emergent goals system is modified, then it, by implication, requires a revaluation of the strategic issues network. This interaction between strategic issues and the goals or aspirations system continues until settlement is reached (remember that an issue will only be an issue if it attacks a goal or negative goal).

The final stage of closure arises when the strategy-making team are clear that they have a realistic and distinctive goals system, and have been able to prioritize strategic issues based upon their interaction with one another, and most importantly, based upon their impact on goals.

As with each of the first two examples of closure, the goals system can be written as a mission statement and the priority strategic issues can be presented as key strategies.

Closure at this stage runs the risk that the goals system is unrealistic because the goals cannot be attained, or alternatively because they are not aspirational enough. Nevertheless, a reasonably clear statement of strategic intent is now possible (albeit without the explication of the business model and so of core distinctive competences). The statement should be coherent and internally consistent as a result of the process followed. The statement will also act as a call to action through the identification of priority strategies. The strategies will not have been checked in relation to the need for stakeholder management or protection from dangerous alternative futures or responses to opportunities presented by a range of alternative futures. But, because they will have been derived from the use of cognitive maps or the OMT, they should be recognizable and meaningful to those required to act with respect to them.

■ The product of closure: emotional commitment to a goals system and key strategies (expressed at a high level, but with some aspects of strategic programmes developed). Taken together these constitute an incomplete, but useful, statement of strategic intent.

Closure Following an Exploration of a Business Model or Livelihood Scheme by Relating Distinctive Competences to Goals (Chapters 6 and 7)

Closure at this stage should provide a sound strategy for the organization. It will still be missing considerations of stakeholder management and alternative futures, a quantitative check and performance indicators, as well as a 'reality check' against the customer's view of distinctiveness. This means that it is, at least, likely some strategies will need continual adaptation to the responses of powerful stakeholders, and also that strategies will be missing the considerations of threats and opportunities that may derive from the environment. Nevertheless, a considerable number of strategy-making teams, in both large and small organizations, have found that closure at this stage can have profound impact on the organization and secures a successful strategic future.

As we have commented in chapter 6, a workshop on distinctive competences is often the most significant workshop. It is also usually the most difficult workshop.

Remember, the principles of the relationship between the goals and distinctive competences are simple.

It says:

'I aspire to . . .'
    'I have competences to do so which are distinctive to me.'
        'They match my aspirations.'
'Or, if they don't, I will develop new distinctive competences, or modify my aspirations.'
'I am assured that there is someone who will:
    (for commercial organizations) buy my product or service,
    (for public or not-for-profit organizations) legitimize my aspirations by providing a mandate and finance.'
        'This support will provide my right to sustain a continuing livelihood, or make a continuing surplus or profit.'

The exploration of the business model by linking distinctive competences, or patterns of competences that are distinctive, to aspirations or goals is what enables the discovery of core distinctive competences. Core distinctive competences are discovered through this process; they are not asserted. This produces a cycle of distinctiveness (Figure 9.1).

The business model shows sustenance, protection and development of existing patterns of distinctive competences, as well as showing continual sustenance for the operational requirements of marketing, sales, production and the facilitative demands of management accounting, HR, etc.[5] When a true business model is created using computer simulation (for example, System Dynamics or Discrete Event simulation methods) it can be possible to

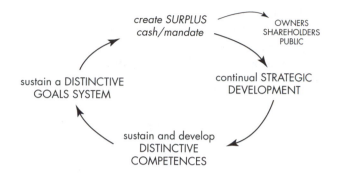

Figure 9.1 The Cycle of Distinctiveness

show numerically how the causal relationships will work over a strategic future.[6]

From the point of view of closure and strategy delivery, the work on distinctive competences should have revealed those competences and distinctive competences that are no longer important for the future of the organization. For them not to be important, remember that some competences may not appear crucial when evaluated singly, but may be absolutely crucial in supporting and sustaining other important competences and distinctive competences. Always remember to check the network of competences, not the list of them. Unimportant aspects of the way the organization does things, and about which the organization feels proud, will have a lesser place in the strategic future of the organization. Because these competences are no longer in need of sustenance there will be a release of energy and resources – sometimes whole departments may be released or outsourced. This release provides important **strategic slack** that enables new strategies to be delivered effectively. But this does need to be done carefully with the consequences (links) examined.

■ The product of closure: emotional commitment to a goals system, business model or livelihood scheme, and key strategies to deliver the goals and sustain and develop the business model, with some more detailed strategic programmes developed. Taken together these constitute a statement of strategic intent.

Reward Systems and Control Systems

At whichever of the above stages closure was seen to be necessary or practical, the issue of subsequent delivery is still paramount, and so devising effective control or reward systems is crucial.

Now read the article by Steven Kerr (support 5).

Kerr is concerned with the dysfunctional effects of reward and control systems. Probably one of the most difficult parts of strategic management is the identification of an appropriate reward system. For strategy implementation the table below represents some key examples of the 'double messages' embedded in reward systems.

We hope for . . .	*But often reward . . .*
■ long term growth; environmental responsibility etc.	■ quarterly earnings
■ teamwork	■ individual effort
■ setting challenging 'stretch' objectives	■ achieving goals; 'making the numbers'
■ downsizing; rightsizing; delayering; restructuring	■ adding staff; adding budget; adding Hay points
■ commitment to total quality etc.	■ shipping on schedule, even with defects
■ candour; surfacing bad news early	■ reporting good news, whether it's true or not; agreeing with the boss, whether or not they are right
■ innovative thinking and risk taking	■ proven methods and not learning
■ intrapreneurial successes	■ only success not effort
■ development of people skills	■ technical achievements
■ employee involvement and empowerment	■ tight control over operations and resources
■ high achievement	■ another year's effort

Note: this table is from Kerr (see support 5) with some additions.

Short term and easily measurable performance indicators dominate organizations. These systems produce the type of outcomes that Kerr warns us of, and are provided in the examples above. Inadequate performance indicators often result from:

■ A 'fascination with an "objective" criterion', which causes goal displacement:

   ■ Simple, quantifiable standards; a resistance to the use of clusters of qualitative performance indicators.[7]
   ■ 'Overemphasis on highly visible behaviours, which miss, for example, team building/creativity'.

■ 'Hypocrisy'.
■ An 'emphasis on morality or equity rather than efficiency'.
■ A focus on action rather than what it's designed to achieve – not managing causality.

- Using lists of actions as a check for strategy delivery encourages a 'tick-box' mentality that ignores the reason why the action must be taken, whereas using maps encourages attention to causality.

- A reluctance to accept that managers are not capable of manipulative behaviour.
- 'Vague and ambiguous mission and goal statements' that are often not even aspirational and certainly not distinctive in relation to competitors.
- A lack of attention to emotional and cognitive commitment – avoiding the role of the strategy-making **process**. (See Kerr, support 5.)

With these warnings in mind 'we must devise processes for monitoring, review, and strategic control which in themselves promote organizational learning, do not stultify strategy, and yet provide respect for a carefully developed strategy and enable operational effectiveness and efficiency to develop' (Eden and Ackermann (1998) p. 158).

This means we must:

- Attend to the causes of reward systems being dysfunctional:

  - Use qualitative as well as quantitative measures.
  - Apply specificity only when appropriate.
  - Reward managing causality.
  - Explicitly recognize systemicity (the interrelationship between strategic actions, strategies, goals).
  - Attend to process management as well as content management.

- 'Explore what types of [rational] behaviour are currently rewarded' and consider what manipulative behaviour can gain rewards.
- Note that 'all organizational behaviour is [not] determined by formal rewards and punishments'.
- Realize that often 'the rewarded is not causing the behaviour but is only a fortunate bystander' – for example, the dilemma of bonus payments to all for the behaviour of a few; rewarding the good performers but not being seen by the good to 'punish' the bad.
- Acknowledge that developing appropriate control or reward systems for delivering strategy is immensely difficult, and so needs constant attention. (See Kerr, support 5.)

Leadership and Closure

John Kotter, a powerful writer on leadership, has produced a helpful list of eight steps towards strategic change. These steps are particularly useful as a reminder of the keys elements that must follow closure. They are set out below, with our comments in square brackets.

John Kotter's Eight Steps to Transforming Your Organization (1995)

■ Establishing a sense of urgency.

　　■ Identifying and discussing crises, potential crises, major opportunities: create crises . . .

■ Forming a powerful coalition [see chapter 2 in this book].

　　■ Assembling a group with enough power to lead change.
　　■ Encouraging the group to work together as a team.

■ Creating vision [see chapters 3 or 4 with chapters 5, 6, 7 and 8].

　　■ Developing strategies for achieving the vision.

■ Communicating the vision [the principles of making strategy that drive the process presented in this book: use of group processes, social, emotional and psychological negotiation].

　　■ Using every vehicle possible to communicate.
　　■ Teaching new behaviours by the example of the guiding coalition [no 'double messages' – see inappropriate reward systems above].

■ Empowering others to act on the vision.

　　■ Getting rid of obstacles to change.
　　■ Changing systems and structures that undermine.
　　■ Encouraging risk taking and non-traditional ideas.

■ Planning for creating short term wins [or 'quick-wins' and 'small wins' – see chapter 8].

　　■ Planning for **visible** improvements.
　　■ Recognizing and rewarding employees involved in major improvements.

■ Consolidating improvements and producing still more change.

　　■ Using increased credibility to change systems.
　　■ Hiring, promoting and developing those who can implement change.

■ Institutionalizing new approaches [bear in mind that the elements of detecting emergent strategizing structures or systems and belief systems are measures of institutionalization; and so, later redetecting of emergent strategizing should detect changes in structures or systems and in beliefs].

- ■ Articulating the connections between new behaviours and strategies and strategic success.
- ■ Encouraging leadership development and succession.

As you move from facilitating strategy workshops to ensuring strategy is delivered, consider in turn each of the bullet points above with particular attention to the last bullet point.

Notes

1. See Eden and Ackermann (1998) pp. 74 and 305 for discussion of the role of strategy making in organizational learning.
2. See Eden and Ackermann (1998) p. 17 and the Scottish Natural Heritage vignette for discussion, and an example of strategy making aiding team building.
3. See Eden and Ackermann (1998) chapter 1, which argues for strategy making being contingent on the particular organization.
4. See Eden and Ackermann (1998) p. 9.
5. See Eden and Ackermann (2000) for further discussion about patterns of distinctive competences discovered through a group workshop.
6. See, for example, Kim Warren's (2002) book on competitive dynamics for an introduction to the use of System Dynamics simulation modelling for competitive strategy analysis.
7. See Eden and Ackermann (1998) p. 445.

Support 1

Analyzing Cause Maps
(adapted from Eden 2004)

Structural Properties Through the Two-dimensional Character of a Map

When a map is relatively complex (typically more than 40–50 nodes and 70+ links) then redrawing the map to an easy-to-read graphical representation will give rise to a pattern, 'shape' or series of patterns depending on the layout. These patterns help reveal emerging characteristics simply by the way in which the structure of the map forces a 'best' way of laying it out in two dimensions. For example, the need to locate linked nodes close to one another, and to keep the number of crossing links to a minimum, whilst adopting a hierarchical layout (for example, all arrows going up the page), will determine a particular layout for the map. This visual structure can be seen in many of the examples of maps shown in this book. Typically maps have been deliberately set out in a hierarchical form with the heads at the top of the map (see Figure S1.1), as this tends to show the clusters of options well (tails) and draws attention to their flow upwards to goals. In addition, the node(s) appearing in the centre of a map is usually significantly central to the way the problem or issue being depicted is seen by the person being mapped.

The analysis methods discussed below are, in effect, more formal examples of detecting the best ways of representing and displaying the map.

The Complexity of a Map

Determining the relative complexity of a map can be helpful because it acts as an appropriate preface to **chunking** analyses (means of working on specific clusters or chunks of the map) that are aimed at determining the nub of the issue (the key elements/nodes).

There are a couple of simple analyses of maps that indicate the central features of a map (which is often referred to as a directed graph). The first of these simple analyses explores the total number of nodes and links; and the second is concerned with the centrality of particular statements.

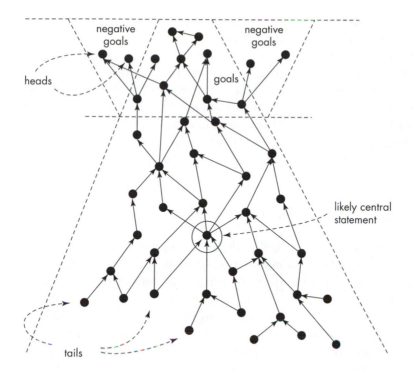

Figure S1.1 The Hierarchical Form of a Map, with the Heads at the Top of the Map

The Extent of the Map

The first of these analyses is based on the premise that the more nodes (or statements) in a map there are, then the more complex the map and so the issue. Here the method of eliciting the statements captured on the map is crucial in determining the validity of such a measure. For structured interviews the number of statements will be affected significantly by a) the structuring provided by the interview itself, b) whether the structure or lack of structure is due to poor interviewing skills or c) the interviewer having a tight agenda of structured questions all of which provide little opportunity for depth and richness. Use of multiple choice or closed questions, and an explicit expectation that the interviewee should be consistent, can have a profound effect on the openness of the interviewee. Interviews designed around pre-prepared agendas will push the number of statements elicited towards an interviewer-determined level. This level will be a function of the number of questions asked and the time given for each answer. Our experience indicates that the number of statements elicited during an interview is dependent upon the length of the interview, the skills of the interviewer and the degree of openness regarding the areas/issues discussed. Poor interviewing skills, such as evaluative non-verbal signals and the interviewer taking too much air-time, will vitally affect the size and shape of a map. Thus analyses that depend upon the number of nodes should be treated with great care.

It is not surprising that the degree of openness in an interview is dependent upon the extent to which the interview is itself a rewarding experience for the interviewee. Interviews can be a cathartic experience that encourages the interviewee on the one hand to be more open, and on the other hand to develop their own thinking about the topic (see chapters 3, 4 and 5 for illustrations of this). The suggestion that we do not know what we think until we hear what we say[1] is particularly significant in relation to the construction of maps.

The Complexity of the Map as a Network

In order to take some account of these concerns about the reliability of using the absolute number of nodes as a measure of the complexity of the map, an alternative analysis of map complexity is to determine the ratio of links to statements. Thus a higher ratio indicates a densely connected map and a higher level of complexity. The robustness of this analysis is dependent upon the coding skills of the mapper. Inexperienced mappers tend to generate a map with a smaller number of nodes than those identified by an experienced mapper and in addition they generate more links.

For example, more links result from coding A causes B, B causes C, C causes D (4 nodes, 3 links) with elaborated links adding A causes C, B causes D, and A causes D (4 nodes and 6 links). Each of the last three links is true as a summary of more detailed paths but does not represent a different causality to the indirect linkage. However, the ratio of links to nodes has increased from 0.75 to 1.25 suggesting an apparent, but incorrect, increase in complexity. We would expect ratios of 1.15 to 1.25 for maps elicited from interviews following the form of mapping introduced in this book.[2]

Idealized Thinking?

Other simple analyses of complexity derive from consideration of the ratio of the number of heads and number of tails to the total number of nodes. So-called **idealized** thinking about a topic tends to generate maps with a small number of heads (ideally a single end/goal/outcome/objective/value – a **pyramid** map). The map depicts someone able to think about situations within the context of a simple hierarchical value system where each value implies another that ultimately implies a single superordinate value.

A person might be judged to be cognitively simple and well organized in relation to the topic when a map takes the form of an idealized pyramid structure. In this case, the person will probably be dealing with a relatively tractable issue. Conversely, a map with a relatively large number of heads indicates recognition of, and a concern for, meeting multiple and possibly conflicting objectives; such a person could be seen as tackling a complex problem. In this case, issue/problem structuring will play a significant role.

The content of the nodes that are heads is also of some significance in this type of analysis, particularly when the same content appears as a tail for one person and a head for another. For example, our work with public policy makers has shown some of them viewing mandates as legitimizing goals (heads) whereas others in the same organization see them as constraints (tails). It is important to be clear about which of these is most helpful in using the map to decide ways forward.

Interpreting the analysis of the ratio of number of tails to total number of nodes is more problematic. The number of tails gives some indication of the range of possible options for acting to alleviate the issue. In general the ratio of tails to total nodes provides an initial indication of the relative **flatness** (see also below for an analysis of shape) of the map structure – a structure is relatively flat where causal arguments are not well elaborated and use short chains of argument.

Exploring the Emergent Properties of a Map: Finding the Nub

If a map is complex then there is a need to use appropriate methods of analyzing for emerging structural properties of the map and then using those emerging properties as a basis for finding the **nub of the issue**.

A map has several structural properties: the property of **hierarchy** and the more general property of **linkage**. Each of these provides opportunities for analysis of structure. The analyses, discussed below, are easier to conduct with the help of a computer and associated software (for example, Decision Explorer®[3]), although all of them can be determined manually or through visual inspection of the map; however, in these instances the validity may be uncertain as it is hard to be as accurate.

This section presents six types of analyses, which when taken together provide a compendium of emergent properties, each of which gives an insight into ways of managing the issue or problem depicted in the map. The analyses are:

1 Islands of themes: clusters – without accounting for hierarchy.
2 Networks of problems: clusters – accounting for hierarchy.
3 Finding 'potent' options.
4 Virtuous and vicious circles.
5 Central statements as the nub of the issue.
6 Simplifying the issue through emergent properties.

Islands of Themes: Clusters – Without Accounting for Hierarchy

At one extreme a map can comprise several clusters of nodes and links that are each disconnected from one another: **islands** of material. In this circumstance the detection of each island as a separate map allows an exploration of the content of each island to identify themes that describe each cluster. At this extreme, the map may contain no links at all between nodes – each node forms an island in a fragmented map. Towards the other extreme, a map may be highly interconnected (most likely when the ratio of links to nodes is high). In this case it is difficult to break apart the map into relatively separable but connected clusters: the map is one island. However, more typically a map is not in the form of islands or a single unbreakable cluster but rather is connected clusters of nodes. In this case the identification of clusters that break the map into a system of interrelated themes becomes worthwhile.[4] However, the identification of themes depends upon seeking out tight interconnection between nodes, and usually pays no attention to the nature of the link.

Thus one important analysis of emerging features relates to the detection of clusters, where a cluster may be more or less separable from other parts of the map. This process helps with managing the complexity of a large map along with giving insights into the themes emerging. One form of analysis follows the principles of something called **simple linkage clustering**[5] by looking at each node and its immediate context of nodes to determine a similarity rating. Clusters are formed gradually by putting relatively similar nodes into the same cluster until a defined level of dissimilarity has been reached. The intention is to attempt the formation of clusters where the nodes in each cluster are tightly linked to one another (similar) and the number of links (or bridges) with other clusters is minimized. In some senses this analysis identifies the 'robust' parts of the map – those parts of the map that are relatively insensitive to small changes in the structure of the map.

Each cluster, so formed, and the interrelationship between clusters form summary characteristics of the overall map. Clearly this type of analysis provides a further insight into complexity, where the proposition suggests that a map which can be broken apart into relatively unconnected smaller maps represents lower complexity than one which is difficult to break apart. In other words, cluster analysis can suggest whether or not (or to what extent) the world has been simplified by a form of categorization.

Although this analysis is easily done using the facilities available in Decision Explorer®, it is possible to see clusters by visual inspection, and in many of the cases in this book examples of visually determined clusters are given.

The purpose of analyzing for clusters is to identify the **system of problems** that makes up the issue being addressed. Thus each cluster, when summarized through a descriptor, represents a relatively separable part of the issue – a problem which may be addressed independently of addressing other parts.

Networks of Problems: Clusters – Accounting for Hierarchy

Alternatively, clusters may be formed by consideration of the hierarchical structure of the map. 'Complexity frequently takes the form of hierarchy and hierarchic systems have some common properties that are independent of the specific content . . . hierarchy . . . is one of the central structural schemes that the architect of complexity uses'.[6] Each node is supported by a 'tree' of other nodes that has implications for the original node of interest. Thus, in general, each node can be inspected for its own hierarchical cluster. However, in order to detect these emerging features of the map, it is more helpful to consider a subset of nodes of particular interest and their hierarchical relationship to one another and to other nodes that are not members of the subset, rather than the entire map. In this way, selected hierarchical clusters may be formed and the thematic content explored in relation to other hierarchically linked, hierarchical clusters. Often determining hierarchical clusters by using the subset 'goals' is helpful because it shows the range of nodes that 'hit' each goal and so form possible options for action to address the goal. Each hierarchical cluster is similar in form to another: it will have a superordinate head which represents the goal for the particular cluster (see Figure S1.2), and tails that represent the most detailed options for addressing that goal. In contrast to the first type of cluster analysis, a hierarchical clustering permits any node (excluding those in the chosen subset) to appear in more than one cluster – and this is a very useful addition to the analysis because, as we shall see below, it suggests options that are most likely to attack the maximum number of goals determined by the subset of nodes used as the basis for the analysis – they are, therefore, 'potent' options. Therefore, if the map has been coded properly, the top part of the map (heads) will depict the goals system, and the bottom part the detailed potential action points or options (Figure S1.1 showed this conceptualization). In attempting to solve problems depicted by a map, the task is to gradually provide the support which enables the network of problems to be translated into portfolios of actions as options are validated as actions.

An additional, helpful and exploratory form of this analysis is often conducted using core, or central, statements (as they are defined below) and heads as the subset of seed nodes. This means that analysis is focused on those statements that are central in linkage terms and those nodes that are, by definition, at the top of a hierarchy. This ensures that all nodes in the map are considered within the analysis, and considered with respect to goals and to central/core statements. The analysis then traces down the tree from each member of the subset and continually pulls nodes into a cluster until another member of the subset is met or the trace reaches a tail. In this way the hierarchical relationship between each hierarchical cluster is noted.

Obviously, the meaning of an analysis for hierarchical clusters is dependent upon the selection of the subset. With care in the choice of content-based seed nodes, interpreting the analysis is likely to be easier when the starting subset

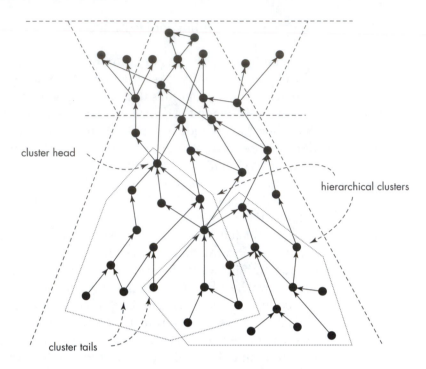

Figure S1.2 Hierarchical Clusters

can be formed with reference to the content of nodes, where the content indicates different topics.

Hierarchical clusters are another view of chunks of the map. Here each chunk is not mutually exclusive of other chunks, but it is representative of that part of the map that relates to any particular goal within the goals system or to central nodes that are descriptive of different content aspects of the problem or issue. Thus once again the analysis suggests that the issue or problem is made up of a system of interrelated subproblems.

Finding 'Potent' Options

The appearance of nodes in a number of hierarchical clusters creates a further emergent characteristic of the map or issue. A node that appears in several clusters is 'potent' for it has ramifications for a large number of hierarchical topics, central statements or goals, depending upon the basis for choosing the subset of seed nodes.

Figure S1.3 shows how an analysis of two possible hierarchical clusters reveals three potent options – tails that are within both clusters.

For problem solving, an important chunk of the map, resulting from this analysis of hierarchical clusters, is that of determining potent options for achieving the goals system.

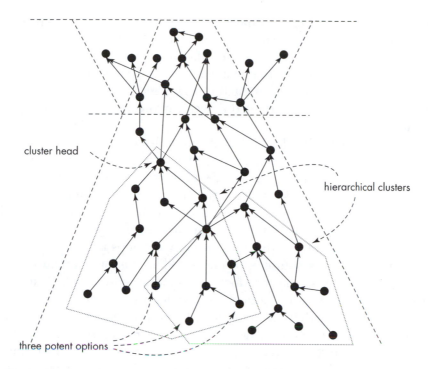

cluster head

hierarchical clusters

three potent options

Figure S1.3 Analysis of Two Possible Hierarchical Clusters Reveals Three Potent Options

Significantly the analysis can also reveal the extent of dilemmas which are a common consequence of recognition of multiple ramifications or goals. Each potent node may have both positive and negative consequences indicating the recognition of a dilemma.

Virtuous Circles, Vicious Circles and Controlling Circles

Within any context of the analysis of maps the existence, or not, of feedback loops will be of interest for two reasons. First, the existence of a loop may be a coding accident that needs correcting. Second, and of greater interest, loops imply the possible existence of dynamic considerations – that is the map indicates the potential for growth, decline or feedback control.

Unintended incorrect coding with respect to loops tends to be common with maps of the sort presented in this book because of the problematic nature of determining what is a cause and what is an effect. Figure S1.4 demonstrates how two different and plausible beliefs about the relationship between 'expanding the range of courses' and 'business experience' result in either a feedback loop or a hierarchy depending on your point of view. For the mapper it is very important to establish which point of view is correct in the particular instance being considered.

The existence of loops will have a significant impact on the results of all of the above analyses by leading to completely erroneous results. In most of the analyses above, every concept on the loop will be accorded the same analytical status. This means that analysis for the existence of loops should usually be undertaken before conducting any other analysis. In this way the coding can be checked and corrected if necessary before any other analysis is conducted.

The formality of coding demands that options lead to outcomes, means lead to ends, the head of an arrow shows the more desired outcome or goal. Without such formality any of the analyses described here is meaningless – this is particularly the case for an analysis to discover loops. Without consistent formal rules of the sort we have introduced throughout this book, loops will be found that are not really vicious circles, virtuous circles or controlling circles.

When analysis results in the existence of true loops then there will be a concern to establish the nature of feedback. When the loop contains an odd number of negative links then the loop is depicting self-control. That is, any perturbation in the state of the nodes in the loop will result in stabilizing dynamics to bring the activity into control. Alternatively, an even number of negative links or all positive links suggests regenerative or degenerative dynamics where a perturbation results in exponential growth or decline. In many studies loops relate to a small number of nodes and it is possible that the implications of the loop are well known to the individual whose issue is depicted. However, where maps contain the views of a number of people then both the identification and exploration of the loops can be of significant interest, as in these cases the loops are not recognized by any one person and can often be counter intuitive.

Figure S1.4 shows a loop recoded as a hierarchy: this recoding depends upon the point of view of the person being mapped.

Interventions which may be considered are:

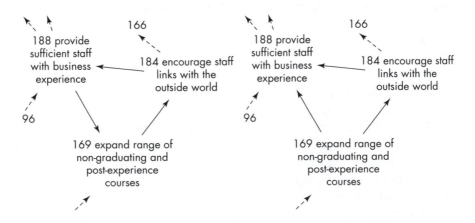

Figure S1.4 A Loop Recoded as a Hierarchy (this recoding depends upon the point of view of the person being mapped)

■ Positive feedback loop:

   ■ Virtuous circle: reinforce one or more of the nodes by exploring influences on each node in turn.
   ■ Vicious circle: 'rub out' one of the arrows by a change in policy or by changing the nature of one of the beliefs (make the loop into a controlling loop (negative) by changing the direction of causation, or destroying the causation); find a number of influences on nodes that can shift the direction of behavior so that a vicious circle becomes a virtuous circle.

■ Negative feedback loop – if the degree of control is undesirable:

   ■ If possible, break the loop by a change in policy; change the direction of causation so that the loop behaves as a virtuous circle.

■ Major strategic change:

   ■ Occurs when the structure of the situation is changed, for example, new loops become dominant, the central core of the map shifts by the deletion of some beliefs (that become insignificant) and others move to prominence when the desired outcomes (goals – those variables with no arrows out of them) change.

Central Statements as the Nub of the Issue

The simplest analysis available for seeking out the nub of the issue is generally known as a **domain analysis** because it calculates the total number of in-arrows and out-arrows from each node, that is its *immediate domain*. Those nodes whose immediate domain is most complex are taken to be those most central. The analysis indicates the richness of meaning of each particular statement. For the purposes of detecting the structural characteristics of issues these analyses can be a first draft of the nub of the issue.

Attending only to the immediate domain of a node the analysis completely ignores the wider context of the node. It is possible to extend the analysis of the structural significance or centrality of single statements within the map by exploring the impact of adding successive layers of domain to the domain count. Intuitively, it seems sensible to give each successive layer of statements a diminishing weight – a distance decay function. For example, each node directly linked to a central node may be given a weight of 1. Nodes in the next layer out are given a weight of 1/2. The next layer is given a weight of 1/3, and so on. Where a node with a high domain score is linked directly to another with a high domain score, then the two will bolster one another's domain score. Thus, for example, if three nodes with equal local domain scores form a row then usually

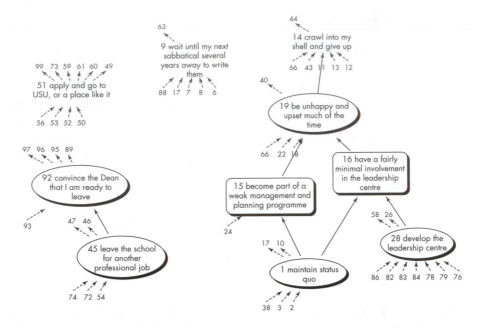

Figure S1.5 Domain Analysis of the Map from Chapter 5. Statements in ovals score high in both analyses, those in rectangles score high in a weighted extended domain analysis, those with no border score high on an immediate domain analysis.

the middle node will score most highly given this form of analysis, indicating greater centrality. This is an important distinction between the output from a simple domain analysis and a weighted extended domain analysis.

A domain analysis that considers more than the immediate context will reveal **bridging nodes**, which if the cross linkage did not exist then the centrality of other local nodes would drop significantly. Thus, within the context of the issue structure, they are worthy of further exploration in any problem-solving attempts.

Whereas the simple domain analysis is easy to undertake visually or manually, the second analysis requires the use of computer software such as Decision Explorer®.

Figure S1.5 shows an example of the difference in the analysis results.

Simplifying the Issue Through Emergent Properties

Simplification, or complexity reduction rather than the management of complexity, is always a dangerous process. Simplification will often lose the subtlety that characterizes the issue. Nevertheless, a highly complex map can be debilitating[7] and the appropriate management of complexity is an important aspect of the added value from mapping detail and subtlety, yet provides summaries that can encompass simplification without losing that which is significant. The detection of systemic, emergent properties is an effective way of ensuring that richness is retained and less necessary detail is lost, and thus the nub of the issue is identified.

When no prior analysis has been conducted, and each node has the same status as all others, the map can be simplified by excluding those causal paths that are simple elaboration. If nodes have one causal link in and one causal link out then the path can be collapsed from two links into a single link by, in effect, merging the node with its tail or head node. Thus, an argument that has been mapped as A→B→C can be reduced to A→C with loss of detail only. Similarly nodes with a single link to other parts of the map can be deleted to strip the map of detail. The process must not be incremental (where each stage assumes no prior stages) as this is likely to lead to the deletion of the whole map; the starting state of the map must be retained and each deletion determined in the light of this initial state. When computer software is used this process can be undertaken with greater assurance that the subtlety of detail contained in argument strings is not lost. The software allows nodes to be merged easily and with attention to content while automatically retaining structure. Without this careful merging process, which is difficult to undertake manually, it is likely that the bridging nodes discussed above would be lost.

The effect of this process of stripping out detail is to collapse the map to include only those nodes with a domain score of three or more – which retains those nodes that sit at branch points and deletes those nodes that are simply a part of extended elaboration.

Conclusions

This support section has introduced a variety of methods for exploring maps. They were all developed within the context of using maps to help individuals[8] and teams to work on complex issues or strategy development.[9]

The analyses provide indications of features of the map and enable emerging features to be detected. It is absolutely crucial to see analysis within the context of a clear theoretical framework, and thus map coding procedure as well as analytical purpose, without which the interpretation of the analysis will be problematic.

An overview is an important aspect of providing complexity reduction and a focus on the most important aspects of the problem or issue. The ability to collapse a map by focusing only on those emerging characteristics of the map discussed above is a powerful analysis in its own right. Thus, the sum of core statements, heads, loop nodes and potent options provides an important overview, or summary, of the map by showing the linkage between key elements of the map. However, the cluster analyses reveal the structural properties of interconnections between the themes detected from an analysis of the content of each cluster. Notably the cluster analysis that does not root itself in a starting subset, and produces clusters with no overlapping nodes, provides the most 'naturalistic' overview of the structure of the map.

Notes

[1] A view expressed by Karl Weick (1979).

[2] This expected ratio does not seem to vary to an extent that could significantly identify differences in cognitive complexity – there are likely to be many other more plausible reasons for this relatively constant ratio, such as the nature of verbal argument in interview conditions.

[3] See *www.banxia.com* and the opportunity, provided with this book, to purchase a version of the software.

[4] Simon's (1981) arguments about the property of near de-composability have relevance here. In many complex, hierarchic systems, intra-component linkages are stronger than inter-component linkages and discovery of where the weakest linkages lie within the system is one basis for the analysis of complexity.

[5] See Gower and Ross (1969) and Jardine and Sibson (1971) for more detail on simple linkage clustering.

[6] From Simon (1981) p. 196.

[7] See Eden et al. (1981) for an interesting discussion of the tension between the need to deal with complexity rather than simplifying to manage the stressful impact of too much complexity.

[8] Initially from the work reported in Eden et al. (1979).

[9] See Eden and Ackermann (1998).

Support 2

The Formalities of Mapping

This support section includes advice on the following:

- Getting the wording of statements right.
- Getting the direction of the arrow (causality) right.

  - Being clear about options and outcomes, means and ends, etc.
  - Dealing with generic statements appropriately.
  - Dealing with assertions and facts.
  - Dealing with feedback loops (see also support 1).

- Goals, negative goals and constraints.

Wording Statements (Nodes)

- Make statements action-oriented by including a verb – without doing violence to what was said where possible.
- Aim for six to eight words as this will ensure that each statement is discrete and yet descriptive.
- If there is likely to be ambiguity then consider including 'who', 'what', 'where' and 'when' in the statement (although this requirement can make the statement too long).
- Exclude words such as 'should', 'ought', 'need', etc (as this makes it more option-like). For example, 'we ought to hire more salespeople' becomes 'hire more salespeople'.
- Avoid using 'in order to', 'due to', 'may lead to', 'as a result of', 'through', 'caused by', etc. as these imply two statements linked together by an arrow.
- When a statement includes several considerations, as, for example, 'postpone writing mapping book, several articles and book chapters, and other books', then it is important to decide whether the statement should become several statements. Ask whether:

- They each have different consequences.
- They each have the same importance.
- They each might involve different types of actions/explanations in order to create the outcome.

Thus, in the example:

- 'Writing article' may be more important than books or chapters, in which case the statement should be separated into two parts.
- 'Postponing the mapping book' may have different consequences because it involves other colleagues, in which case it should be separated.
- 'Writing other books' may require large chunks of time whereas others can be done using small intervals, in which case it should be a separate statement.

Therefore, watch the use of 'and' as this might suggest two options rather than one. For example, split 'increase and improve services' into 'increase services' and 'improve services' as these might lead to different outcomes and have different explanations.

Using Contrasting Poles in a Statement (Node)

- The **meaning** of a statement is often best discovered by listening for the contrast. For example, the meaning of 'warm rather than hot weather' is different from 'warm rather than cold weather', 'buy two computers rather than six computers' is different from 'buy two computers rather than hire more staff', etc.
- Difficulties arise when each contrast is an option in its own right, and there might be several options. When the contrast illustrates meaning by suggesting a possible alternative outcome, circumstance, etc. (often contrasting past with now, past with future, now with future) then use the contrast as a part of the statement; when the contrast is a clear option then make it a separate statement (sometimes linked without an arrowhead to other options).

Getting the Link Right: Causality

■ The direction of the arrow should indicate the direction of causality and influence: means to ends, options/actions to outcomes.

■ One person's means can be another person's ends: A→B might be correct for one person, whereas B→A might be correct for another.

 ■ For example, 'turning things around means we have to win every battle in the next five years' may be coded with 'winning every battle' as the desired outcome from 'turning things around', or alternatively 'winning every battle' is required in order to 'turn things around', depending on the desired ends of the interviewee.

■ Bear in mind some 'objective' truths might be subject to debate.

 ■ For example, 'putting more police on the beat will reduce crime' may be an objective truth to one person, nevertheless another person might argue the objective truth to be that more crime leads to more police on the beat.

■ Sometimes A→B can be treated as so consensual that it need not be debated.

 ■ For example, 'obvious' arithmetical relationships: more sales causes more sales revenue.

■ Means to ends are most difficult to judge when considering a hierarchy of criteria, values and goals.

 ■ For example, is 'be unhappy and upset much of the time' more disastrous than 'crawl into my shell and give up'? That is, does 'be unhappy' lead to 'into shell' or vice versa? This can only be judged by the person being mapped, or this choice must be open to consideration.

 ■ It sometimes helps to work with a hierarchy of goals, such as 'objectives' lead to 'goals' which lead to 'ideals or values'. So, objectives are shorter term and more easily measurable, whereas goals are expressions of desirable longer term outcomes, whereas ideals or values are unlikely ever to be attained but guide purposeful behaviour.[1]

■ Avoid mapping time sequences that are not causal relationships (as this will produce flow diagrams or process maps that are not amenable to the same sort of analysis or meaning as cause maps).

■ Ensure that the map does not contain duplication of links.

 ■ For example, where the map shows A→B→C→D along with A→C and

C→D and A→D ensure that the latter three links show different causal chains (through additional material).

■ Avoid double headed arrows as these are implicit feedback loops suggesting either:

  ■ Muddled thinking that can be resolved by determining means and ends.
  ■ A legitimate feedback loop consisting of additional statements that might provide more intervention options.

Dealing with Generic Statements

■ It is best to ensure that all members of a category are subordinate to the statement expressing the generic category. For example, 'buy more saucepans' should in most circumstances lead to 'buy more kitchen equipment' – that is, the specific leads to the generic.
■ When a subcategory has different consequences from those of other members of the category, then it will need its own out-arrow to other consequences (along with the link to the generic).
■ Sometimes the generic statement may not be necessary because there are no specific consequences that follow from it, rather they all follow from specific subcategory statements.

Dealing with Assertions and Facts

■ We presume that when someone makes an assertion then they have a reason to do so, and that it is intended to suggest an implied action is required. Thus, if someone states that 'Glasgow has a population of over 500,000 people' then we ask why this assertion is being made – what is its meaning in action terms? For example, they might know that it was 600,000 last year and so the statement 'obviously' implies that the 'Council will be short of taxes next year', which also is stated as a 'fact' with implied consequences.
■ Thus, assertions tend to be at the bottom of a map, with consequences following from them.

Goals, Negative Goals and Constraints

■ Goals are desired outcomes that are 'good in their own right' (so much so that they are hardly seen as optional by the interviewee).
■ Negative goals are undesired outcomes that are bad in their own right, for example, 'become bitter'.

■ Constraints are often stated as if they were goals, but will be subordinate and have consequences that constrain actions, goals, issues, etc. For example, 'attaining minimum levels of shareholder return' may act as a constraint on management behaviour, rather than act as a goal (even though shareholders would wish to see it expressed as a goal).

Note

[1] Based upon the Ackoff and Emery typology (Ackoff and Emery (1972) p. 1345), see also discussion on values in Eden et al. (1979) p. 1467.

Support 3

MBA Student Project Case Study

This case study reviews the application of the strategy-making methodology presented in this book in developing a business strategy for a small or medium enterprise (SME). The intervention was facilitated by Ian Brown (one of the authors) while he was a part-time student on the Strathclyde MBA programme. It discusses the experiences of a student facilitating an intervention using this methodology for the first time, making use of the information provided in *Strategy Making: The Journey of Strategic Management* (Eden and Ackermann, 1998) as the primary guide.

Fitzpatricks is a long-established professional company specializing in the law and practices relating to the protection, enforcement and renewal of intellectual property rights world-wide, providing professional services relating primarily to patents, trade marks, designs and copyright.

At the time of the intervention, the company had been under the control of three generations of one family and had, therefore, been subject to their influence and value needs. It was being run as what might be called a 'benevolent autocracy', with control firmly in the hands of the owner. As a result, there was little or no articulation of strategic intent, resulting in individual managers being left very much to their own devices. The lack of any clear vision caused people to pull in different directions, leading to fragmented activities and making it difficult to co-ordinate work and to ensure the effective deployment of resources.

The company was also in the midst of a 'friendly' management buy out (MBO) at the time of the intervention. During the course of the MBO, it became clear that changes would have be made at a fundamental level when the responsibility for running the business moved into the hands of a management team. The MBO team were, therefore, keen to create a strategic plan that would help them to attain their joint objectives. This, combined with the fact that a group of shareholders would also have a keen interest in the performance of the company, suggested that a number of different views of the future would have to be considered.

This story is told by Ian Brown, the facilitator and an employee of the organization. At that time, Ian was head of Information Services and had worked with the company for over twelve years. His role, along with his length of service, meant that he had a detailed knowledge of both the company and the industry. He is now a director of the company.

Background

I developed an interest in causal mapping during the early stages of my MBA. I found that mapping helped me to organize my thoughts and I made use of this technique throughout the course. When this concept was re-introduced in relation to strategy development, I felt that it had real potential and I began to experiment with some of the techniques described by Eden and Ackermann in their book *Strategy Making: The Journey of Strategic Management.*

These experiments involved running group workshops making use of the oval mapping technique, using the book as a guide.[1] I started working in my own department where I felt relatively 'safe'. As my confidence grew, I gradually extended the concept into other functional areas within the company and into more critical areas of the business. When the MBO began to experience some difficulties, I realized that it was a potential opportunity to put what I had learned to good use.

My first challenge was to convince the then owner of the business and those who were leading the MBO team to allow me to facilitate an intervention using the methodology. I knew that this was an alien concept to all of the people concerned and I expected to encounter resistance from some of those involved. Consequently, I spent time discussing the methodology and its benefits with the owner and with one of the 'directors in waiting' whom I knew would be most receptive to my ideas. I was sure that, if I could persuade them to let me proceed, they would be able to win over the other members of the management team.

This worked well and I was given the task of designing and facilitating an intervention, the aim of which was to generate a strategic intent document for the first three years of operation of the new company. My 'clients' also indicated that they wanted to use the intervention to start to break down some of the functional barriers that existed and to build a team spirit around common goals. In addition, they were keen to ensure that the resulting strategy had credibility with potential funders, as well as within the company itself.

Designing the Intervention

I was aware of the fact that it was essential for the new management team to reach agreement as to how the company should progress. Consequently, I felt that it was important to design the intervention in such a way that the views of each powerbroker were considered (see chapter 2), leading to the development of strategy built on consensus, rather than compromise. I was, therefore, keen to achieve the following objectives:

- To ensure that everyone had an equal say, thus guaranteeing that procedural justice[2] was not only done but was seen to be done.
- To surface as many relevant issues as possible.
- To ensure that there was depth as well as breadth to the issues surfaced (see chapter 3 and support 1).
- To promote team building and increase organizational learning.[3]

After much deliberation based on previous experience of working with the stakeholders, I came to the conclusion that a group-based workshop (see chapter 4) would not have been the best way to initiate this intervention for a number of reasons, including:

- The members of the new management team had limited experience of working together as a team.
- There was a high probability that one or two individuals, who had strong personalities and had demonstrated in previous meetings that they were 'opinion formers', would dominate a workshop or group meetings.
- The group was experiencing some difficulties at the time and this might have had a negative effect on the workshop, with interpersonal problems resulting in the suppression of a number of issues.

The time taken up by the process was another important factor when persuading people to participate (see chapter 3). It is interesting that while people tend to be willing to spend time in an endless series of meetings, they are very reluctant to give up a day, or even half a day, from their diaries. This is especially true in a professional company where time is directly related to revenue and involves what can be a high opportunity cost to the company.

Due to these difficulties, I decided to initiate the intervention with a series of individual interviews involving the key stakeholders. I felt that, in the circumstances, the relative anonymity would encourage the participants to discuss issues more freely than would have been the case in a group workshop. I also felt that the interviews would enable the elicitation of deeper knowledge, as well as the expression of their values and beliefs (see chapter 3).

The aim of these interviews was to gather information on emergent strategic issues and to link them to form a cognitive map for each person. The individual maps were subsequently entered into the Decision Explorer® computer system and merged to form a group map (see support 1). This map was analyzed using the tools which are available within the software in order to identify important issues and emergent goals.

The Interviews

A series of eight interviews were held with the senior and professional staff in the company. The discussions centred upon exploring the ways in which the business ought to develop over the next few years and what might get in the way. They were also designed to:

■ Gain an insight into the knowledge that individuals had about the company and its industry.
■ Elicit ideas on how the company could progress.
■ Surface problems that the participants felt would have to be dealt with.
■ Develop an understanding of each individual's own aspirations and their aspirations for the company.

The interviews were scheduled to take account of political weighting, with the most senior people being interviewed first (see chapter 3). This enabled me to feed some of the key issues raised by senior management into the subsequent interviews, which had a number of advantages. First, it ensured that the group model would, to some extent, be moulded around the thoughts of the people who would ultimately be entrusted with running the business. Second, it helped to start the process of consensus building by encouraging people to discuss (and therefore think about) issues that were important to the group. Finally, it helped the process of creating an aggregated group map by providing common themes or 'hooks', which were subsequently used to weave the individual maps together.

In general, I found that the interviewees were happy to talk, although they were inclined to stay within their own functional boundaries and tended to resist attempts to persuade them to talk about more general issues. They consistently started the interview with topics that were at the forefront of their minds. These issues were normally short term and operational in nature. I found letting them get 'today's issue' out of their system before moving the interview forward from there worked best. I made use of the technique of laddering (see chapter 3) to elicit the emergent goals from the people involved. This technique involves encouraging the interviewee to elaborate on the issues that they raise by asking 'so what?' type questions. This helped to generate causal relationships in a way that moved them away from current issues and uncovered information about their aspirations or goals and concerns or negative goals (see chapter 5).

During the interviews, the amount of information that was forthcoming was often difficult to manage (an average of 100 statements were captured for each person). Once people became engaged in the process (which happened very quickly) they had a great deal to say, which made capturing and linking their statements quite challenging. While I was able to record what was being said, I regularly had difficulty finding the opportunity to discuss the linkages between the statements with the interviewee. While many of the links tended to follow the flow of the conversation, I found that I often had to simply draw lines between concepts in an attempt to keep up with what the interviewee was saying. This meant that I had to return to them later to discuss the cause and effect relationships (i.e. to determine the direction of the arrow). Finding a balance between asking for clarification and trying to avoid breaking the interviewee's train of thought was tricky at times.

The fact that I was working within my own organization helped with the process because I knew what the interviewees were talking about and was, therefore, able to understand the causal relationships. I was, however, aware of the importance of recording what the interviewees meant as well as what they said. Consequently, I was concerned that there was a danger that I would make implicit assumptions about what was being said, based on my own knowledge and belief system, thereby adding my meaning to their statements. Being aware of these risks helped me to take steps to avoid making assumptions during the interview. I was also careful to feed the information back to the interviewee as often as possible in order to have them validate the information that I had captured.

In general, all of those involved in the interview process found it useful. As with any group, some found it more useful than others and some would not admit to how useful it had been, although their actions indicated that they took a great deal from it. Each interview lasted longer that its allotted one hour, with most stretching (with the agreement of the participant) to one and a half hours.

While a wide variety of seemingly diverse opinions relating to a number of different aspects of the business were raised, subsequent analysis of the group model (see below) revealed that a great deal of commonality of thinking existed within the group. This provided a basis on which a consensus view of the strategic future of the company was built.

My Learning Points

In general, I found the interview process to be a very valuable part of the intervention and one that is suited for use in a company where either the culture or the circumstances are not conducive to team working. The fact that it gives the individuals involved much more 'air time' than they would have in a group situation means that it is also useful in situations where a greater depth of information is required. It should, however, be noted that it places a significant time burden on the facilitator and also generates a great deal of material, which can cause some difficulties with the analysis of the aggregated group model.

Analyzing the Strategy Model

Having completed the interviews, I entered the individual maps into the Decision Explorer® model. The individual maps were then merged to form an aggregated model that represented the thinking of the group as a whole (see support 1). I found that the most efficient way of creating the combined map was to enter each individual map into a single model and subsequently to merge the maps by topic areas. I also found that entering all of the material over a sustained period was beneficial because it helped me to remember the major subject areas, as well as many of the statements that people had made.

The interview process generated a great deal of material which gave an insight into the interviewee's aspirations, elaborated their ideas and captured their knowledge. This resulted in a large volume of data being generated (over 1000 statements and 1400 links), which I found to be very distracting, making it difficult for me to locate the important issues.

When working with such a large model, I found that it is important to tidy it before starting the analysis as this avoids reworking later (see support 1). This involved locating statements which were not properly linked into the model and then making the relevant links where appropriate. Duplicate concepts were also located and these were merged to form one concept, having first made certain that the concepts being merged were contextually similar.

Having tidied the map, I proceeded to use the tools which are available within the Decision Explorer® software to identify the key statements (see support 1). I found that this was by far the most difficult part of the intervention to work on from the book. This was primarily due to the fact that you have to get a feel for the data in order to analyze it properly. This is not possible unless you have a good understanding of what you are trying to achieve. Working blind, using only the book as a point of reference, would not have allowed me to develop the necessary level of comprehension.

I found that I became bogged down in the detail and found myself having to abandon the analysis and start again on at least three occasions. Through trial and error, I discovered that one of the keys to analyzing this model was gaining an understanding of the hierarchical nature of the strategy model, as shown in Figure S4.1. This acted as a constant point of reference during the analysis, helping to keep me on track.

I found that it was useful to concentrate on locating these basic building blocks of the strategy model and I used the way in which the concepts were interconnected to provide some clues about the nature and importance of key statements. I used the Decision Explorer® software to locate the patterns shown in Figure S4.2, which allowed me to identify the key concepts in the model.

Having identified the key statements, I felt that the remaining concepts were obstructing the completion of the analysis. Consequently, I decided to isolate them from the main group model, splitting it into manageable chunks by extracting the strategically important issues from the main model, as shown in Figure S4.3. This reduced the complexity and helped me to derive a greater understanding of the information contained within the model.

Leaving the main group model intact allowed me to 'drill down' into the base data when more detailed information was required.

Figure S4.1 Representation of the Hierarchical Structure of the Strategy Model

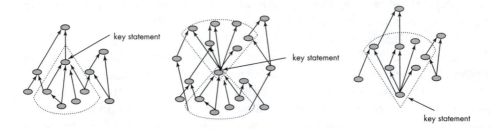

Figure S4.2 Patterns that Help in Identifying Key Constructs in the Strategy Map (the Decision Explorer software can be used to locate these patterns)

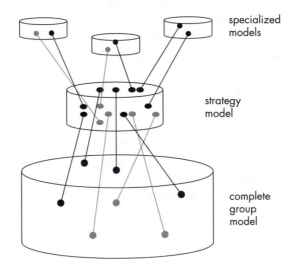

Figure S4.3 Sub-models Taken from the Main Group Model Retaining Links to Subordinate Models

It was interesting to note, however, that two of the concepts that had been discussed by most of the participants had not been picked up by this analysis as being of significance (because they were not very well articulated). A good example of this was a statement that was made by a few of the participants that we should 'improve the cost controls on jobs', which had only one link to a statement about improving the profit generated per job. On the face of it, this was a relatively insignificant statement and was not picked up by the analysis because it was not 'busy'. In reality, this has become a key part of our strategic action programme and we have devoted a great deal of time and resources to obtaining a suitable job costing system. We believe that this system will have a major impact on a number of areas of the business and will play an important role in attaining many of our objectives.

This clearly highlights the limitations of this process, which is heavily dependent on the degree of articulation surrounding the concepts, and confirms our view that some validation by the group is imperative. It also suggests that you should not rely on the analytical tools of the software alone and that, as a facilitator, you must bring your own intuition and knowledge to the process.

My Learning Points

Don't try to be too exact. I got caught up in trying to over-analyze the data and this cost me a considerable amount of time. I came to realize that this is not an exact science and that it is important to understand that the purpose of the analysis is to inform the decision-making process, not to find solutions.

The volume of data that had been generated acted as a distraction, making it difficult to see the wood for the trees. The keys to the evaluation of the group model were to gain an understanding of the hierarchical nature of the strategy model and to extract the strategically important issues from the main model.

Workshops

Due to a number of internal difficulties, the intervention stalled for four months. Interest was re-ignited when a consultant was brought in to help negotiate a way forward for the business. I worked closely with him and, after weeks of discussions, we succeeded in persuading the management team to attend a group workshop, effectively resurrecting the MBO process.

Eden and Ackermann suggested that the time between the interviews and the workshop should be no more than a 'psychological week' (ten days). I was, therefore, concerned that the time which had elapsed between the interviews and the first workshop would result in the information that was gathered during the interviews being rendered unusable because the participants would have forgotten the discussions. I was, however, sure that the work that had been carried out was still valid and could be used productively with the group. Consequently, I was keen to make a link between the interviews and the workshop.

I achieved this by pulling out the key issues, the potential goals and the strategies that were identified in the analysis of the group model. These were written on to ovals which where made available to the participants during an OMT workshop. The participants were told that they could use any or all of them as well as creating new ones. It was interesting to note that, in addition to adding new material, the participants used all of the material that was surfaced during the interviews.

The success of this experiment enabled me to design many of the subsequent sessions in a similar way. Not only did this allow the group to complete the very important process of validating the work that had been done previously but it also helped to make the workshops much more productive than they may otherwise have been.

In the end, we held a total of seven group workshops with each one focusing on a different area of the strategic plan. Most of the workshops involved members of the management team although some sessions were devoted to other members of staff who we felt were important to the future success of the company. We felt that involving them at an early stage in the process would help to ensure their support for the new management team.

I facilitated the workshops with the help of the consultant who was not familiar with the tools and techniques being used. This, combined with the fact that it was the first time that I had worked with a co-facilitator, meant that I had to put a great deal of time and effort into the preparation for each workshop. This proved to be invaluable as, through careful design, we were able to circumvent many of the problems that we had anticipated might arise within the group as a whole and with certain individuals, who we identified as potential saboteurs (see chapter 2).

An agenda was prepared for the participants for each workshop and this was distributed one day in advance. The intention was to give them just enough information to ensure that they knew the general areas on which they would be working while making certain that they did not arrive with too many preconceived ideas.

I created a 'facilitator's timetable' which guaranteed that we each knew what the other was supposed to be doing and when.[4] A set of facilitator's notes was also prepared for each item on the agenda. These were used to help us to prepare for the task in hand, to ensure that we knew what our role was and also to act as a checklist during the workshop itself.

Outcomes

These workshops proved to be very successful, enabling the team to create a goals system that was supported by a set of key strategic options, which were, in turn, supported by a portfolio of strategic actions. The workshops also created a strong consensus within the group of how best to grow the business and helped to develop a team spirit within the management group.

A business plan, which was based almost entirely on the material that was surfaced during the intervention, was written and used successfully to secure funding for the MBO. The backbone of this business plan was a goals system that everyone in the group was committed to achieving.

After many months of negotiation, we successfully completed the management buy out. The strategy-making methodology takes much of the credit for this success as it played a very important part in breaking the deadlock that existed within the group. It also created a strategic plan that the management team believed in and were focused on achieving. The methodology was subsequently used to develop detailed programmes of action that were designed to deliver the agreed goals.

The organization has continued to use the strategy model as a point of reference to help to guide the decision-making process. In doing so, we have continued to refine and improve it. It is, in effect, a living model reflecting our thinking at any given point in time. We have identified and prioritized action programmes which will help us to attain our goals. A project brief has been created for each one. This brief sets out the aims of the project and links it to the relevant concepts within the model.

We recently held our annual strategic planning meeting. Many of the strategy-making tools and techniques were used during this process but with a slightly different focus. We are now working to tie our goals into a performance measurement system based on the balanced scorecard.[5] It is hoped that this will help to communicate our strategy to everyone in the company in a way that will focus attention on the key actions and activities that need to be undertaken in order to deliver the goals.

Conclusions

This book lays the foundations and provides the reader with the tools that are required to begin the methodology. You must not only learn which tools to use, and when, but also understand when to adapt the tools to cope with changing circumstances.

The versatility of this methodology allows it to be adjusted to fit many different situations and the work that I have done shows that it is even adaptable during the process itself. It is a very powerful tool that has a number of important benefits, including:

- It creates enhanced ownership of the issues within the group.
- It increases the general level of understanding within the organization.
- It creates organizational history.

- It enables a wide range of knowledge and expertise to be acquired within the organization.
- It results in a robust well-articulated strategy.
- It facilitates a company-wide awareness of and commitment to the objectives of the organization.

This methodology encompasses all aspects of strategy making from initial idea generation through to the development of portfolios of strategic actions and the management of individual projects. It enables people from all levels of the organization to understand and participate in what can often be seen as a complex and rather abstract area of business management.

In Summary

- Use the book as a starting point and a constant point of reference.
- Start small, think big.
- Gain the support of a senior person within the organization.
- When designing the intervention, consider:

  - The culture of the organization.
  - The personalities of the participants.
  - The time taken up by the process.

- Remember that the analysis of the data is a means to an end, not an end in itself.
- Group workshops are a critically important part of the intervention, helping to gain consensus and build mutual respect and trust.

Notes

[1] Eden and Ackermann (1998) chapter 3 describe the OMT process in detail, giving a step-by-step guide to setting up and running an OMT workshop.
[2] Eden and Ackermann (1998) pp. 53–5 discuss the concept of procedural justice.
[3] Eden and Ackermann (1998) pp. 74–8 discuss the concept of organizational learning.
[4] See Eden and Ackermann (1998) p. 382.
[5] Kaplan and Norton (1996); Kaplan and Norton (2001).

Support 4

Issues in Working With External or Internal Facilitators

Internal Staff as Facilitators

Advantages

- They know the organization and group members well through involvement in the day-to-day management of the organization.
- They can have a continuing relationship with the projects and develop approaches to match each phase.
- They are on site and able to provide support in a timely way, and also catch up on local gossip about the project.

Disadvantages

- In being part of the system they will be unable to take a detached view beyond a certain point. They may know the organization too well and so impose their own, rather than the client group, view of the world as they interpret data.
- They will often be junior to those they are facilitating and this can constrain effectiveness because of a fear of being forceful when required.
- Their exposure to a variety of situations in teams will be low and this may reduce flexibility and resourcefulness.

External Consultants as Facilitators

Advantages

- They are detached from the system and can take a more detached/objective view of both the content and the process.
- They can usually overcome status problems through a peer relationship with the key client.

- They have more experience to draw on through familiarity with a variety of organizational cultures. As trust develops this experience can be shared.
- They can bring powerful interventions to crucial projects where both the risk and the pay-off are high.
- They may pass on knowledge and skills that help develop internal facilitators.
- Staff may be more frank with an external facilitator than an internal one.

Disadvantages

- They may not have time or insight to tune in to the situation and understand its dynamics.
- The overhead of briefing the external consultant can be expensive in time (but this stage may be useful to the client).
- They may struggle to understand the language of the culture, especially its hidden language that is crucial to read in facilitation situations.
- They can have difficulty in being accepted as a confidant.
- They may be seen as not responsible and accountable for their actions and advice.

On the Folly of Rewarding A, While Hoping for B

An Academy Classic

Steven Kerr

Whether dealing with monkeys, rats, or human beings, it is hardly controversial to state that most organisms seek information concerning what activities are rewarded, and then seek to do (or at least pretend to do) those things, often to the virtual exclusion of activities not rewarded. The extent to which this occurs of course will depend on the perceived attractiveness of the rewards offered, but neither operant nor expectancy theorists would quarrel with the essence of this notion.

Nevertheless, numerous examples exist of reward systems that are fouled up in that the types of behavior rewarded are those which the rewarder is trying to discourage, while the behavior desired is not being rewarded at all.

Fouled Up Systems

In Politics

Official goals are 'purposely vague and general and do not indicate . . . the host of decisions that must be made among alternative ways of achieving official goals and the priority of multiple goals . . .'[2] They usually may be relied on to offend absolutely no one, and in this sense can be considered high acceptance, low quality goals. An example might be 'All Americans are entitled to health care.' Operative goals are higher in quality but lower in acceptance, since they specify where the money will come from, and what alternative goals will be ignored.

The American citizenry supposedly wants its candidates for public office to set forth operative goals, making their proposed programs clear, and specifying sources and uses of funds. However, since operative goals are lower in acceptance, and since aspirants to public office need acceptance (from at least 50.1 percent of the people), most politicians prefer to speak only of official goals, at least until after the election. They of course would agree to speak at the operative level if 'punished' for not doing so. The electorate could do this by refusing to support candidates who do not speak at the operative level. Instead, however, the American voter typically punishes (withholds support from) candidates who frankly discuss where the money will come from, rewards politicians who speak only of official goals, but hopes that candidates (despite the reward system) will discuss the issues operatively.

In War

If some oversimplification may be permitted, let it be assumed that the primary goal of the organisation (Pentagon, Luftwaffe, or whatever) is to win. Let it be assumed further that the primary goal of most individuals on the front lines is to get home alive. Then there appears to be an important conflict in goals – personally rational behavior by those at the bottom will endanger goal attainment by those at the top.

But not necessarily! It depends on how the reward system is set up. The Vietnam war was indeed a study of disobedience and rebellion, with terms such as 'fragging' (killing one's own commanding officer) and 'search and evade' becoming part of the military vocabulary. The difference in subordinates' acceptance of authority between World War II and Vietnam is reported to be considerable, and veterans of the Second World War were often quoted as being outraged at the mutinous actions of many American soldiers in Vietnam.

Consider, however, some critical differences in the reward system in use during the two conflicts. What did the GI in World War II want? To go home. And when did he get to go home? When the war was won! If he disobeyed the orders to clean out the trenches and take the hills, the war would not be won and he would nor go home. Furthermore, what were his chances of attaining his goal (getting home alive) if he obeyed the orders compared to his chances if he did not? What is being suggested is that the rational soldier in World War II, whether patriotic or not, probably found it expedient to obey.

Consider the reward system in use in Vietnam. What did the soldier at the bottom want? To go home. And when did he get to go home? When his tour of duty was over! This was the case whether or not the war was won. Furthermore, concerning the relative chance of getting home alive by obeying orders compared to the chance if they were disobeyed, it is worth noting that a mutineer in Vietnam was far more likely to be assigned rest and rehabilitation (on the assumption that fatigue was the cause) than he was to suffer any negative consequence.

In his description of the 'zone of indifference,' Barnard stated that 'a person can and will accept a communication as authoritative only when . . . at the time of his decision, he believes it to be compatible with his personal interests as a whole.'[3] In light of the reward system used in Vietnam, wouldn't it have been personally irrational for some orders to have been obeyed? Was not the military implementing a system which rewarded disobedience, while hoping that soldiers (despite the reward system) would obey orders?

In Medicine

Theoretically, physicians can make either of two types of error, and intuitively one seems as bad as the other. Doctors can pronounce patients sick when they are actually well (a type 1 error), thus causing them needless anxiety and expense, curtailment of enjoyable foods and activities, and even physical danger by subjecting them to needless medication and surgery. Alternately, a doctor can label a sick person well (a type 2 error), and thus avoid treating what may be a serious, even fatal ailment. It might be natural to conclude that physicians seek to minimise both types of error.

Such a conclusion would be wrong. It has been estimated that numerous Americans have been afflicted with iatrogenic (physician caused) illnesses.[4] This occurs when the doctor is approached by someone complaining of a few stray symptoms. The doctor classifies and organises these symptoms, gives them a name, and obligingly tells the patient what further symptoms may be expected. This information often acts as a self-fulfilling prophecy, with the result that from that day on the patient for all practical purposes is sick.

Why does this happen? Why are physicians so reluctant to sustain a type 2 error (pronouncing a sick person well) that they will tolerate many type 1 errors? Again, a look at the reward system is needed. The punishments for a type 2 error are real: guilt, embarrassment, and the threat of a malpractice suit. On the other hand, a type 1 error (labeling a well person sick) is a much safer and conservative approach to medicine in today's litigious society. Type 1 errors also are likely to generate increased income and a stream of steady customers who, being well in a limited physiological sense, will not embarrass the doctor by dying abruptly. Fellow physicians and the general public therefore are really rewarding type 1 errors while hoping fervently that doctors will try not to make them.

A current example of rewarding type 1 errors is provided by Broward County, Florida, where an elderly or disabled person facing a competency hearing is evaluated by three court-appointed experts who get paid much more for the same examination if the person is ruled to be incompetent. For example, psychiatrists are paid $325 if they judge someone to be incapacitated, but earn only $125 if the person is judged competent. Court-appointed attorneys in Broward also earn more – $325 as opposed to $175 – if their clients lose than if they win. Are you surprised to learn that, of 598 incapacity proceedings initiated

and completed in the county in 1993, 570 ended with a verdict of incapac-
itation?[5]

In Universities

Society hopes that professors will not neglect their teaching responsibilities
but rewards them almost entirely for research and publications. This is most true
at the large and prestigious universities. Clichés such as 'good research and
good teaching go together' notwithstanding, professors often find that they must
choose between teaching and research-oriented activities when allocating their
time. Rewards for good teaching are usually limited to outstanding teacher
awards, which are given to only a small percentage of good teachers and usually
bestow little money and fleeting prestige. Punishments for poor teaching are also
rare.

Rewards for research and publications, on the other hand, and punishments
for failure to accomplish these, are common. Furthermore, publication-oriented
résumés usually will be well-received at other universities, whereas teaching
credentials, harder to document and quantify, are much less transferable.
Consequently it is rational for university professors to concentrate on research,
even to the detriment of teaching and at the expense of their students.

By the same token, it is rational for students to act based upon the goal
displacement[6] which has occurred within universities concerning what they
are rewarded for. If it is assumed that a primary goal of a university is to transfer
knowledge from teacher to student, then grades become identifiable as a
means toward that goal, serving as motivational, control, and feedback devices
to expedite the knowledge transfer. Instead, however, the grades themselves
have become much more important for entrance to graduate school, successful
employment, tuition refunds, and parental respect, than the knowledge or lack
of knowledge they are supposed to signify.

It therefore should come as no surprise that we find fraternity files for exam-
inations, term paper writing services, and plagiarism. Such activities constitute
a personally rational response to a reward system which pays off for grades
rather than knowledge. These days, reward systems – specifically, the growing
threat of lawsuits – encourage teachers to award students high grades, even if
they aren't earned. For example:

When Andy Hansen brought home a report card with a disappointing C in
math, his parents . . . sued his teacher. . . . After a year and six different appeals
within the school district, another year's worth of court proceedings, $4000
in legal fees paid by the Hansens, and another $8500 by the district . . . the C
stands. Now the student's father, auto dealer Mike Hansen, says he plans to
take the case to the State Court of Appeals . . . 'We went in and tried to make a
deal: They wanted a C, we wanted an A, so why not compromise on a B?' Mike
Hansen said. 'But they dug in their heels, and here we are.'[7]

In consulting

It is axiomatic that those who care about a firm's well-being should insist that the organisation get fair value for its expenditures. Yet it is commonly known that firms seldom bother to evaluate a new TQM, employee empowerment program, or whatever, to see if the company is getting its money's worth. Why? Certainly it is not because people have not pointed out that this situation exists; numerous practitioner-oriented articles are written each year on just this point.

One major reason is that the individuals (in human resources, or organisation development) who would normally be responsible for conducting such evaluations are the same ones often charged with introducing the change effort in the first place. Having convinced top management to spend money, say, on outside consultants, they usually are quite animated afterwards in collecting rigorous vignettes and anecdotes about how successful the program was. The last thing many desire is a formal, revealing evaluation. Although members of top management may actually hope for such systematic evaluation, their reward systems continue to reward ignorance in this area. And if the HR department abdicates its responsibility, who is to step into the breach? The consultants themselves? Hardly! They are likely to be too busy collecting anecdotal 'evidence' of their own, for use on their next client.

In Sports

Most coaches disdain to discuss individual accomplishments, preferring to speak of teamwork, proper attitude, and one-for-all spirit. Usually, however, rewards are distributed according to individual performance. The college basketball player who passes the ball to teammates instead of shooting will not compile impressive scoring statistics and is less likely to be drafted by the pros. The ballplayer who hits to right field to advance the runners will win neither the batting nor home run titles, and will be offered smaller raises. It therefore is rational for players to think of themselves first, and the team second.

In Government

Consider the cost-plus contract or its next of kin, the allocation of next year's budget as a direct function of this year's expenditures – a clear-cut example of a fouled up reward system. It probably is conceivable that those who award such budgets and contracts really hope for economy and prudence in spending. It is obvious, however, that adopting the proverb 'to those who spend shall more be given,' rewards not economy, but spending itself.

In Business

The past reward practices of a group health claims division of a large eastern insurance company provides another rich illustration. Attempting to measure and reward accuracy in paying surgical claims, the firm systematically kept track of the number of returned checks and letters of complaint received from policyholders. However, underpayments were likely to provoke cries of outrage from the insured, while overpayments often were accepted in courteous silence. Since it was often impossible to tell from the physician's statement which of two surgical procedures, with different allowable benefits, was performed, and since writing for clarifications would have interfered with other standards used by the firm concerning percentage of claims paid within two days of receipt, the new hire in more than one claims section was soon acquainted with the informal norm: 'When in doubt, pay it out!'

This situation was made even worse by the firm's reward system. The reward system called for annual merit increases to be given to all employees, in one of the following three amounts:

1   If the worker was 'outstanding' (a select category, into which no more than two employees per section could be placed): 5 percent
2   If the worker was 'above average' (normally all workers not 'outstanding' were so rated): 4 percent
3   If the worker committed gross acts of negligence and irresponsibility for which he or she might be discharged in many other companies: 3 percent.

Now, since the difference between the five percent theoretically attainable through hard work and the four percent attainable merely by living until the review date is small, many employees were rather indifferent to the possibility of obtaining the extra one percent reward. In addition, since the penalty for error was a loss of only one percent, employees tended to ignore the norm concerning indiscriminant payments.

However, most employees were not indifferent to a rule which stated that, should absences or latenesses total three or more in any six-month period, the entire four or five percent due at the next merit review must be forfeited. In this sense, the firm was hoping for performance, while rewarding attendance. What it got, of course, was attendance. (If the absence/lateness rule appears to the reader to be stringent, it really wasn't. The company counted 'times' rather than 'days' absent, and a ten-day absence therefore counted the same as one lasting two days. A worker in danger of accumulating a third absence within six months merely had to remain ill – away from work – during a second absence until the first absence was more than six months old. The limiting factor was that at some point salary ceases, and sickness benefits take over. This was usually sufficient to get the younger workers to return, but for those with 20 or more years' service, the company provided sickness benefits of 90 percent of normal salary, tax-free! Therefore . . .). Thanks to the U.S. government, even the reporting of wrongdoing has been corrupted by an incredibly incompetent reward system that calls for whistleblowing employees to collect up to thirty percent of the amount of a fraud without a stated limit. Thus prospective whistleblowers are encouraged to delay reporting a fraud, even to actively participate in its continuance, in order to run up the total and, thus, their percentage of the take.

I'm quite sure that by now the reader has thought of numerous examples in his or her own experience which qualify as 'folly.' However, just in case, Table 1 presents some additional examples well worth pondering.

Table 1 Common management reward follies

We hope for . . .	But we often reward . . .
■ long-term growth; environmental responsibility	■ quarterly earnings
■ teamwork	■ individual effort
■ setting challenging 'stretch' objectives	■ achieving goals; 'making the numbers'
■ downsizing; rightsizing; delayering; restructuring	■ adding staff, adding budget; adding xx points
■ commitment to total quality	■ shipping on schedule, even with defects
■ candor; surfacing bad news early	■ reporting good news, whether its true or not; agreeing with the boss, whether or not (s)he's right

Causes

Extremely diverse instances of systems which reward behavior A although the rewarder apparently hopes for behavior B have been given. These are useful to illustrate the breadth and magnitude of the phenomenon, but the diversity increases the difficulty of determining commonalities and establishing causes. However, the following four general factors may be pertinent to an explanation of why fouled-up reward systems seem to be so prevalent.

1 **Fascination with an 'objective' criterion**
   Many managers seek to establish simple, quantifiable standards against which to measure and reward performance. Such efforts may be successful in highly predictable areas within an organisation, but are likely to cause goal displacement when applied anywhere else.

2 **Overemphasis on highly visible behaviors**
   Difficulties often stem from the fact that some parts of the task are highly visible while other parts are not. For example, publications are easier to

demonstrate than teaching, and scoring baskets and hitting home runs are more readily observable than feeding teammates and advancing base runners. Similarly, the adverse consequences of pronouncing a sick person well are more visible than those sustained by labeling a well person sick. Team-building and creativity are other examples of behaviors which may not be rewarded simply because they are hard to observe.

3 **Hypocrisy**
In some of the instances described the rewarder may have been getting the desired behavior, notwithstanding claims that the behavior was not desired. For example, in many jurisdictions within the U.S., judges' campaigns are funded largely by defense attorneys, while prosecutors are legally barred from making contributions. This doesn't do a whole lot to help judges to be 'tough on crime' though, ironically, that's what their campaigns inevitably promise.

4 **Emphasis on morality or equity rather than efficiency**
Sometimes consideration of other factors prevents the establishment of a system which rewards behavior desired by the rewarder. The felt obligation of many Americans to vote for one candidate or another, for example, may impair their ability to withhold support from politicians who refuse to discuss the issues. Similarly, the concern for spreading the risks and costs of wartime military service may outweigh the advantage to be obtained by committing personnel to combat until the war is over. The 1994 Clinton health plan, the Americans with Disabilities Act, and many other instances of proposed or recent governmental intervention provide outstanding examples of systems that reward inefficiency, presumably in support of some higher objective.

Altering the Reward System

Managers who complain about lack of motivation in their workers might do well to consider the possibility that the reward systems they have installed are paying off for behavior other than what they are seeking. This, in part, is what happened in Vietnam, and this is what regularly frustrates societal efforts to bring about honest politicians and civic-minded managers.

A first step for such managers might be to explore what types of behavior are currently being rewarded. Chances are excellent that these managers will be surprised by what they find – that their firms are not rewarding what they assume they are. In fact, such undesirable behavior by organisational members as they have observed may be explained largely by the reward systems in use.

This is not to say that all organisational behavior is determined by formal rewards and punishments. Certainly it is true that in the absence of formal reinforcement some soldiers will be patriotic, some players will be team oriented, and some employees will care about doing their job well. The point, however, is that in such cases the rewarder is not causing the behavior desired but is only a fortunate bystander. For an organisation to act upon its members, the formal reward system should positively reinforce desired behavior, not constitute an obstacle to be overcome.

Postscript

An irony about this article's being designated a management classic is that numerous people claim to have read and enjoyed it, but I wonder whether there was much in it that they didn't know. I believe that most readers already knew, and act on in their non-work lives, the principles that underlie this article. For example, when we tell our daughter (who is about to cut her birthday cake) that her brother will select the first piece, or inform our friends before a meal that separate checks will be brought at the end, or tell the neighbor's boy that he will be paid five dollars for cutting the lawn after we inspect the lawn, we are making use of prospective rewards and punishments to cause other people to care about our own objectives. Organisational life may seem to be more complex, but the principles are the same.

Another irony attached to this 'classic' is that it almost didn't see the light of day. It was rejected for presentation at the Eastern Academy of Management and was only published in *The Academy of Management Journal* because Jack Miner, its editor at the time, broke a tie between two reviewers. Nobody denied the relevance of the content, but reviewers were quite disturbed by the tone of the manuscript, and therefore its appropriateness for an academic audience. A compromise was reached whereby I added a bit of the great academic cure-all, data (Table 1 in the original article, condensed and summarised in this update), and a copy editor strangled some of the life from my writing style. In this respect, I would like to acknowledge the extremely competent editorial work performed on this update by John Veiga and his editorial staff. I am grateful to have had the opportunity to revisit the article, and hope the reader has enjoyed it also.

Notes

[1] Originally published in 1975, *Academy of Management Journal*, 18, 769–783.
[2] Charles Perrow, 'The Analysis of Goals in Complex Organisations,' in A. Etzioni (ed.), *Readings on Modern Organisations* (Englewood Cliffs. NJ: Prentice-Hall. 1969), 66.
[3] Chester I. Barnard, *The Functions of the Executive* (Cambridge, MA: Harvard University Press, 1964), 165.
[4] L.H. Garland, 'Studies of the Accuracy of Diagnostic Procedures.' *American Journal Roentgenological Radium Therapy Nuclear Medicine*, Vol. 82. 1959, 25–38; and Thomas J. Scheff, 'Decision Rules, Types of Error, and Their Consequences in Medical

Diagnosis,' in F. Massarik and P. Ratoosh (eds.), *Mathematical Explorations in Behavioral Science* (Homewood, IL: Irwin, 1965).

[5] *Miami Herald*, May 8, 1994, 1a. 10a.

[6] Goal displacement results when means become ends in themselves and displace the original goals. See Peter M. Blau and W. Richard Scott, *Formal Organisations* (San Francisco, CA: Chandler, 1962).

[7] *San Francisco Examiner*, reported in *Fortune*, February 7, 1994, 161.

About the Author

Steven Kerr (Ph.D., City University of New York) is a visiting professor of management in the University of Michigan business school, and has recently assumed the position of Vice President, Corporate Management Development, for General Electric Co. (managing Crotonville). He has been on the faculties of Ohio State University and the University of Southern California (where he was Dean of the Faculty from 1985–89), and was President of the Academy of Management from 1989–90.

Support 6

Additional Resources

Although the chapters in this book aim to cover all of the immediate requirements when undertaking making strategy, below are a few extra resources,
which we believe might help in getting started.

Additional Reading

Surfacing Issues Through Mapping

Ackermann, F. and Eden, C. (2001) 'SODA – Journey Making and Mapping in Practice',
in J. Rosenhead and J. Mingers (eds), *Rational Analysis in a Problematic World
Revisited*, London: Wiley, pp. 43–61.

Ackermann, F. and Eden, C. (2004) 'Using Causal Mapping: Individual and Group:
Traditional and New', in M. Pidd (ed.), *Systems Modelling: Theory and Practice*,
Chichester: Wiley, pp. 127–45.

Bryson, J. M. and Finn, C. B. (1995) 'Creating the Future Together: Developing and Using
Shared Strategy Maps', in A. Halachmi and G. Bouckaert (eds), *The Enduring
Challenges in Public Management*, San Francisco: Jossey-Bass, pp. 247–80.

Bryson, J., Ackermann, F., Eden, C. and Finn, C. (2004) *Visible Thinking*, Chichester:
Wiley.

Eden, C. (1988) 'Cognitive Mapping: a Review', *European Journal of Operational
Research*, 36: 1–13.

Eden, C. and Ackermann, F. (1998) *Making Strategy: the Journey of Strategic Management*,
London: Sage.

Distinctive Competences/Business Model

Eden, C. and Ackermann, F. (2000) 'Mapping Distinctive Competences: a Systemic
Approach', *Journal of the Operational Research Society*, 51: 12–20.

The Strategy Journey

Bryson, J. (1995) *Strategic Planning for Public and Nonprofit Organizations* (3rd edn), San Francisco: Jossey-Bass.

Eden, C. and Ackermann, F. (1993) 'Evaluating Strategy: Its Role within the Context of Strategic Control', *Journal of the Operational Research Society*, 44: 853–65.

Eden, C. and Ackermann, F. (2001) 'A Mapping Framework for Strategy Making', in Huff, A. and Jenkins, M. (eds), *Mapping Strategy*, London: Wiley, pp. 173–95.

Eden, C. and Ackermann, F. (2003) 'Cognitive Mapping for Policy Analysis in the Public Sector', *European Journal of Operational Research*, 152(3): 615–30.

Analysis of Maps

Eden, C. (2004) 'Analyzing Cognitive Maps to Help Structure Issues or Problems', *European Journal of Operational Research*, forthcoming.

Eden, C. and Ackermann, F. (1998) 'Analysing and Comparing Idiographic Causal Maps', in C. Eden and J.-C. Spender (eds), *Managerial and Organizational Cognition*, London: Sage. pp. 192–209.

Eden, C., Ackermann, F. and Cropper, S. (1992) 'The Analysis of Cause Maps', *Journal of Management Studies*, 29: 309–24.

Software

Decision Explorer® is produced by Banxia Software® (*www.banxia.com*). This software was developed expressly for cause mapping, with in-depth analytical and presentation capabilities. Indeed, the authors of this book have contributed significantly to the development of the software over the years, incorporating new analytical routines and presentation possibilities as they were developed. A demonstration version of Decision Explorer® can be obtained from Banxia's web site.

Other Resources

■ There is a 'Structuring Argument' video on CD-ROM available from Banxia. The CD comprises three parts. The first part focuses upon some basic background to mapping (both individually and in groups) and the second part demonstrates the technique live in an interview. Here viewers are able to either watch the interview process unfold alongside the map or have a go at mapping directly. Commentary on the map is given during the interview. The third part is a basic tutorial on the use of the mapping software Decision Explorer®.

■ Oval Mapping Equipment:

■ Ovals: these can be obtained from *www.ovalmap.com*. While they are not as cheap as the standard Post-it® notes, as we explain in chapter 4, there are advantages in using ovals. First, they provide participants with more room to capture each statement thus encouraging larger writing. This helps in enabling other participants to be able to read their contributions and potentially 'piggy back' off them. The second reason for using ovals is that they ensure that when structuring material the clusters take the form of teardrops rather than, as is often experienced, columns and rows. They also work better than 'hexagons' because text forms a rectangle not a circle.

■ Pens: make sure you have the right pens. There are two types. The first set is for the facilitator and these are usually water-based flipchart pens (we recommend Berol®). Have a range of colours so as to be able to mark key issues, number ovals, draw in links, etc. The second set or type of pens is for participants. Here you want a set of the same colour, with a reasonably thick nib so as to encourage large writing (about six to ten words that are legible a couple of metres away) and again water-based.

■ Blu®tack: have a plentiful supply of Blu®tack and flipchart paper, so as to be able to have at least 14 sheets of paper attached to the wall, giving participants and the facilitator lots of room with which to work. Blu®tack is undoubtedly the best of the sticky putty products but masking tape and various other putties do work.

References

Ackermann, F. (1996) 'Participants' Perceptions on the Role of Facilitators Using Group Decision Support Systems', *Group Decision and Negotiation*, 5: 93–112.

Ackermann, F. and Eden, C. (1994) 'Issues in Computer and Non-computer Supported GDSSs', *International Journal of Decision Support Systems*, 12: 381–90.

Ackermann, F. and Eden, C. (2001a) 'Contrasting Single User and Networked Group Decision Support Systems for Strategy Making', *Group Decision and Negotiation*, 10(1): 47–66.

Ackermann, F. and Eden, C. (2001b) 'SODA – Journey Making and Mapping in Practice', in J. Rosenhead and J. Mingers (eds) *Rational Analysis in a Problematic World Revisited*, London: Wiley, pp. 43–61.

Ackermann, F. and Eden, C. (2003) 'Stakeholders Matter: Techniques for Their Identification and Management', *Proceedings of the Academy of Management Conference*, Seattle, Best Paper Award.

Ackoff, R. L. (1974) *Redesigning the Future: a Systems Approach to Societal Problems*, New York: Wiley.

Andersen, D. F. and Richardson, G. P. (1997) 'Scripts for Group Model Building', *System Dynamics Review*, 13(2): 107–30.

Axelrod, R. (1976) *Structure of Decision*, Princeton: University of Princeton Press.

Beer, S. (1966) *Decision and Control*, London: Wiley.

Belbin, R. M. (1981) *Management Teams: Why They Succeed or Fail*, Oxford: Heinemann.

Bostrom, R. P., Anson, R. and Clawson, V. K. (1993) 'Group Facilitation and Group Support Systems', in L. M. Jessup and J. S. Valacich (eds) *Group Support Systems: New Perspectives*, New York: Macmillan, pp. 146–68.

Bryson, J. M. (1995) *Strategic Planning for Public and Nonprofit Organizations*, San Francisco: Jossey-Bass.

Bryson, J. M. and Crosby, B. C. (1992) *Leadership for the Common Good: Tackling Public Problems in a Shared-power World*, San Francisco: Jossey-Bass.

Bryson, J. M. and Roering, W. (1988) 'The Initiation of Strategic Planning by Governments', *Discussion Paper No. 88*, May, Strategic Management Research Center, University of Minnesota.

Bryson, J., Ackermann, F., Eden, C. and Finn, C. (2004a) *Causal Mapping: What to Do When Thinking Matters*, Chichester: Wiley.

Bryson, J., Ackermann, F., Eden, C. and Finn, C. (2004b) *Using Cause Maps to Understand What You Want and How to Get It*, Chichester: Wiley.

Buzan, T. and Buzan, B. (1993) *The Mind Map Book*, London: BBC Books.

Calori, R., Lubatkin, M. and Very, P. (1998) 'The Development of National Collective Knowledge in Management', in C. Eden and J.-C. Spender (eds) *Managerial and Organizational Cognition*, London: Sage, pp. 147–67.

Campbell, A. and Tawadey, K. (1990) *Mission and Business Philosophy*, Oxford: Heinemann.

Dalkey, N. and Helmer, O. (1963) 'An Experimental Application of the Delphi Method to the Use of Experts', *Management Science*, 9: 458–67.

De Wit, B. and Meyer, R. (eds) (1998) *Strategy: Process, Content, Context: an International Perspective* (2nd edn), St Paul, MN: Thomson Learning.

Delbecq, A. L., Van de Ven, A. H. and Gustafson, D. H. (1975) *Group Techniques for Program Planning*, Glenview, IL: Scott Foresman.

Eden, C. (2004) 'Analyzing Cognitive Maps to Help Structure Issues or Problems', *European Journal of Operational Research*, forthcoming.

Eden, C. and Ackermann, F. (1998) *Making Strategy: the Journey of Strategic Management*, London: Sage.

Eden, C. and Ackermann, F. (2000) 'Mapping Distinctive Competences: a Systemic Approach', *Journal of the Operational Research Society*, 51: 12–20.

Eden, C. and Ackermann, F. (2001a) 'A Mapping Framework for Strategy Making', in A. Huff and M. Jenkins (eds) *Mapping Strategy*, London: Wiley, pp. 173–95.

Eden, C. and Ackermann, F. (2001b) 'SODA: The Principles', in J. Rosenhead and J. Mingers (eds) *Rational Analysis for a Problematic World*, London: Wiley, pp. 21–42.

Eden, C. and Ackermann, F. (2003) 'Cognitive Mapping for Policy Analysis in the Public Sector', *European Journal of Operational Research*, 152(3): 615–30.

Eden, C., Jones, S. and Sims, D. (1979) *Thinking in Organisations*, London: Macmillan.

Eden, C., Jones, S., Sims, D. and Smithin, T. (1981) 'The Intersubjectivity of Issues and Issues of Intersubjectivity', *Journal of Management Studies*, 18: 37–47.

Forrester, J. (1971) 'Counter-intuitive Behaviour of Social Systems', *Technology Review*, January: 53–68.

George, W. (2001) 'Medtronic's Chairman William George on How Mission Driven Companies Create Long-term Shareholder Value', *Academy of Management Review*, 15(4): 39–47.

Gower, J. C. and Ross, G. J. S. (1969) 'Minimum Spanning Trees and Single Linkage Cluster Analysis', *Applied Statistics*, 18: 56–64.

Hamel, G. and Prahalad, C. K. (1993) 'Strategy as Stretch and Leverage', *Harvard Business Review*, March/April: 75–84.

Haveman, H. (1992) 'Between a Rock and a Hard Place: Organizational Change and Performance Under Conditions of Fundamental Transformation', *Administrative Science Quarterly*, 37: 48–75.

Hickling, A. (1990) '"Decision Spaces": a Scenario About Designing Appropriate Rooms for Group Decision Management', in C. Eden and J. Radford (eds) *Tackling Strategic Problems: the Role of Group Decision Support*, London: Sage. pp. 169–77.

Huxham, C. (1990) 'On Trivialities in Process', in C. Eden and J. Radford (eds) *Tackling Strategic Problems: the Role of Group Decision Support*, London: Sage, pp. 162–8.

Huxham, C. (1996) *Creating Collaborative Advantage*, London: Sage.

Huxham, C. and Eden, C. (2001) 'The Negotiation of Purpose in Multi-organizational Collaborative Groups', *Journal of Management Studies*, 38(3): 373–91.

Insinga, R. C. and Werle M. J. (2000) 'Linking Outsourcing to Business Strategy', *Academy of Management Executive*, 14: 58–70.

Janis, I. L. (1972) *Victims of Group Think*, Boston: Houghton Mifflin.

Jardine, N. and Sibson R. (1971) *Mathematical Taxonomy*, New York: Wiley.

Johnson, G. and Scholes, K. (2002) *Exploring Corporate Strategy* (6th edn), Hemel Hempstead: Prentice-Hall.

Kaplan, R. and Norton, D. (1996) *The Balanced Scorecard*, Harvard, MA: Harvard Business School Press.

Kaplan, R. and Norton, D. (2001) *The Strategy-focused Organization*, Harvard, MA: Harvard Business School Press.

Kelly, G. A. (1955) *The Psychology of Personal Constructs*, New York: Norton.

Kim, W. C. and Mauborgne, R. A. (1995) 'A Procedural Justice Model of Strategic Decision Making', *Organization Science*, 6: 44–61.

Kim, W. C. and Mauborgne, R. A. (1997) 'Fair Process: Managing in the Knowledge Based Economy', *Harvard Business Review*, 75(4): 65.

Kotter, J. (1995) 'Leading Change: Why Transformation Efforts Fail', *Harvard Business Review*, 73(2): 59–67.

Kotter, J. (1996) *Leading Change*, Harvard, MA: Harvard Business School Press.

Lindblom, C. E. (1959) 'The Science of Muddling Through', *Public Administration Review*, 19: 79–88.

Lynch, R. (2003) *Corporate Strategy* (3rd edn), Harlow, Essex: Prentice-Hall.

Mintzberg, H. and Waters, J. A. (1985) 'Of Strategies, Deliberate and Emergent', *Strategic Management Journal*, 6(3): 257–72.

Mintzberg, H., Ahlstrand, B. and Lampel, J. (1998) *Strategy Safari: the Complete Guide Through the Wilds of Strategic Management*, New York: The Free Press.

Pascale, R. T., Milleman, M. and Gioja, L. (2000) *Surfing on the Edge of Chaos: the Laws of Nature and the New Laws of Business*, Crown Business.

Pettigrew, A., Whittington, R., Melin, L., Sanchez-Runde, C., Van den Bosch, F. A. J., Ruitgrok, W. and Numagami, T. (2003) *Innovative Forms of Organizing*, London: Sage.

Rosenhead, J. and Mingers, J. (eds) (2001) *Rational Analysis in a Problematic World Revisited*, London: Wiley.

Rowe, G. and Wright, G. (1999) 'The Delphi Technique as a Forecasting Tool: Issues and Analysis', *International Journal of Forecasting*, 15: 353–75.

Schwarz, R. M. (1994) *The Skilled Facilitator: Practical Wisdom for Developing Effective Groups*, San Francisco: Jossey-Bass.

Simon, H. A. (1962) 'The Architecture of Complexity', *Proceedings of the American Philosophical Society*, 106: 467–82.

Simon, H. A. (1981) *The Sciences of the Artificial* (2nd edn), Cambridge, MA: MIT Press.

Smith, K. and Grimm, C. (1987) 'Environmental Variation, Strategic Change, and Firm Performance: a Study of Railroad Deregulation', *Strategic Management Journal*, 8: 363–76.

Spender, J. C. (1989) *Industry Recipes, an Enquiry into the Nature and Sources of Managerial Judgment*, Oxford: Basil Blackwell.

Van der Heijden, K. (1996) *Scenarios: the Art of Strategic Conversation*, Chichester: Wiley.

Van der Heijden, K., Bradfield, R., Burt, G., Cairns, G. and Wright, G. (2002) *The Sixth Sense: Accelerating Organizational Learning with Scenarios*, Chichester: Wiley.

Vygotsky, L. S. (1962 [1934]) *Thought and Language*, Cambridge, MA: MIT Press.

Warren, K. (2002) *Competitive Strategy Dynamics*, Chichester: Wiley.

Weick, K. E. (1979) *The Social Psychology of Organizing*, Reading, MA: Addison-Wesley.

Williams, K., Harkins, S. J. and Latane, B. (1979) 'Many Hands Make Light the Work: the Cause and Consequences of Social Loafing', *Journal of Personality and Social Psychology*, 37: 822–32.

Williams, T., Ackermann, F. and Eden, C. (2003) 'Structuring a Delay and Disruption Claim: an Application of Cause-mapping and System Dynamics', *European Journal of Operational Research*, 148(1): 192–204.

Index

Please note that page references to Figures and other non-textual material are in *italic* print; references to footnotes are in **bold** print